S0-BYW-965

NEWS

NEWS

THE POLITICS OF ILLUSION

SECOND EDITION

W. Lance Bennett
University of Washington

Longman
New York & London

News: The Politics of Illusion, Second Edition

Copyright © 1988 by Longman Inc. All rights reserved.
No part of this publication may be reproduced, stored
in a retrieval system, or transmitted in any form
or by any means, electronic, mechanical, photocopying,
recording, or otherwise, without the prior permission
of the publisher.

Longman Inc., 95 Church Street, White Plains, N.Y. 10601

Associated companies:
Longman Group Ltd., London
Longman Cheshire Pty., Melbourne
Longman Paul Pty., Auckland
Copp Clark Pitman, Toronto
Pitman Publishing Inc., New York

Senior editor: David J. Estrin
Production editor: Halley Gatenby
Text design: Lynn Luchetti
Cover design: Joseph DePinho
Production supervisor: Judith Stern

Library of Congress Cataloging-in-Publication Data

Bennett, W. Lance.
  News, the politics of illusion.

  Includes index.
  1. Journalism—Political aspects—United States.
I. Title.
PN4888.P6B46 1988   302.2'34   86-32203
ISBN 0-582-28664-6 (pbk.)

Compositor: Best-Set Typesetter Ltd.
Printer: R.R. Donnelley & Sons Company

  88 89 90 9 8 7 6 5 4 3 2

Contents

Acknowledgments

It is gratifying to work on this book again. As time passes and political reality becomes ever more "mediated," it is increasingly important to understand and to respond critically to the news. Toward these ends, concepts and definitions have been expanded and clarified throughout the text, particularly in chapters 1 and 2. The concluding chapter has been reworked to provide both citizens and journalists with detailed practical strategies for responding to their respective news dilemmas. Examples have been updated and sharpened in all the chapters. In making these changes, I have been mindful of the advice from those supportive readers who urged me to preserve the basic argument of the book. This edition was written in the same spirit that guided the first, with the intention of pointing out where our mass information system does not serve the ideals of American democracy, while offering constructive suggestions for improving the situation.

My sense of how people react to the news has been deepened through research funded by grants from the Spencer Foundation and the National Science Foundation (#SES 8025046). Some specific results of this research are reported in chapter 5, and the time made available by these grants for study and reflection has yielded ideas that appear throughout the book.

In addition to the people acknowledged for their contributions to the first edition, I would like to thank the following for their more recent input. Steve DeTray has provided excellent criticism and research assistance. Thanks, also, to Steve Livingston, Matt Hirshberg, Lynne Gressett, and John Gilliom for many hours of good conversation about the news. The Lake Wilderness Conference on media effects organized by Kurt and Gladys Lang generated interesting ideas about the problems of politics and mass communication. The Seattle Central America Media Project (SCAMP) has provided a refreshing model for effective citizen response to the media. Discussing the book at a meeting of the Pacific Northwest Association of Journalism Educators gave me a much better sense of the issues inside the journalism classroom. Special thanks go to all the teachers and students who have used the book and taken the time to send me their reactions (hats off to Rob Sahr and class for the detailed evaluation). As usual, Jerry Manheim provided sage advice about what to change and what to leave alone. David Estrin handled the editing duties with style and grace, not to mention amusing letters. Word-processing honors this time around go to Carole Davison-Mulligan, Cheryl Mehaffey, Vicky Lee, and Jackie Brady. The "stickler for detail" award goes to Julie Harrison, who has done the indexing of both editions.

Last, but not least, I would like to thank the Madison, Wisconsin, Organization for Reporters and Editors (MORE) for inviting me to play "Scrooge" at their annual Christmas party.

ACKNOWLEDGMENTS TO THE FIRST EDITION

I am indebted to a number of people for helping me to think more clearly about the political implications of the news. Due to their patience and generosity, the time spent writing this book has been both personally enjoyable and intellectually satisfying. First, a word of thanks goes to my colleagues at the University of Washington who endured all those fuzzy discussions about what I thought I was trying to do. I am particularly grateful to Bill Haltom, Jude Tomamichel, Dan Lev, Stu Scheingold, Alex Edelstein, David Olson, Don McCrone, Liz McHale, Paul Peretz, Jonathan Pool, and Don Matthews. An award for showing me how to spend hours in front of the television without going crazy goes to Martha Feldman, who does the best instant news analysis of anyone I know. I am also indebted to Kathleen Hance for bringing me back to earth on a regular basis by persistently asking me that dreaded question: "What are you trying to say?" Don Morrissey helped me answer that question during our Thursday night explorations of life and politics. Murray Edelman has been a continuing inspiration for my thinking about politics. I am indebted to his wise comments on the parts of the argument that I presented to his NEH summer seminar at the University of Wisconsin. Lloyd Bitzer also made the stop in Madison a rewarding experience. The Department of Rhetoric and Communication and the Department of Political Science at SUNY Albany provided another valuable opportunity to take this show on the road before its official debut. A sabbatical year granted by the University of Washington made the research and writing a real pleasure. The unsung secretarial heroics of Sharon Clark, Mary Pierce, and Brahmi Warich turned my questionable longhand into a thing of typographical beauty.

Working with the people at Longman has been a joy. Irv Rockwood not only read the drafts but knew precisely what to say and how to say it (the Editor of the Year Award to Irv). Jerry Manheim proved to be the perfect critic. His comments always hit the mark, and his enthusiasm for the project made the revision process almost tolerable.

Finally, a special thanks goes to Miss Nancy Ann Searcy, my third-grade teacher. She first introduced me to the world of news with a subscription to *My Weekly Reader*. The world seems much different to me now than it did then, but somehow the news remains much the same.

Introduction:
The News Puzzle

> I really look with commiseration over the great body of my fellow citizens who, reading newspapers, live and die in the belief that they have known something of what has been passing in the world in their time.
>
> —*Harry Truman*

We can only imagine what Harry Truman might have said about the fates of modern Americans who live in a news world dominated by television, not newspapers—Americans who are exposed to ever-simpler images of an ever-more-complex world—Americans who are the targets of increasingly sophisticated communication techniques designed to control the balance of power on the important issues affecting their lives. It is little wonder that the news is one of the most controversial subjects of our time. Mentioning the news is likely to trigger strong views on matters such as the political biases of reporters, the latest threat to the freedom of the press, and whether television can ever really replace newspapers.

Despite the multitude of positions taken by journalists, scholars, politicans, and the public, the news remains a puzzle. On the one hand, few things are as much a part of our lives as the news. With the advent of sophisticated mass communication, the news has become a sort of instant historical record of the pace, progress, problems, and hopes of society. On the other hand—and here's the puzzle—the news provides, at best, a superficial and distorted image of society. From the tremendous number of events occurring in America each day, the typical news fare covers only a narrow range of issues, from the viewpoints of an even narrower range of sources, with emphasis placed on drama over depth, human interest over social significance, and formula reporting over perceptive analysis. The puzzle, put simply, is this: How can anything so superficial be so central to our lives?

The search for an answer to this question takes us on a behind-the-scenes tour of American politics and mass communications. This exploration reveals that the three major actors in the news process—politicians, journalists, and the public—occupy quite different positions in both the political structure and the mass communication system. Despite the vast differences in these actors' political worlds, each contains certain conditions that reinforce the same superficial news. This means that problems with the news are not minor, accidental, or temporary departures from American norms about freedom of information in a democracy. Flaws in the news are the results of structural conditions in our political system.

Consider, briefly, the "news politics" of politicians, journalists, and the public. From the standpoint of politicians, it has always been clear that power and influence in a democratic society depend on the control and strategic use of information. The battle for information traditionally has been intense among interest groups, government, and the public. However, the public is increasingly losing ground to public officials and economic interests who have helped perpetuate the belief that major policy areas of government, like economic planning and national security, are well beyond the knowledge and judgment of the average citizen. The fact that these issues also seem to be beyond the knowledge and judgment of average politicians and bureaucrats does not alter the remarkably low levels of accountability surrounding their decisions. As long as information control is essential to the accumulation of power, and as long as information control is tacitly justified by fears of an informed public, political actors will never be compelled to release candid news of their political dealings.

The politics of information, power, and decision making also carry gloomy prospects for journalistic reforms. As long as the distribution of power is narrow and decision processes are closed, journalists will never be free of their dependence on the small group of public-relations experts, official spokespersons, and powerful leaders whose self-serving pronouncements have become firmly established as the bulk of the daily news.

The prospects for an enlightened citizenry are not much brighter than the hopes for noble politicians or crusading journalists. As long as the public has little political access and even less power, there will be little substance behind the familiar democratic rhetoric that equates all decisions of state with the public interest. Even though the masses of people never participate directly in the actual decisions that affect their lives, they receive through the news the constant impression that American democracy, despite its flaws, still works better than any other brand of government. The "advertisements for authority" that dominate the news are surrounded by other reports that convey fearful images of violent crime, economic insecurity, and nuclear war. Such images reinforce public support for political authorities who promise order, security, and responsive political solutions.

None of this means that people are "brainwashed" or turned into unconscious zombies by their exposure to the daily news. Studies show, for example, that many people recognize the influence that powerful institutions have over news content. And some people turn to the news more for entertainment and companionship than for serious political information. Yet for all its recognized flaws—and here is the problem—mass media news remains our only broadly shared window on reality. Turning our back on this window isolates us from the only commonly experienced reality we have as a people. When people overlook the flaws and accept the basic terms of news reality, they gain the satisfaction of participating, albeit vicariously, in the life of the nation and the world beyond.

Not surprisingly, most Americans report that they tend to believe what they see through the news window. This belief may not be fanatical, but the legitimacy and maintenance of a political system do not require fanaticism. Passive acceptance will do. Even minimal acceptance of basic assumptions about political reality is enough to keep conflict at manageable levels and to discourage most people from participating actively in the political process.

If maintaining power and privilege while limiting popular participation were the goal, the news should be given an award for "best supporting role" in the daily dramatic series "Maintaining the Status Quo." However, with the media playing a supporting role in the system, it becomes important to ask: *Who is in charge of evaluating the effectiveness of policies and the fairness of the system itself? Who is making sure that the United States is on a sound course in the world?* The answer is surely not the majority of the people in their uninformed, passive state. People are ill-equipped to monitor and guide their own destiny when they look through a news window and see a world of scattered happenings, sketched with stereotype and colored by ideology. The news, in short, reproduces and sometimes creates the illusions we hold about ourselves rather than challenging those illusions and helping us see if they have any grounding in the world beyond. Illusion is a poor basis for critical thought and action, particularly in a nation helping to chart the course of world history.

But is any of this trouble with democracy really the fault of the news media and the journalists, who, after all, are merely delivering the daily political messages from on high? Why blame the messenger for the content of the message? The point is that the media and journalists have choices about whom to carry messages for. Instead of running a messenger service for the rich and powerful, the media could become a forceful voice in their own right or even on the people's behalf. At the very least, if the news media really wanted to play "fair," journalists would be trained and empowered to analyze and "decode" the daily propaganda to help people figure it out. Choosing to be neither advocate of the people nor interpreter-teacher, the mass media pass along (with little other than editorial comment) the daily garble of political debate, fearful threats, and the stream of sometimes threatening, sometimes reassuring, public-relations images pumped out by governments and powerful political organizations.

No wonder people don't understand what is happening to them, much less what to do about it. When viewed through the news window, the complexities of terrorism and revolution dissolve into simple good-guys-versus-bad-guys melodrama. Economic crisis is always lurking in the shadows until it springs, unpredictably, on the hapless public. Hopes for peace are dashed time and again behind the closed doors of summit conferences—doors that are opened only long enough for leaders of both sides to come out, hold a press conference, and blame each other for the latest breakdown.

It would be a happier prospect if the news were merely an entertainment medium—a sort of theater of the daily absurd hosted by friendly media personalities. Unfortunately, behind the images in the news are real political developments that have profound effects on our lives: the rise and fall of leaders, increasing militarism at home and abroad, tragic and dangerous wars throughout the Third World, the growing and fortified maze of government secrecy, the expansion of domestic and foreign intelligence agencies, dizzying spirals of debt and budget deficits, support for "friendly" dictators, government cutbacks in social benefits, the retreat of "Middle America" into suburban shopping mall enclaves, and the widening gap between rich and poor.

The list of the world's problems is a long one. Yet who knows where these troubles come from, or, for that matter, where they go when they disappear, mercifully, from the news for awhile? Few people who turn to the news as their main source of information can offer useful explanations for what is going on in the world. It is no wonder that citizen understanding is at such a low ebb. The virtual absence of explanation or analysis in the news leaves the origins of events shrouded in mystery. Items seem to be pushed onto the social agenda by the hidden hand of "the economy," "the government," or good old "human nature." When it comes to safer subjects, like Communists and terrorists, the media can drop the veil of mystery and explain how good people (like us) are preyed upon by bad people (like Communists and terrorists) who just seem to want to destroy us. Surely the good-guys-versus-bad-guys explanation is too simple to be true or useful, but just ask the average American news consumer which side is responsible for escalating the arms race every year.

When it descends from the realms of mystery and melodrama, the best that popular journalism offers is painless rationalization for what is happening. The classic story is that the latest government policy is the result of reasoned arguments considered on their own merits and decided by officials with the "public interest" in mind. If, as often seems to be the case, people are upset with the results, they are reminded that there are bound to be winners and losers in the democratic process. Even when the majority of people are the losers, the instant rationalization is that the authorities and the experts have a better-developed sense of what is in the "public interest" than do the people. Reporters, of course, don't make up these rationales—they don't have to. Journalists merely pass along, without comment, the daily reassurances offered by politicians. It is thus regrettable that militarism is our fate ("We don't bear nuclear weapons because we like it," said a recent secretary of state), but it is the only rational response to the aggression of our Communist/terrorist enemies. It is also unfortunate that social programs must be cut, but they create inflation, feed budget deficits, and threaten higher priorities like military spending.

Mysteries, melodramas, and rationalizations are all poor substitutes for explanations, since none provides a solid basis for critical thinking or effective action. It is no wonder that few Americans become involved politically, and most cannot imagine how they could make a political difference. About the only choice available to the average citizen is purely psychological: either accept the available rationalizations for what is happening in the world, or reject them and live in confusion and isolation. Of course, one can also choose to read history books and specialized publications, but those who take the time to do so may find themselves unable to communicate with the majority who remain trapped on the other side of the wall of mass media imagery.

It is just easier to accept what one encounters in the daily news, and pass over in silence the parts that don't make sense. After years of exposure to the litany of slogans and rationalizations in the news, it becomes second nature to adopt them, and heretical not to pronounce them, when in doubt. Yet, if you will pardon the heresy, how do we know that the Russians are really as hostile and deceitful as our leaders have made them out to be for the last thirty years? Or that we are as well-intentioned, peaceable, and pure as our public-relations doctrines imply? When viewed apart from political images, both superpowers seem to act in very similar ways in the world: supporting corrupt regimes, building spheres of influence, tolerating human oppression, pursuing economic advantage, and alternating between postures of reconciliation and aggression whenever it suits their purposes to do so. The images that each side attaches to these behaviors are quite different, however. One side's aggressive behavior evokes the other's defensive posture. Such has been the enduring historical script for "moral" war and "justifiable" human destruction. Thus the news images of the political world can be tragically self-fulfilling. *Dominant political images, when acted upon, can create a world in their own image—even when such a world did not exist to begin with.*

The foregoing ideas and others to be developed in these pages are not easy for many Americans to think about, much less to accept. Before most of us were able to think or reason for ourselves, we were taught to believe that America is the world's greatest democracy and that freedom of the press is one of its main foundations. This makes it hard for us to see either the power gap between authorities and the public, or the degree of information control that traps the news-hungry press.

When faced with a choice between confronting an unpleasant reality and defending a set of comforting and socially accepted beliefs, most people choose the latter course. For example, it is common to hear people defend the news as an accurate and useful reflection of society and politics (never mind its domination by the "news factories" of government, business, and interest groups). It is also easy to rationalize the flaws in the news merely by affirming that, whatever its problems, it is still better than in Russia. (This is true, but what is gained from comparing something to the worst imaginable case?) Some people make excuses by condemning the superficiality of mass news sources like television but noting the existence of excellent journals and magazines for those who care to take their news seriously. (What credibility do such "highbrow," low-readership sources have when pitted against the mainstream news corps of respected journalists who represent the latest official pronouncements as objective news for the masses?) Other people even take the offensive and criticize the news as too antiauthority due to the left-wing bias of journalists. (Leaving aside the obvious news production edge held by the government and influential "right-wing" figures, just how much subversion really lives in the hearts of reporters who are, at their most extreme, professional, upper-middle-class, civic-minded, liberal Democrats?)

Perhaps the most significant response to news is the one that is missing: the virtual absence of credible public figures pointing out the flaws in the news and explaining those flaws in terms of the realities of power and information in American politics. Since the news is a major source of what people regard as true, objective, and real in the world around them, it would not serve the separate purposes of politicians, press, or public to accept news that undermines itself. However, it is not very comforting to know that people pay such a high price for the comforts of an "objective reality" that is the illusory product of a vicious cycle of news and politics. In this cycle, "official" versions of reality are legitimized because they dominate news content, and the news, in turn, seems "objective" because official versions of events fall into such familiar, standardized patterns.

The first step toward understanding this news politics problem is to gain an appreciation of how serious a problem it really is. Chapter 1 is devoted to explaining the differences between the mass media and other information sources in society, pointing out the key political role played by journalists in the mass media. Chapter 2 examines the information biases of the daily news and shows why this sort of "information" is of little use to the citizen interested in participating in the political process. Following the overview of the problem in the first two chapters, the core of the book looks at the three sets of actors responsible for news politics. Chapter 3 shows how powerful political actors attempt to control news content. Chapter 4 explains how journalists unwittingly promote the propaganda of those political actors. Chapter 5 addresses the question of why the American people remain attentive to the illusory, but dramatic, political images contained in the news. Based on this analysis of how the news is produced, communicated, and consumed, the concluding chapter explores the problem of why the news persists in its present form and shows how the concerned citizen can make better use of (that is, "decode") the information provided by the mass media. In the interest of sharing the responsibility for changing the balance of power, participation, and information in the United States, there are also some words of advice about what journalists can do to make their reporting more useful to "we, the people."

A Note to the Reader

- Why is a society that is so rich in information populated with people who are so confused about politics?
- Is it possible for journalism to be objective as it is practiced in America?
- Is the news mainly an "advertisement for the system," or is it a valuable citizen resource?

These are just a few of the questions you will encounter in this book. In the final analysis, it is up to you to draw conclusions about them. In order to stimulate your thinking, the book presents a perspective that is critical of the news—a perspective intended to provoke thought and reaction. I have chosen to present a broad, alternative point of view for a simple reason: There would be little gained by going over the story of the free press in America for yet another time. As an American citizen you already know by heart the saga of "A Free Press and a Free People." True, you may have forgotten a few characters or some of the episodes. Nevertheless, memorizing those missing facts once again would not change the plot about how the enduring struggle for freedom of speech and information has created the foundation for democracy in America. Since you know this story already, you should use it in thinking about the argument in this book. Don't feel that you must accept either the story of the free press or the perspective in this book in its entirety. Use the two perspectives to challenge each other and to help you draw your own conclusions. After all, the capacity to think independently, without fear or insecurity, is the foundation on which our political freedom rests.

NEWS

CHAPTER 1

Mass Media News, Mass Mediated Politics

> Journalism must give mankind a picture of the world on which it can act....I wonder if we haven't missed that goal....There isn't a sense of cohesion in a lot of editing of the papers and the production of the programs. We have failed in some way to get across to the public the essence of the craft, which is to enable people in a democracy to make decisions based on information.
>
> —*John Chancellor*

Americans live in a vast information and communication empire. The number of media outlets is staggering. By the latest count, there are some 1,700 daily newspapers in the United States, with a combined circulation of more than 60 million. There are also more than 7,000 weekly papers and countless periodicals aimed at audiences like college students, ethnic groups, religious sects, foreign-language speakers, and business and professional groups. The broadcast bands are equally crowded, with nearly 5,000 AM radio stations and some 4,000 commercial and 1,300 educational FM channels. As for television, there are more than 1,100 commercial and 600 educational and public TV channels.[1] The national addiction to mass media is perhaps best captured by the fact that more American homes have television sets than flush toilets.

The abundance of such information sources would seem to lend credence to the old adage that there is no excuse for people to be uninformed about the world in which they live. It is, after all, tempting to conclude that if members of a "mass mediated" society like ours are ignorant of politics and world affairs, then they simply have not bothered to become informed. Yet many people are not informed. Opinion research indicates that many citizens—perhaps the majority—live in a state of confusion and ignorance about government and political issues. What are we to make of this paradox that one of the most sophisticated communication societies in the world is populated by poorly informed individuals?

Before leaping to the conclusion that the fault resides with apathetic citizens, consider the possibility that the problem lies primarily with the nature of the news itself. Despite the common assumption that professional news organizations provide clear, informative, and fairly objective pictures of the world, there is a growing body of evidence to the contrary. Recent research is beginning to paint a portrait of the news as fragmented, analytically superficial, hard to remember, and difficult to use meaningfully. Only rarely does the news contain solid explanations, and even less often does it present clear conclusions about events. It is also becoming apparent that the media are far from "objective" in their coverage. We shall see, for example, that the views of powerful political and economic figures dominate the news, while the concerns of groups outside the mainstream are typically ignored or presented in negative ways.

In view of these and other problems with the news, the citizen's best efforts to become informed may be counterproductive: The more news consumed, the more narrow and stereotypical the resulting understanding may become. But how can such a situation exist when there are so many free and competitive information channels in the United States? In order to answer this important question, we must first distinguish mass media channels from more restricted information sources and then separate the quantity of information from its quality.

First, it must be acknowledged that there are hundreds, if not thousands, of small publications, listener-sponsored radio and television stations, and public access cable channels that offer a broad range of clear and detailed perspectives on public affairs. However, for reasons that will be discussed later, news sources that exist outside the mass media are not credible in the eyes of most Americans. Diverse viewpoints matter little if they are not taken seriously. We are, like it or not, prisoners of mass media. Therefore, it is the nature of mass media news that we must understand.

Even if the mass media dictate the terms of accepted political reality in America, it would seem that there are so many different mass media outlets transmitting so much sheer information that the concerned citizen should be able to assemble an accurate and sophisticated view of the world. It is true that media organizations differ considerably in terms of the quantity of information they transmit and the range of topics they cover. Nevertheless, underneath these differences in information quantity and subject matter lies a common core of remarkably similar political messages.

How can the basic political messages of mass media news be pretty much the same whether we listen to the two minutes of headlines every hour on our favorite radio station or spend the week trying to digest the ten-pound Sunday edition of the *New York Times*? Technical answers to this question will be presented later in this book when we explore the interworkings of journalism and politics. For now, let's start with a simple, common-sense distinction between the form and the substance of news. Much can be learned about a product by distinguishing the packaging from the contents.

In what sense is the news a "product"? It surely differs from corn flakes and underarm deodorants. Yet the news shares one important thing in common with most commercial products: It is marketed effectively through the creation of product images. Such images promote the illusion of distinctiveness while blurring the underlying reality of the product. One brand of corn flakes conveys an image of crunchiness, another exudes healthiness, while still another promises a fantasy of family togetherness at the breakfast table. Similarly, if our desire is to keep in touch with world events, we are invited to do so by becoming an "eyewitness," taking an adventure into the world of "action news," turning ourselves over to a respected "news authority," or sitting down with the serious purpose of reading "All the News That's Fit to Print." While there is no doubt that the consumer of mass media has choices, the important question is whether those choices differ in any meaningful way.

Have you ever wondered why Pontiac, Chevrolet, and Buick sell very similar car models with different names and at different prices? It is, to put it simply, much more profitable to mass produce the same product and sell it in personalized packaging than it is to produce many distinctive products. If the marketing goal is to capture large segments of the mass buying public, it is more efficient to sell everyone pretty much the same thing than to undermine profits by designing something different for everyone. This is where packaging comes in. Packages convey images. They dress products up or down. They give off signals about the social status (real or desired) of the people who use particular products. Packages even fit products into the life-styles of consumers—the pace, taste, zest, zip, rush, whoosh (and let's not forget those springtime moments) of life itself.

The news is, above all, a consumer good. It would not exist in the diverse forms that we know it without the marketing strategies that deliver (or, better put, "sell") news audiences to advertisers. Perhaps, as NBC reporter Linda Ellerbee has claimed about TV news, the most important product in the news business is not the news itself, but the audience sold at a price to the sponsor:

> In television the product is not the program, the product is the audience and the consumer of that product is the advertiser. The advertiser does not "buy" a news program. He buys an audience. The manufacturer (network) that gets the highest price for its product is the one that produces the most product (audience)....The value of any news program is measured by whether it increases productivity; the best news program, therefore, is the one watched by the greatest number of people....Altruists do not own television stations or networks, nor do

they run them. Businessmen own and run them. Journalists work for businessmen. Journalists get fired and cancelled by businessmen. That is how it is.[2]

In order to sell audiences to sponsors, the news must be "sold" to the audience in the first place. That is, the news product must fit into the audience's social image, life-style, and daily schedule. Much of what passes for diversity in mass media news is largely a matter of packaging designed to deliver a product to market. Once this packaging is removed, it is possible to see that behind the various forms of news, there is a remarkable uniformity of content.

FORM TRIUMPHS OVER SUBSTANCE: NEWS STYLES AND LIFE-STYLES

It is hard to imagine anything, short of the air we breathe, that has become easier to consume than news. The saturation of everyday life with news is no small feat, considering the diversity of American life-styles. Differences in age, wealth, education, occupation, religion, social customs, and leisure pursuits all have effects on the way in which people receive, interpret, and use news information.[3] Despite such differences in American society, the news reaches most people one way or another. Forms of news are designed to fit most personal schedules. People who drive the freeways to and from work can tune their car radios to morning and evening "drive time" news. People who spend early-morning hours at home can choose among the big-budget "news and features" programs produced by the major television networks. Newspapers and magazines reach wide readerships and offer people considerable choice about where and when to read them. Local evening news programs on television often run for two or three hours in order to accommodate different work and dinner schedules. Any gaps that may exist in this news barrage are filled by other sources like an all-news cable television network (CNN), all-news radio stations, regular newscasts scattered throughout radio and television entertainment programming, late-night radio talk shows, and the news-in-review features of weekend radio, television, and newspapers. People who somehow elude this incredible communication net will often make contact with friends or strangers who ask the familiar question, "Did you hear the news about ———— ?" It is virtually impossible to avoid the news.

Since news delivery is so individualized, it is easy to see why people think there are choices available to the information-seeking public; yet the choices are matters of style, not substance. The formats of newspapers cater to information appetites ranging from the serious to the sensational. Early-morning network television programs offer viewers strikingly different presentations of much the same information. One program invites the audience in for morning coffee with a folksy host—a former television actor—who sits and chats with guests in a living-room-like set. On another channel viewers can watch an affable newsman and a glamorous co-host present news and interviews. The third network offers a cast of bubbly-but-credible personalities who read the news, clown through the weather, and exchange quips on a set that could double for a late-night talk show. Even the pace and mood of a day are captured by the news. Compare the slow, leisurely feel of the Sunday newspaper with the frantic pace—intensified by constant reminders of the exact time of day—of a weekday "rip-and-read" newscast on an all-news radio station. When people tune into the late-night local television news, it is no accident that they encounter a lighter, slower-paced format than the one used in the early-evening news. It has become a law of the late-night news to close with an upbeat feature story that sends people off to bed reassured that, despite its problems, the world is still a safe and positive place.

The marked differences in news formats indicate how much a part of everyday life the news has become. People may be exposed to the same disaster stories or the same grim reports on the economy, but it helps to receive the information in ways that minimize the gap between the stark realities of the world and the familiar routines of private lives. The media have adopted increasingly sophisticated market research techniques to pitch the same news items to different audiences. For example, beginning in 1968, ABC broke up its homogeneous radio news network and created four network services: Contemporary, Entertainment, Information, and FM. With the advent of satellite transmission in the 1980s, ABC added two more networks, Direction and Rock, resulting in three news formats for different market segments of the twenty-five-to-fifty-four-year-old age bracket and three formats for young adults under the age of twenty-five. Here are the ways in which some of these ABC services covered a flood in California:

- The Information Network opened its broadcast with 100 words of spoken text before cutting to a 20-second capsule summary by a reporter on the scene.
- The Contemporary Network began the story with a dramatic clip of a law-enforcement official calling for help with a broken levee.
- The FM Network announced that "choppers" are "movin' " people "a ways north of San Francisco."

According to Kathy Lavinder, general manager of news programming for the ABC radio network, "We do a lot of research when we decide how to target our newscasts. We select a core group of listeners and try to choose news that's appropriate, relevant and interesting to them and deliver it with an announcer who sounds like he fits in with the listeners."[4]

Market studies also show that people personalize their relations with favorite television newscasters. Many people prefer to hear the news from someone they identify as a concerned friend, an image that made former CBS newscaster Walter Cronkite the most preferred news source in America. In fact, when Cronkite retired, CBS fell from first to last place in the network nightly news ratings. The dramatic drop in audience share was attributed to the fact that fewer people were attracted to Cronkite's replacement, Dan Rather, who projected a more distant and less friendly image.[5] CBS repaired Rather's image, along with his ratings, by dressing him in sweaters that made him look "warmer" and less aloof. To go along with its "warmed-up" anchorman, CBS then began to personalize and emotionalize its news scripts. According to a prominent news critic,

> CBS is by far the most emotional of the three networks. When there is joy, CBS celebrates. When there is sadness, CBS consoles. When man overcomes adversity, CBS is there to marvel. And when the emotions are mixed, CBS tries to sort them out. Thus, when the national Christmas tree was lit on the same day on which 256 [American servicemen died in an air crash near Gander, Newfoundland], Dan Rather signed off with this epiphany: "Tragedy knows no season; but today's tragedy is especially painful. It comes at a time of traditional joy and celebration, celebration of rebirth of faith, celebration of the miracle of the flame that refused to be snuffed out: the trappings of joy all around us today for the season; the national Christmas tree lighting tonight by the President. But now, added to the traditional trappings, the unexpected symbols of grief, unfurled and half staffed, on flagpoles and on faces, in a season of faith, remembering that those who died in the service of their country today were coming home from a mission of peace in the Sinai."[6]

As the facelifts at ABC radio and CBS TV indicate, news formats change with the times. Even the idea of a national newscast is a comparatively modern phenomenon born largely of network radio news coverage of World War II. During the six years of that fateful world conflict, radio listeners tuned to the national network for war news. Trusted radio war correspondents like Edward R. Murrow, Charles Collingwood, Howard K. Smith, and others went on to pioneer the first generation of national television network news in the 1950s. In the 1960s and 1970s, increasingly elaborate local television news formats emerged to tap audience concerns about community affairs and local life-styles. Local news, like national, has gone through various changes over the years from the "Good News," happy-patter formula of the mid-1970s to the present-day "Action-Eyewitness News" approach.[7]

What is in line next to keep the news geared to consumer life-styles? The broadcast media seem headed toward more "integrated" delivery systems that will run national feeds through local broadcasts. NBC Television News president Lawrence Grossman has hinted that he may allow the local affiliates to fashion the "Nightly News" around local tastes. Under the new format, the network would feed the locals through a 90-minute "news wheel," permitting the "blend" to be mixed according to the tastes of the affiliates.[8] Initial affiliate reaction to this idea was mixed, but it is clear that further changes will result from increasingly aggressive (and expensive) network and affiliate efforts to capture the TV news market. With the advent of the Cable News Network and the ability of local affiliates to receive direct satellite feeds on world news events, network news organizations face increasing competition from all sides. Preservation of the big nightly news shows will require format changes at the networks. The question is whether new formats will improve the quality of information.

Newspapers, too, seem headed toward faster, more lively delivery styles, keeping pace with the TV generation. The national paper *USA Today* is even sold from vending machines resembling TV sets. *USA Today* also gears itself to local concerns through heavy coverage of sports, weather, consumer trends, and a daily capsule summary of happenings in every state of the union. Daily papers across the nation have expanded their city, county, and state coverage while introducing more departments like "Home," "Life-style," "Consumer Hints," and "Arts and Leisure." The "hard news" is still there but it occupies an increasingly smaller space amidst all of the pretty packaging.[9]

Keying information delivery to American life-styles through marketing research has expanded the profits of news organizations. TV news, once a network "loss leader," is now a big moneymaker. Increased profits provide incentives for more sophisticated marketing and audience-targeting through stylized delivery formats. In recent years the journalistic product has invaded everyday life to the point where it has become associated with things that people build their identities around, including self-image, status concerns, and sense of community. For example, a leading national news magazine ran an advertising campaign that equated reading the magazine with social respect, prestige, and personal competence. A major national newspaper devoted to business and economic affairs suggested that a subscription was a sign of good business sense and future career success. Local television news programs emphasize, both in advertising and program formats, the display of local symbols, landmarks, and themes of community pride. Viewers are encouraged to see the local TV news as a caring and watchful eye on the community they love.

The integration of news with everyday life is not just a one-way street. Not only are news forms responsive to individual life-styles, but the news can also shape the pace and concerns of social life. It is easy and appealing for people to get caught up in the real-life dramas that unfold on the world stage. There seems to be a steady stream of long-playing news events such as wars, government scandals, economic crises, social changes, and political conflicts. These news "serials" can capture the attention and shape the emotions of the public.

When society becomes captivated by one of these sagas, it is hard to tell whether the news is a reflection of social life or whether the pace and mood of daily life are set by the news. For example, when the government corruption scandal "Watergate" reached its dramatic climax with the implication of President Nixon and his top aides, millions of Americans became addicted to the daily media installments. One report on the Watergate audience of 1973 indicated that average Americans adjusted their lives to the year-long media spectacle:

> ...contrary to any picture of middle Americans tending their lawns and dialing out on the news, our panels paid close—even avid—attention to the Watergate scandals throughout the summer....The blue-collar workers on the second shift at the Delco-Remy plant in Anderson, IND.,...spent the day watching the televised Ervin committee hearings...and then discussed Watergate at work....One Portland business executive delayed going to his office until the morning hearings adjourned around 12:30 Washington time (9:30 on the West Coast)....
> In western Massachusetts, of ten panelists, seven read about Watergate daily in the newspapers and four watched the hearings regularly, especially the rebroadcasts at night on public television. Attention to the hearings was unexpectedly high among Nixon voters. In the engineering department of a large manufacturing plant in Dayton, there was only one McGovern voter in a group of 17 men holding managerial and foreman jobs; but a large majority of the group followed and approved of the hearings.[10]

A similar social preoccupation with the news occurred when Iranian rebels stormed the U.S. embassy in Tehran in 1979 and held the occupants captive. The media launched a 444-day series of dramatic updates on the situation. Even though there was very little "news" to report each day, the story continued to develop. As the unchanging political circumstances became monotonous, the focus of journalistic attention began to shift to the "home front." The news audience was bombarded with human interest stories of hometown vigils, public displays of concern, and Christmas back home with the hostages' families. These human interest stories quickly became self-perpetuating news, with little or no connection to the political importance of the actual situation. It was as though a closed-circuit camera had been turned on the entire country. Millions of anonymous Americans became media stars for a day through their participation in patriotic rallies and demonstrations. The attention paid to these rallies spawned more and more of them, creating an always available formula news story. The saturation of the news with stories about public concern produced a saturation in society of more displays of public concern. It became impossible to attend a sporting event, a concert, or a public meeting without hearing something about the hostages. The proliferation of public concern added credibility to the increasingly standardized news stories, while the news stories fed on the diffusion of concern about the hostages.[11]

Stories like the hostage crisis and Watergate show how easily the news can capture the social imagination. Moreover, as the hostage crisis indicates, this captivation may have little to do with any objective properties of an event. As we shall see in the coming pages, these lessons apply even to news in its more mundane forms of government pronouncements, daily disasters, and heartwarming, real-life melodramas. Although the news appeals effectively to diverse sectors of the public, there is an underlying uniformity to the political messages it transmits. Recognizing the narrow range of content packaged in a broad range of communication styles is a key to understanding mass media news.

THE POINT

Why is it important to understand that the seemingly broad range of information in the news is really a wide assortment of packaging for much the same information? *The point is that the news we are given is not fit for a democracy; it is superficial, narrow, stereotypical, propaganda-laden, of little explanatory value, and not geared for critical debate or citizen action.* The next chapter spells out the nature of these information biases and illustrates their various political effects. For now, the reader is just invited to consider this possibility: Even though the United States has the most sophisticated communication capacity on earth, the American people would have to create another forum for the exchange of information if they wanted to become involved directly in their own government!

THINKING DIFFERENTLY ABOUT THE NEWS

Despite the superficiality of mass media information, it is widely believed that ignorance is the fault of people who don't bother to become informed. It is important to understand why this belief persists in order to comprehend the profound psychological effects of superficial news described in chapter 2. Why does the myth of individual responsibility persist? For one thing, the strong strain of individualism in this culture encourages people to blame themselves for their own shortcomings and problems. There is nothing wrong with being self-critical, but there is nothing productive about criticism that goes so far as to "blame the victim" for problems that are well beyond individual control. People need specific changes in their political environments (namely, changes in institutions like government, press, and schools) if they are to overcome problems of ignorance and political passivity.

Compounding this cultural individualism are the effects of news marketing techniques on perceptions of product quality. Good marketing can blur the distinction between form and substance or between a package and its contents. Successful advertisers and marketers are often effective because they induce people to identify with, and then buy, a standardized product in a personalized package. It is easy to fall prey to superficial distinctions and conclude that one product must be substantially different from another. Yet, when we look closely, the obvious distinctions between different media have little to do with the underlying messages they transmit. For example, it is easy to think that since newspapers have more words than television, they must contain more "information." Yet experiences with other kinds of products show that quantity may have little to do with quality. It is possible to say very little with many words and to say a great deal with a few words. And what about pictures on television, don't they count as information, too? A picture may not be worth a thousand words but it can convey strong impressions when placed in context by a few selected words. In short, reasoning that "newspapers have more words, so they must convey more information than TV" does not hold up on close inspection. One beach may have more grains of sand than another, but that is usually not the dimension along which we rate the quality of beaches.

Journalists themselves probably do more than anyone to perpetuate the belief that there are meaningful choices available within the American mass communication system. There is continuing debate among respected journalists and media executives about the differences among various information channels. The hottest debate is—you guessed it—whether newspapers are more informative than television. To their dying day, the print media will maintain that they are informationally superior to radio and TV. It has become part of the national mythology that newspapers are more stubborn, investigative, detailed, and just plain informative than the other media. And print journalists do more than anyone to keep this mythology alive. Never mind the evidence showing newspapers going the way of all media with increased features and special departments and reduced space for national and international affairs coverage.[12] What matters is that print journalists continue living out the historical fantasy that they are crusading advocates for the people, while the people continue to have a soft spot in their hearts for the mythology that the press will somehow rise to defend their freedom. And so the debate over media differences continues, and as long as it continues, there is a chance that people will take it seriously. Let's drop in on a recent round of the Great Media Debate.

THE GREAT MEDIA DEBATE: PERPETUATING
THE MYTH OF INFORMATION DIFFERENCES

The latest round of debate over whether newspapers are superior to broadcast media was kicked off when an outgoing president of the American Society of Newspaper Editors leveled a strong charge that television, not the newspaper, was responsible for the low state of public awareness and the latest "crisis of democracy." In his presidential address, Creed Black said, among other things:

> On one hand, most thoughtful students of the American press agree that our newspapers are doing a better job today than ever before in this nation's history. On the other, we are buffeted almost daily with new pronouncements of a crisis of public confidence which—in the words of that familiar TIME magazine cover story—threatens "one of the foundations of the country's democratic system."
>
> Finally, I come to what I have become increasingly convinced is one of the major reasons our public standing seems to have declined while our performance as an institution has improved.
>
> It is that the public lumps the printed press and the television together in something called "the media" and makes little if any distinction between the two. The result is that we are blamed for the sins and shortcomings of what television—which remains basically an entertainment medium—calls news.[13]

Needless to say, this bold accusation produced an outcry from television journalists who were eager to establish that TV may be different from, but surely not inferior to, newspapers. The controversy raged over the merits and substantive differences of TV versus newspapers until a major foundation decided to hold a conference to give the matter even more serious attention. The conference sponsored by the Poynter Institute for Media Studies drew a long list of luminaries from television, newspapers, the wire services, and political science. Creed Black opened the proceedings by reissuing his previous inflammatory statement. Moderator and political scientist James David Barber called for a response from the television industry. Ready on the firing line was none other than CBS News' Van Gordon Sauter (the man responsible for the earlier discussed "facelift" at CBS). Sauter turned the tables on Black and encouraged the venerable newspaperman to look into his own backyard before being critical of the neighbors':

Let me take you to, of all places, Fayette County, Kentucky, home of the city of Lexington, the *Herald-Leader* and its chairman and publisher, Creed Black. They like the media down there. And while Creed may find this fact distressing, I have to report that they liked television more than they liked their newspaper.

Less than two weeks ago, we conducted a telephone interview with a random sample of 670 adults in Fayette County who read the newspaper and watch television. Nearly all those individuals consider the Lexington *Herald-Leader* as their main newspaper. They said quite clearly that television is their principal source of news. If faced with the choice of having only one source of news, more would choose television than a newspaper. Television was the first choice of both those who regularly watch television and those who regularly read newspapers. This cross section of Fayette County also regards television as being more serious and professional. It considers television stories clearer and more understandable. Television also leads newspapers, but by a narrower margin, at being fair in its reporting. They also feel the newspaper is more likely to make mistakes than television. However, they believe that the newspaper is more willing to correct its errors. Perhaps they have just had more experience with newspaper errors. Either way, Creed, you do quite well down there on both sides of the error category.

But if Fayette County is representative of the larger world, and I have no doubt its national sales representative contends that to be the case, then there is encouraging news. A great majority believe that quality of reporting has improved both in newspapers and on television. Eighty-seven percent of the people said television news reporting is fair. Eighty-four percent said newspaper reporting is fair. Seventy-nine percent said newspaper stories and television stories have the facts straight. Discussing stories where they had a personal knowledge of the events, 81 percent of the respondents said television news is accurate, and 79 percent said the newspaper is accurate.

On the basis of this survey, I would say to you, Creed, that it is myopic, self-serving, and ultimately self-destructive to dash about the country proclaiming that television news is damaging the credibility of newspapers. There is no credible evidence of this. If anything, the evidence speaks to the reverse.[14]

Around and around they went. Only one exchange touched on the question of whether any brands of the mass media presented information in forms people could use as a basis for critical thought and democratic action. During the second day of the Great Debate, NBC commentator John Chancellor issued the challenge used as the epigraph for this chapter:

Journalism must give mankind a picture of the world on which it can act. . . . I wonder if we haven't missed that goal. We've gotten tied up in other perceptions of the world, and the readers and viewers don't think that we're trying to give them that picture of the world on which they can act. There isn't a sense of cohesion in a lot of the editing of the papers and the production of the programs. We have failed in some way to get across to the public the essence of the craft, which is to enable people in a democracy to make decisions based on information.[15]

In response to Chancellor's call to look at the political quality of news information, Don Hewitt, executive producer of CBS's "60 Minutes," replied that the role of the media, particularly television, was to bring political events directly, without analysis, into the living room. In Hewitt's view, people at home are saying, "Hey, I watched it. I saw it. Shut up. I'll make up my own mind. I don't need John Chancellor to tell me anything about that. I was there. I was at the same event he was at."[16]

Despite this failed attempt to explore the issue of information quality, the conference closed on a high note. *Boston Globe* editor Martin Nolan recalled the words of turn-of-the-century newspaper commentator Finley Peter Dunne, who spoke through his fictional Irish bartender, Mr. Dooley: "The newspaper does everything for us. It runs the police force and the banks, commands the militia, controls the legislature, baptizes the young, marries the foolish, comforts the afflicted, afflicts the comfortable, buries the dead and roasts them afterwards...."[17] The conference closed on Nolan's stirring paraphrase of Mr. Dooley:

> That phrase I love, "comforts the afflicted and afflicts the comfortable." Well, whatever our ethics problems are, whatever our credibility problems are, we're going to have no trouble if we remember that it is our duty to "comfort the afflicted and afflict the comfortable." Thank you. (Applause)[18]

A nice idea, to be sure, but during the two-day debate there was little discussion devoted to just how journalists might go about presenting information in ways that would "comfort the afflicted and afflict the comfortable." So large is the gap between this noble ideal and the daily practice of journalism that the conferees might have found this issue, along with John Chancellor's challenge, difficult to address. Taking the hard look (see chapter 2) might, of course, end the debate about which medium is superior, as none comes out looking very good. More important, a hard look at information quality shows that far from "comforting the afflicted and afflicting the comfortable," the mass media play a major political role by not taking sides at all. In theory it seems fair for the media to be neutral. *In practice, however, journalistic neutrality means that groups with the loudest, best financed, and most rehearsed voices get their messages across more effectively and more often. The result of journalism's unwillingness to develop a voice for democracy is that the news has become virtually a direct pipeline for propaganda from powerful organizations to the people.* In practice, then, media neutrality must be a great comfort to the already comfortable and an additional affliction to the already afflicted. Understanding this key political role of the news media sets the stage for the argument of the rest of the book.

MAINTAINING THE STATUS QUO:
THE MASS MEDIA AS GATEKEEPER

It is often said that the news media play the crucial role of "gatekeeper" in the American political system. With the above concerns about information and democracy in mind, let's see what the media gatekeeper role is all about. *The first important political observation about the American mass media is that to an important extent they regulate the content of public information and communication in the U.S. political system. Mass mediated images of reality set the limits on who in the world we think we are as a people, and what in the world we think we are doing.* As the only national public forum and most generally accessible public record around, the news becomes a surrogate conscience of the people. True, we are still free to register our disagreements in private or, for that matter, in large angry mobs. But complaining in private changes nothing, and the voices of angry mobs are filtered through political imagery that the mob surely has no editorial control over. *That is what the mass media do: translate the complex and multi-voiced reality of our times into another, symbolic realm of simpler images and fewer voices.*

As if living in a world of simplistic illusion were not enough, *the media add a second dimension to their political role by exercising considerable discretion over whose illusions, hopes, and dreams are admitted through the gate and into public consciousness.* Gates, to extend the metaphor, swing open in two ways: to let people on the inside out, and people on the outside in. *In the American system, the media gate is opened frequently to put the messages of political insiders onto the public record. However, the gate opens much less frequently for the large number of outsiders who would speak if only someone gave them the opportunity.*

True, the media gate swings two ways for the Republicans and the Democrats. This is what gives the impression that the system is "fair." But can we truly convince ourselves that the Republicans and Democrats are the only two kinds of people in the world who count? When it comes to the more important democratic categories of "power holders" versus "powerless" or "insiders" versus "outsiders," the Republicans and Democrats begin to look like a powerful inside minority given vast media preference over any number of outsiders who might wish to challenge their privileged position. When it comes to maintaining the existing balance of power and enforcing the existing rules of the game, the media play gatekeeper with a selective eye.

A third consequence of the way the media play their gatekeeper role is that the one-way communication system described above lacks what communication theorists call "feedback." It is important for ideas in a democracy to be criticized, modified, and reacted to by the general public. In place of two-way communication, the news gives us one-way images justified largely on the grounds that the officials who make the news are elected by the people and therefore really do speak for those on the outside. It would seem far more sensible not to take on faith this key principle on which the whole system rests. Instead, why not introduce a broader range of voices into the news, to make sure many views are registered before decisions are made? Democracy requires two-way (better yet, multi-sided) communication with feedback.

Media Power: What Is It and How Does It Work?

By regulating the flow of "who" and "what" passes through the public information gate, the media hold enormous power in the system. Imagine how much impact you would have in any situation if you controlled who spoke, how long they could talk, how credibly they were introduced, and what they could talk about. People would call you a tyrant or a dictator. Yet the news is seldom perceived as tyrannical or dictatorial. *Journalists play their gatekeeper role (or, if you prefer, exercise their power) in a low-key way that seems to avoid taking sides.* The appearance of neutrality is achieved by scripting the news in terms of traditional American political beliefs. As mentioned above, politicians can be given preferential treatment because they are defined traditionally as servants of the people. Similarly, U.S. interventions abroad are never called "invasions" or "aggressions" because of traditional beliefs that American actions represent only the noblest, defensive purposes.

Linguist and political critic Noam Chomsky has used the term "historical engineering" to describe the media practice of fitting ongoing reality to preconceived images drawn from the national mythology. The idea of historical engineering originated when a group of American historians joined forces during World War I to explain the issues in the war in ways that would mobilize popular support for a U.S. victory. Now, argues Chomsky, "such 'engineering' extends beyond outright war to affairs of state more generally and to the interests of the corporate institutions that dominate society."[19]

The practice of filtering political events in keeping with the national self-image is not common just in "lowbrow" media like television and the wire services. Chomsky points to a long succession of cases in which the *New York Times*, the flagship of the U.S. mass media, has led the way in placing rose-colored lenses over dubious national policies. The *Times* has gained a liberal reputation for launching the careers of a number of investigative reporters and for allowing its reporters during the later years of the Vietnam War to file stories that challenged government propaganda efforts. Despite these critical moments, the general tendency at the *Times* has been to protect U.S. policies and interests from public scrutiny. Such protective imagery served up by the media is easy to miss through the haze of right-wing accusations of media liberalism.

For example, the now-established tradition of CIA subversion and overthrow of other governments got off to a quiet and uncriticized start in 1954 when the *New York Times* led the U.S. media in disguising U.S. intervention in Guatemala behind reports of a popular local political uprising. Entirely ignored in *Times* coverage was the instrumental role of the United Fruit Company, whose profitable Guatemalan operations were protected through powerful company connections to the CIA and the State Department. Instead of being at the center of the news story, United Fruit remained behind the scenes, where it provided the media with scripts for the stories that did make the news. As Chomsky tells it:

> When the U.S. government was preparing to overthrow Guatemalan democracy in 1954, the public relations department of the United Fruit Company brought the *Times* on board in what United Fruit's director called "a first-class public relations coup," which included a series of fraudulent stories and the entire flimsy pretense that the U.S. was not involved, swallowed whole by the *Times*. He commented later that "it is difficult to make a convincing case for manipulation of the press when the victims proved so eager for the experience." That is the real point. The *Times* understands its role: creating an acceptable history, while preserving enough of the truth about the real world to serve those whose decisions require a taste of reality.[20]

In more recent years, dozens of examples illustrate this tendency to filter reality through comfortable images of U.S. goodness. The human rights atrocities of "enemy" nations receive far more media attention than the inhuman practices of U.S. "friends." The grinding war in El Salvador disappeared behind an image of hope and democracy when the *Times* withdrew a correspondent who filed more stories from the Salvadoran people's point of view than the U.S. embassy, right-wing media lobbies, and, ultimately, *Times* editors could tolerate. And on the local front, a popular commentator on New York City politics was fired following a series of articles that criticized development projects supported by *Times* editorials and challenged the *Times* for devoting more attention to the trials and tribulations of wealthy suburban homeowners than to the city's crises of homelessness and poverty.

Whether the filtering of daily reality through rose-colored "Middle-American" glasses is conscious or not is beside the point. Later, we will see that the media may be consciously conservative at the highest management levels, while being institutionally or bureaucratically moderate at the lower reporting levels. *What matters in any event is that the media fail to wield their enormous potential power for criticism and expression of grass-roots sentiments, while compounding the sway of the powers that be by rationalizing most of the established interests and policies of the day.*

As a result of the "reality filtering" done by the news media, public policy debates are presented in narrow, predictable terms, not because those terms are useful or realistic ways to understand what is going on, but because they reflect the values and beliefs that America is thought to stand for. *Journalists, therefore, are not perceived as being autocratic in the ways they open and close the information gate, because they do it quietly and in keeping with "Middle-American" norms about who ought to be given voice in the public record, and what they should be allowed to say.*

Before applauding the press for single-handedly preserving American myth and tradition, we should ask what the consequences are of a gatekeeper who pays more attention to the outward appearance of those passing through the information gate than to who or what may be disguised beneath the cloak of propriety and tradition. A good gatekeeper should pay attention to who really "goes there" in the name of familiar, invited guests. *In its unstated mission to preserve the hallowed values and beliefs of the country, the press may have lost its critical eye for judging whether or not there is any substance behind the familiar political symbols.* Surely one of the most important traditions in America is that of criticizing the government and the governors. The founders of the country regarded the press as essential to making sure that basic values were not just empty images.

The tradition of a critical gatekeeper goes back to the trial of Peter Zenger in the year 1735 and the political battles over the Alien and Sedition acts around 1800. At one time, the idea of "afflicting the comfortable and comforting the afflicted" was not just a self-serving slogan. *With the rise of a commercial mass media, the press may have abdicated its most important political function: to keep the flow of ideas moving in many directions and to make sure there is reason to take politicians at their word. The existence of a "passive press" reduces the quality of political life for the majority on the outside who are forced to accept what they are told. And it is doubtful that anyone, including the powerful minority, is better off in the long run living in a world where decisions and actions are cloaked in imagery, and more energy is spent maintaining illusions than understanding reality.* There is no doubt that the modern press would take a lot of heat if it acted on its own traditional ideals, but nobody said that being a critical gatekeeper would be an easy or appreciated task.

What to Do with a Nearsighted Gatekeeper

Rather than continue blaming apathy and "human nature" for the ills of democracy, it makes more sense to define the problem in terms that permit a solution. Since the press plays an identifiable role in the flow of information and ideas, we can point to concrete institutional changes that could alter the political balance before the people become relegated to permanent spectators in their own life drama. For example, American society is the most advanced in the world in terms of its *capability* for placing useful information at our fingertips and for helping people to use that information by developing creative schemes for direct, democratic participation. If the average household watches eight hours of TV a day, isn't it conceivable that people would give up, say, an hour of sitcoms and soaps for a chance to participate *meaningfully* in the decisions that affect their lives? The key word here is "meaningfully." It is no wonder that public affairs programs, as currently presented, generate little audience interest. They are not connected in any obvious ways to political action. Why should people gather information they can't use?

It is simply too convenient to condemn the public for ignorance and apathy. Until they are given a realistic opportunity to participate actively in their own governance, nobody can say what the people are capable of. The truly revolutionary idea of trusting the people with the responsibility for their own government has remained in the wings of American politics, untried and untested, since Thomas Jefferson proposed it over 200 years ago. Now, with the advent of home computers, video display systems, and satellite-fed technology, we have the capability to put democracy to a serious test.

Unfortunately, in place of a crusading press pushing for democratic reforms, we have a media establishment that promotes popular ignorance by producing news with an ignorant public in mind. The vicious circle of ignorance and apathy will not be broken until journalism rises above "lowest-common-denominator" news. Chapter 2 explores the information biases in the news that set the daily tone for American politics by defining the who, what, where, when, how, and why of political life. These biases must be reckoned with by scholar, citizen, and journalist alike if the balance of information power is to be tilted in favor of the people.

NOTES

1. The data on print media are from *Editor and Publisher International Yearbook: 1986* (New York: Editor and Publisher, 1986), "Ready Reckoner of Advertising Rates and Circulation." The data on broadcast media can be found in the *Statistical Abstract of the United States: 1986* (Washington, D.C.: U.S. Department of Commerce, 1986), p. 547.
2. From Linda Ellerbee, *"And So It Goes": Adventures in Television* (New York: Putnam, 1986). Quotation excerpted in a review by Neil Hickey, "Funny Business," *Columbia Journalism Review*, July/August 1986, p. 55.
3. See, for example, Jay G. Blumler and Denis McQuail, *Television in Politics: Its Uses and Influences* (Chicago: University of Chicago Press, 1969); Lee B.

Becker, "Two Tests of Media Gratifications: Watergate and the 1974 Election," *Journalism Quarterly* 53, no. 1 (1976): 26–31; Mark R. Levy, "Television News Uses: A Cross-National Comparison," *Journalism Quarterly* 55 (Summer 1978): 334–37; and Mark R. Levy, "Watching TV News as Para-Social Activity," *Journal of Broadcasting* 23 (Winter 1979): 69–80.

4. Eric Zorn, "The Specialized Signals of Radio News: Giving Listeners What They Want," *Washington Journalism Review*, June 1986, p. 32.

5. Based on marketing studies of TV news personalities reported in Gerald M. Goldhaber, "The Charisma Factor: Why Dan Rather May Be in Trouble," *TV Guide*, 2 May 1981, pp. 4–6.

6. Michael Massing, "CBS: Sauterizing the News. Go for the Moment! Get Out to the People! A Look at How Van Gordon Sauter Is Changing the News Agenda," *Columbia Journalism Review*, March/April 1986, p. 32.

7. See Desmond Smith, "You Can Go Home Again: The New Attractions of Local News," *Washington Journalism Review*, June 1986, pp. 44–47.

8. *Ibid.*, p. 47.

9. Leo Bogart, "How U.S. Newspaper Content Is Changing," *Journal of Communication*, Spring 1985, pp. 82–90.

10. Edwin Diamond, "The Folks in the Boondocks: Challenging a Journalistic Myth," *Columbia Journalism Review*, November/December 1973, p. 58.

11. A fascinating historical study showing how news events can take on a social life of their own is John William Ward's *Andrew Jackson: Symbol for an Age* (New York: Oxford University Press, 1955).

12. See Bogart, "How U.S. Newspaper Content Is Changing."

13. Quoted in Don Fry, ed., *Believing the News* (St. Petersburg, Fla.: The Poynter Institute, 1985), pp. 226, 229.

14. *Ibid.*, pp. 17–18.

15. *Ibid.*, p. 166.

16. *Ibid.*, p. 167.

17. *Ibid.*, p. 171.

18. *Ibid.*

19. Noam Chomsky, "All the News That Fits," *Utne Reader*, February/March 1986, p. 56.

20. *Ibid.*, p. 65.

CHAPTER 2

News Content:
Messages for the Masses

> "Eyewitless" news contains little in the way of useful information...of ongoing, integrated issues and concerns, of attempts to dig beneath the surface for more enduring truths and subtle shadings—a twinkie of the airwaves.
>
> —*Ron Powers*

This chapter takes a close look at the problems with news content. *The specific concern here is with information biases that make news hard to use either as a guide to political action or as an aid to seeing the "big picture" in which daily events take place.* Most debates about journalistic bias are concerned with the question of ideology—namely, whether the news has a liberal or conservative, a Democratic or Republican, drift. Let us concede at the outset that the media probably do suffer some ideological drift from time to time. Not only is it hard to set exactly the same tone for both sides of every story, but the political coloring of the news tends to drift along with climates of opinion in the country. Thus, journalism of the late 1960s had a slightly liberal flavor, while the news of the 1980s followed, to a degree, the national swing to the right. One problem with looking for ideological bias in reporting is that by the time enough cases have been documented to warrant a charge against the media, the trend is likely to be drifting back in the other direction again.

An even bigger problem with allegations of ideological bias is that they are exaggerated by the ideology of the beholder. Many liberals see the media as inherently conservative, even during periods like the 1960s when a glimmering of socially critical journalism emerged. Similarly, many conservatives are convinced that "media liberalism" consistently spills over into news content. Criticism from conservative media watch groups like "Accuracy in Media" has never been stronger than during the 1980s, a period in which spokespersons for conservative causes have gained a great deal of media access. In general, opinion research shows that perceptions of media bias correspond to one's own political bias, with people in the middle (roughly half of the population) seeing the media as generally fair, while those on the left (roughly one quarter of the public) complain that the news is too conservative, and those on the right (another quarter of the public) think the news has a left-leaning bias. Overall, slightly under half (45 percent) of the public feel that news organizations introduce political bias into reporting, and slightly over half (53 percent) feel that the media tend to favor one side over the other in dealing with political and social issues.[1]

Around and around the debate over ideological bias goes, and wherever it stops there is a loud chorus of disagreement. Indeed, the debate cannot be resolved satisfactorily as long as the parties on both sides hold their own different ideological biases. Meanwhile, other, more fundamental information biases in the news are going neglected and undetected. Whether the media are drifting left or right, it is possible that there are some underlying information problems that remain constant across all political shadings. *A more sensible approach to news bias is to look for these universal information problems that hinder the efforts of most citizens, whatever their ideology, to take part in political life.*

Even when we lift the veil of ideology, it still may be difficult to see the fundamental obstacles that news information presents for democracy. In addition to their ideological blinders, many people carry at least a trace of the mythology, learned as children, that the free press in America is the cornerstone of democracy. Our expectations and idealizations of the quality of public information are rather high. Most of us grew up with history books full of journalistic heroism in the name of truth and free speech. We learned that the American Revolution was inspired by the political rhetoric of the underground press and by printers' effective opposition to the British Stamp Act. The lesson from the trial of Peter Zenger has endured through time: The Truth Is Not Libelous. The goal of these and many other history-book journalists was as unswerving as it was noble: to guarantee for the American people the most accurate, comprehensive, critical, coherent, illuminating, and independent reporting of political events.

Yet Peter Zenger would probably not recognize, much less feel comfortable working in, a modern news organization. Like it or not, the news has become, increasingly, a mass-produced entity, bearing little resemblance to history-book images. Mass communication technologies beginning with the wire services and progressing to satellite feeds have combined with corporate profit motives to create a new form of "lowest-common-denominator" information, lacking both critical perspectives and coherent organizing principles. The illusion of coherence and relevance has been achieved in part, as described in the chapter 1, through packaging the news in emotionally appealing formats geared to the psychological tastes of different segments of the market audience.

The implication of this introductory discussion is that we must look beyond ideology, beyond mythology, and beyond the packaging of our favorite news program or paper in order to see the remarkable similarities that run through most mass media content. In particular, there are four characteristics of news that stand out as reasons why public information in the United States does not advance the cause of democracy.

FOUR INFORMATION BIASES IN THE NEWS: AN OVERVIEW

First of all, the mass media almost always retreat from opportunities to explain the power structures and political processes that lie behind the issues that pop, mysteriously, onto the public agenda. In place of power and process, the media concentrate on the people engaged in political combat over the issues. It is easy for the news audience to react for or against the actors in these *personalized*, emotional human-interest stories. When people are invited to "take the news personally," they can find a certain private, emotional meaning in it. However, the meanings inspired by personalized news are not the shareable, critical, analytical meanings on which a healthy democracy thrives. *Personalized news encourages people to take an egocentric rather than a socially concerned view of political problems. Moreover, the focus on attractive political personalities encourages a passive attitude among a public inclined to let those personalities do their thinking and acting for them.* In general, the media preference for personalized human-interest news creates a "forest-for-the-trees" information bias in which it becomes hard to see the big (institutional) picture that lies beyond the multitude of actors crowding center stage to catch the eye of the news camera.

Compounding the information bias of personalization is a second reporting tendency, which involves selecting those aspects of events most easily *dramatized* in short, capsule "stories." *With actors at their center, news dramas emphasize crisis over continuity, the present over the past or future, and the impact of scandals on personal political careers rather than on the institutions of government that harbored them.* Lost in the news drama—"melodrama" is the more appropriate term—are the persistent problems of our time, such as inequality, hunger, resource waste, staggering levels of military spending, and political oppression. Under its current information format, the news simply cannot play the people's advocate, lobbying governments for relief from the wearying problems that burden large numbers of people who currently have no public voice.

Serious though these problems may be, they just aren't dramatic enough on a day-to-day level to make the news.

Chronic conditions become news only when they reach astounding levels that threaten large-scale cataclysm through famine, depression, war, or revolution. The "crisis cycle" portrayed in the news is classic dramatic fare, with rising action, falling action, sharply drawn characters, and, of course, plot resolutions. By its very definition, crisis is something that will subside and be resolved, for better or worse. Unfortunately the crisis cycles that characterize our news system only reinforce the popular impression that high levels of human difficulty are inevitable, and therefore acceptable. Crises are resolved when situations return to "manageable" levels of difficulty. Seldom if ever are underlying problems treated and eliminated at their source. The news is certainly not the cause of these problems, but it could become part of the solution if it dropped dramatic coverage of symptoms in favor of continuing illumination of causes.

The emphasis on personal and dramatic qualities of events feeds into a third information characteristic of the news: the isolation of stories from each other so that information in the news becomes *fragmented* and hard to assemble into a big picture. *The fragmentation of information begins by emphasizing individual actors over the political contexts in which they operate. Fragmentation is then heightened by the use of dramatic formats that turn events into self-contained, isolated happenings. News stories would become undramatic and too complicated to grasp if their plots were strained to include multiple issues and explanations of larger institutional processes. The fragmentation of information is exaggerated still further by the severe space limits imposed by nearly all media for fear of boring readers and viewers with too much "information." Thus, the news comes to us in sketchy dramatic capsules that make it difficult to see the connections across issues or even to follow the development of a particular issue over time.*

Passing for depth and coherence in this system of personalized, dramatized, and fragmented information is a fourth journalistic tendency to seek out the reassuring, authoritative voices of officials who offer *normalized* interpretations of the otherwise threatening and confusing events in the news. *Official responses to the mysterious crises and problems of society tell us that things will return to "normal" again, if only we will trust those officials to act in our interest. And when officials are unable to establish the right tone of normalcy, journalists are ever-ready to raise the question of alarm ("Should we be alarmed about this?")—a question sure to trigger an outpouring of reassurance from officials eager to seem in charge. The scripts of both official statements and reporter-provided accounts in the news are filled with popular beliefs, values, and norms (expectations) about what the problem or crisis is all about, what caused it, and what actions are appropriate to return the situation to normal.*

The assurances that leap from the tongues of those in power not only personalize journalistic accounts but provide basic dramatic themes at the same time. Among the most common story lines used by journalists is one that goes like this: "Something has gone awry in the world today, but officials are hopeful that the situation will return to normal soon. And now, for a report from the scene, we go to. . . ." The plot thickens when different officials disagree about what measures are appropriate to the restoration of normalcy. But the outcome is almost always the same: Some official action wins out, the day is saved, and the story ends with a return to "normal." As crisis symptoms subside (as they always will, one way or another), popular tolerance for an "acceptable" level of social distress masks the underlying causes of problems, and the news returns the world's problems to their "normal" state: chronic-but-unreported. This normalizing cycle in the news invites people to draw the conclusion that "the system worked." In fact, it is really the mass information system that worked dramatically to normalize another crisis and sweep another unsolved problem from the stage of public attention—at least until the next crisis leaps from the headlines and sets another normalizing information cycle in motion.

It is no wonder, given this information system, that people are unprepared for the steady stream of "bad news" that pours forth from the media. Bad news is, after all, surprising: "Didn't we just solve this problem?" Normal news thus sows the seeds of its own discontent. If people accept the dramatic resolution to a news story, they implicitly adopt at the same time the expectation that things have somehow returned to "normal" and are OK. This expectation helps the audience resolve the immediate news drama, but it is poor preparation when the same or a similar issue resurfaces later.

People thus have good psychological justification for being angry at the media for reporting so much "bad news." However, the popular plea for the media to report more "good news" is a thoroughly misguided solution to the bad-news problem. In the end, more good news would only create more unrealistic expectations about a "normal world"—expectations that would bring even greater shock and despair when upsetting realities became unavoidable. A more sensible prescription for good—meaning high-quality—news would involve replacing the current system of *personalized, dramatized, fragmented,* and *normalized* information with perspectives that were more *institutional, analytical, historical,* and *critical* in their orientation. Under such information conditions people might be better equipped to understand the problems of society and more motivated toward (perhaps even insistent on) participating in their solution. In such a world, bad news might turn into good because problems were actually being addressed and resolved in realistic ways.

FOUR INFORMATION BIASES IN THE NEWS: AN IN-DEPTH LOOK

These criticisms are not new. In fact, there is a sizable literature that reads like an inventory of problems and failings with the news.[2] Fortunately, a blow-by-blow review of this literature is unnecessary due to the remarkable degree of consensus among the critics. Virtually all the reported failings of the news can be summarized under the four general categories introduced above. According to the majority of the critics, mass media news tends to be *personalized, dramatized, fragmented,* and *normalized.* It is important to be able to recognize each of these news characteristics in action.

Personalized News

Following the overview above, *personalized news* can be defined as *the journalistic bias that gives preference to the individual actors and human-interest angles in events while downplaying institutional and political considerations that establish the social contexts for those events.* Getting people to tune into issues on a purely egocentric level may be worse than no public involvement at all. The nightly glimpses of powerful figures and factions locked in mortal combat directs public attention to the surfaces of politics: the scandals, careers, personal wins and losses, prestige and status, and the mysterious congressional vote tallies that determine the new rules we must obey if we wish to continue playing the political game. Some of this information in the news (like new rules of the game) is not trivial. What is missing is the context beyond the actors that would help us understand what it all means and what to do about it.

If they operated under a general commitment to critical reporting and continuing public education, journalists would minimize attention to the individual power struggles, the personal motives and fortunes of leaders, and the human crisis or disaster area of the moment. Instead, news would report on the evolution of issues, the powerful institutions involved, and the factions—like lobby groups, special interests, and powerful bureaucracies—with motives that might be hard to reconcile with the public interest. A public-interest media would stop inviting people, through personalized news, to take distant and persuasive politicians at their word. Journalism for democracy would challenge people to think about any values, interests, and consequences that the newsmakers might have neglected to mention in their prepared news releases.

Despite its superficiality, personalized news is popular. This doesn't mean that different and more relevant forms of news wouldn't be popular also; it just means that the media have settled on a formula that is popular yet not terribly helpful to the people who consume it. Since personalized news is popular, it must be understood as a factor shaping the consciousness of the American people. *What accounts for the popularity of personalized news?* The same thing that makes it so dangerous to public political health: The focus on individual actors who are easy to identify with positively or negatively invites members of the news audience to project their own private feelings and fantasies directly onto public life. Mass journalism, both broadcast and print, appeals to the ego and conditioned emotions first and to the intellect and critical capacities second, if at all. For many people, it is hard to deny the attraction of a direct, personal, emotionally charged appeal. Direct emotional bonding with distant political figures can result in highly egocentric (not to mention inarticulate and ethnocentric) views of the world. *The news gives people a "me-first" view of the world in which "my" well-being, "my" group and "my" country are emphasized over social realities that differ from one's own. Even the "two-sided" format used in most reporting usually offers one side that is much "closer to home" than the other.* Since the news provides little help in bridging the gap between conflicting (or simply new) realities, the path to easy understanding is to pick the reality that most closely resembles one's initial beliefs and prejudices. When the ego is thus engaged, it is easy to ignore or rationalize any facts or moral claims that don't fit the prior images that people carry around.

The personal emotional appeal of a news story can be magnified further by the use of story angles based on psychological themes of security and reassurance. The news is filled with images of threat, fear, conflict, uncertainty, catastrophe, surprise, and reassurance. The use of such psychological themes represents the implicit reporting policy of most news organizations. So important is the private, individualized appeal of the news that it has even been written down as formal policy in at least one organization, as indicated by this memo from an executive producer of ABC News to his staff:

> The Evening News, as you know, works on elimination. We can't include everything. As criteria for what we do include, I suggest the following for a satisfied viewer: (1) "Is my world, nation, and city safe?" (2) "Is my home and family safe?" (3) "If they are safe, then what has happened in the past 24 hours to help make that world better?" (4) "What has happened in the past 24 hours to help us cope better?"[3]

The personalized content of the news fits comfortably with the personalized styles of news delivery discussed in chapter 1. In fact, the news is becoming increasingly like an intimate conversation between friends, where a message geared to personal concerns is delivered by a caring and respected messenger. It is no accident that a key ingredient of "life-style news" is the image of the columnist, reporter, or anchor who delivers the story. This trend toward personalized reporting is likely to grow as the media rely more and more on the advice of professional news consultants. These "news doctors," like Philip McHugh of the influential firm McHugh and Hoffman, regard personalization of both content and delivery as the best way to sell the news: "There has to be an emphasis on human interest and human beings. You have to have an anchorman who can establish rapport with the audience. . . . It takes a very special kind of personality."[4]

Examples of personalized coverage of events can be found in virtually any paper, magazine, or broadcast. Consider, for instance, a *Wall Street Journal* report on a government decision to terminate a large-scale public employment program. Despite the numerous "big-picture" social, political, and economic themes that could have been used to frame the report, the opening paragraph of the story was this one:

> SAN FRANCISCO — As the chill, first light breaks on a Haight-Ashbury curbside, a street sweeper stops to gather the gutter's yield of leaves, litter, and dog waste. "This job's the best thing ever happened to a poor man," he says. "It's feeding babies. When it's over, I'll be putting cardboard in my little girl's shoes, like my mama did me."[5]

Although there is a journalistic law that stories should be organized with the most important information first and the least important facts last, the article made no mention of large-scale social, political, or economic implications of the program cuts until paragraphs 8, 9, and 10, and these brief passages were followed immediately by a return to the heart-rending story of the street sweeper's fate. Are we to infer from the proliferation of such stories that personal angles have replaced broader concerns as the most important information in the news?

Personalizing the Reagan Presidency. Personalized treatments are not reserved just for obscure events that people would otherwise have trouble relating to. The coverage of even the most important political events suggests that personal themes have indeed attained first place on the list of reporting priorities. As Paletz and Entman observed, "Prime news generally involves prominent, powerful people in action, or, more desirable from the media's point of view, in conflict."[6] A case in point is press coverage of Ronald Reagan's years in office. From the outset of his presidency, Reagan initiated many domestic and foreign policies of great national and international importance. However, the news formula that quickly emerged in most of the stories about those historic actions was the theme of whether Reagan was personally "winning" or "losing" in his battles with Congress, the bureaucracy, business leaders, and foreign governments. This theme reduced momentous political issues to engrossing but trivial questions about Reagan's personal power, his political "scorecard," and his risks of public embarrassment. The personal focus on Reagan so dominated the news that he was able to manipulate and enhance his news coverage simply by emphasizing his personal stake in policy decisions. When he began defining his policies as tests of personal power, the news was locked into a vicious cycle of the sort that emerged during the Iranian hostage crisis discussed in chapter 1: A news theme had become artificially injected into real life, thereby creating the illusion that the news was, indeed, mirroring the real world.

An early example of personalization based on the "winning-losing" theme was the reporting of Reagan's controversial "AWACS deal." AWACS is an acronym for a sophisticated U.S. Air Force radar and battle command aircraft. The Reagan administration proposed selling this plane, along with a large package of weaponry, to Saudi Arabia. The Senate had to approve such a sale, and many senators raised objections about selling sophisticated military equipment to an unpredictable nation in a volatile area of the world. There were, indeed, many serious political questions that could have dominated news coverage: Would the sale unbalance an already unstable region? How could the administration guarantee that the equipment would not be used for offensive purposes? Would the sale alienate Israel, whose cooperation was vital to American efforts to settle long-standing disputes in the region? Was this all a thinly disguised power ploy designed to gain future U.S. control of precious oil fields?

Although some attention was paid to these important questions, the bulk of press coverage quickly fell into personalized formulas. To begin with, the story became reduced to the "AWACS affair," even though AWACS was just one part of a larger arms package and even though the major political issues went well beyond the sale of a particular kind of military equipment. The focus on the fate of AWACS fit nicely with the personal theme of the president winning or losing, since an eventual vote in the Senate would decide the sale of the airplane. Focusing on the "up" or "down" vote allowed the news plot to pit the president directly against powerful opponents in the Senate. Thus the distorted emphasis on the AWACS vote in the Senate conveniently narrowed the whole issue to its purest personal form: the clash of individual power and human egos at the highest levels of government. The measure of this power and status was the simplistic matter of how the Senate would vote.

The emergence of this classic news formula was no accident. Long before AWACS came to its dramatic conclusion with a narrow, eleventh-hour Reagan victory, a sage Washington observer had predicted that the larger issues would be lost in the preoccupation with the personalities involved. Peter Osnos, then national editor for the *Washington Post*, saw the early signs that AWACS had all the makings of a "Great Washington Drama."[7] It involved powerful figures locked in mortal combat. Power and reputations were on the line. There would be fascinating political maneuvering to report as the issue made its way through the formal processes of government. Moreover, there would be a guaranteed moment of climax (the vote) in which either possible outcome would be equally exciting (namely, Reagan would either "win" or "lose").

True to its self-fulfilling form, the AWACS saga dominated news headlines for over a month. The story gained prominence as it appeared that Reagan would lose his first political battle. However, in a last-minute session of wheeling and dealing, the President put everything on the line—and won! Not surprisingly, the last installment of this news serial placed the overwhelming emphasis on the "personal victory" theme. Here is a sampling of how various news outlets presented the last chapter of the story:

A local TV newscast from a big-city CBS affiliate station:
Local anchor opens program: *"Good Evening. President Reagan's AWACS deal gets Senate approval."*

Cut to the program introduction and return to the anchor: *"Now it's on to the next battle for the Reagan administration. President Reagan has won his toughest battle since taking office. It was a down-to-the-wire, come-from-behind win. . . ."*

Cut to a report from CBS national correspondent Leslie Stahl, who does a voice-over report on a videotape showing Reagan's top political aides tallying the votes during the Senate roll call. She tells the viewers that the top aides who engineered the big win had vowed not to "gloat" over the victory. The report ended with Stahl saying that Reagan's first act after the victory was to call his wife Nancy and tell her the good news.

Cut to a report on the favorable impact the sale would have on a local aircraft company.

Cut to a network report showing a parallel negative effect on the British aircraft business that had hoped to sell its plane to Saudi Arabia if the AWACS deal fell through.

Cut (at last, and, therefore, least) to CBS Israeli correspondent Bob Fall reporting briefly from Jerusalem to say that the effects of the AWACS sale on U.S.-Israeli relations could be negative.[8]

NBC network television 9 P.M. evening news update following the final game of the world series:
Anchor opens with a recap of the just-completed, come-from-behind series victory of the Los Angeles Dodgers.

After announcing himself as John Shubek reporting from L.A., he continues: *"Another Californian came from behind to win a big one today. The Californian, of course, is Ronald Reagan, who received a vote of 52–48 from the Senate on the AWACS arms sale to Saudi Arabia."*[9]

ABC network television "Nightline," 11:30 P.M.:
Program opens with dramatic close-up of the host, Ted Koppel, who announces, *"The President wins on the AWACS sale, but what happens next?"*

Following the introduction of the program, the host returns with: *"Good evening. The President put his own prestige on the line and he won. He lobbied hard all day with key senators. . . ."*

Shots of senators who changed their minds on the issue. Followed by shots of Senate Minority Leader Alan Cranston on the phone *"trying hard to hold his opposition coalition together."*

Cut to White House with shots of aides tallying the votes.

Cut back to the Senate chamber with comments from elated supporters and dejected opponents after the vote.

Cut to interview with a senator who stresses that he voted for the president, not for AWACS.

Finally, the host asks the question *"What next?"* and introduces a series of political observers who discuss the political consequences of the arms sale.[10]

A big-city newspaper:
Banner headline: PRESIDENT WINS AWACS.

Opening two paragraphs of story under headline:

"WASHINGTON — President Reagan, displaying extraordinary muscle, scored a major foreign policy victory yesterday as the Senate voted 52–48 to allow the sale of AWACS radar planes and other military hardware to Saudi Arabia.

The tally that defeated a resolution to disapprove the $8.5 billion package represented a stunning turnaround of Senate opinion. Friend and foe alike said Reagan's personal persuasion was the crucial ingredient in building the winning coalition behind the largest single foreign military sale in U.S. history."[11]

The "winner" theme continued to dominate press coverage throughout the Reagan years. Well into Reagan's second term *Newsweek* published a curious analysis piece under the heading: "Is This Any Way to Make Foreign Policy?"[12] The question referred specifically to the president's most recent "victory" over Congress—this time a twelve-vote margin of victory in the House of Representatives on a funding bill to continue the U.S. "Contra" war against Nicaragua. The writer, Gloria Borger, expressed concern that the emphasis on winning and losing might make it hard for Americans to see that U.S. foreign policy was in a shambles. Making too much of narrow personal victories distracted public attention from the weakness of bipartisan support and the virtual absence of well-articulated goals behind administration maneuvering abroad. The article also expressed concern that the United States was dangerously out of step with its allies on many issues and that Congress seemed to have abdicated any leadership role in foreign policy to the White House. These important questions all seemed to be driven off the public agenda by the national preoccupation with one man's personal scorecard.

While the *Newsweek* article raised a number of thoughtful and important concerns about the pitfalls of personalized politics, it is curious that the editors and writers for *Newsweek* did not go the obvious extra step to ask: Who, if not the magazine itself (along with the rest of the mass media), had created the misleading illusion of a president presiding over a "winning" foreign policy? Perhaps this question would have been too painful to answer, as the editors needed only turn to the prior page and read their own coverage of the "contra war" in Nicaragua. Beneath a headline that read "Rekindling the Magic: Reagan Wins a Congressional Victory to Aid the Contras" was a story with this opening paragraph:

> The cause was a matter of deep conviction, his own credibility was on the line—and Ronald Reagan, defying the widespread belief that he must sooner or later succumb to lame-duckery, pulled out all the stops. In a lobbying blitz targeted on 50 wavering congressmen, the president worked his septuagenarian magic to build a decisive victory on what may be the single most controversial foreign-policy issue of his administration: by 12 votes, the House of Representatives approved U.S. military aid to the contra rebels for the first time. "His optimism and his commitment are simply contagious," a senior White House staffer marveled. "Not a bad week's work for an old lame duck," another aide chortled. "Maybe one of these days he'll fall apart, but I wouldn't start laying any bets just yet."[13]

It is distressing that *Newsweek* did not see that at least some of the "foreign policy" problem it described was of its own making. Such blindness is an indicator of a press trapped by a reporting formula that introduces recognized defects into the news, but that is, at the same time, too sacred to change. *Indeed, the media may have created a monster in devoting so much attention to the movements and pronouncements of one actor.* An ABC News vice president once lamented to this author the costs, in resources and lost coverage of other issues, of the "obligatory" practice of keeping a full-time "body watch" on the president. At the time, there were seventeen television news crews and many more newspaper and radio correspondents assigned full-time to cover the resident of 1600 Pennsylvania Avenue. With such a commitment of resources, something the president says or does each day, no matter how trivial, is likely to make the news.

Personalized News as Corporate Policy: The Case of the CBS Evening News. When the journalistic imperative is to report something about the person, or to find the human-interest angle no matter what the larger political significance, the news has left the realm of information that people "need to know" and entered the business of psychological massage. As the line between news and entertainment, reality and ego, dissolves, it is enough for news reports to create emotional "moments" of unknown significance. As mentioned in chapter 1, former CBS News President Van Gordon Sauter steered his organization toward a more personalized, emotional format for the 1980s. The face-lift at CBS was based on his theory of the "news moment." According to Sauter, "Moments relate to how you tell stories. Not every story has a moment, but some stories do. If you're able to seize the right moment of video, if you capture that quality that makes a story live in people's minds and memory, then you have a moment."[14]

Sauter lamented the fact that CBS had missed "the moment" in its coverage of a memorial ceremony for American troops killed in a Christmas Eve air crash:

> There was a scene where Mr. and Mrs. Reagan turn down the aisle. Mrs. Reagan dabs a tear from her eye. It was a remarkably telling moment. It said so much about the couple, about the moment. And we missed it. Then Mrs. Reagan leaned over to embrace two young children. It was a marvelous moment—and we missed it. It was very annoying. Here was a story filled with emotion, and we failed adequately to capture it.[15]

It is remarkable that Sauter criticized his organization for insufficiently personalized coverage in light of how CBS actually portrayed the event. As the news cameras closed in on the president, a choir in the background sang "Amazing Grace," and CBS anchor Dan Rather pronounced the following solemn words: "In the experiment that is America, a president, any president, is many men—head of state, head of government, commander-in-chief, and, in days such as this, comforter and head of the national family."[16]

Personalized news can be powerful and moving and, at the same time, pointless and uninformative. Lost in the emotional shuffle is journalistic responsibility to stir the conscience and intellect of the audience with information they ought to have about the world. The theory of the news moment assumes that what people "need" is emotional release, not information. A CBS senior producer recalls the early days of Sauter's regime at CBS: "Sauter would look at a story and say, 'Why should any American care about that?' And we'd say, 'Because it's important.' And he'd ask, 'Why?' If it were a foreign story like a parliamentary election in England, we'd say that people should know about foreign affairs. And he'd persist, asking, 'But why do they need to know about *this?*' "[17] And so, the themes of news coverage are often removed from the political issues at hand. News themes tend to heighten the emotional impact of the moment by emphasizing opportunities for emotional projection over opportunities for critical thinking and action.

The Political Effects of Personalized News. In the meantime, somewhere beyond the moment, there is a reality being forged in the world, and it is likely to be poorly understood and monitored. The greatest risk of an information system like ours is that people remain largely unaware of what they are doing and are therefore unable to detect or correct their mistakes.

Perhaps in ten or twenty years a few students of history will argue that it was a mistake to sell arms to both sides in the volatile Middle East. Perhaps other historians will conclude that it was a mistake not to pursue a course of reconciliation with Nicaragua. But such voices could have been heard at the time these fateful actions were taken. They just didn't have any institutional standing in an illusory world of winners and losers. In effect, these voices of caution "lost" the news debate, and so they just didn't count at the time. Meanwhile, the people who backed the "winner" became caught up in the moment, marching blindly to an unknown destiny.

The tendency to personalize the news also gives the news audience a distorted view of power and its political consequences. As Paletz and Entman have concluded: "Power seems to be understood in a limited sense by the media....Stories emphasize the surface appearances, the furious sounds and fiery sights of battle, the well-known or colorful personalities involved—whatever is dramatic. Underlying causes and actual impacts are little noted nor long remembered."[18] Without a grasp of power structures, it is virtually impossible to understand how the political system really works. As a result, the political world becomes a mystical realm populated by actors who either have the political "force" on their side or do not.

The absence of attention to power further encourages the audience to abandon political analysis in favor of casting their political fates with the hero of the moment. *The world of personalized politics is thus a fantasy world.* Like any fantasy world of play, sport, or fiction, it can involve people intensely on the basis of catharsis, escape, hope, or sheer entertainment. Unfortunately, the world of personalized politics is one in which meaningful political understanding and effective political access are limited severely. Aided by the news, American politics is a world in which today's heroes are tomorrow's fools. The primary substance in this world is the occasional moment when the public rises up and banishes the latest fool to make way for the newly elected hero.

The news fantasy offers us a broad cast of characters with whom we can establish vicarious psychological relationships: from the president to the people in the street; teachers, lawyers, doctors, factory workers, criminals, terrorists; friends and enemies, rich and poor, men and women, black and white. It is not, however, the same cast of characters we are likely to meet in real life. We are likely, for example, to see more men in the news than women, more rich than poor, many more terrorists and criminals than we will ever encounter in real life, and far more white, professional, well-educated spokespeople than exist in any random sample of society. *Thus, the social world presented in the news is anything but a dispassionate bird's-eye view of social reality. It is a view from "Middle America" with preference given to white, articulate, successful men. It is a world colored by an almost obsessive fear of crime, communism, and terrorism. Above all, it is a social world in which the first and last words are usually granted to public officials who are implicitly portrayed as representing "the people." Rather than challenging the fears and fantasies of "Middle America," personalized news plays right into them.*

Dramatized News

The potential for drama is a virtual guarantee that an event will become a major news story. *It is no secret that reporters and editors search for events with dramatic properties and then emphasize those properties in their reporting.* Consider, for example, the following policy memo from the executive news producer of a major television network to his editors and reporters:

> Every news story should, without any sacrifice of probity or responsibility, display the attributes of fiction, of drama. It should have structure and conflict, problem and denouement, rising action and falling action, a beginning, a middle, and an end. These are not only the essentials of drama; they are the essentials of narrative.[19]

The weight of such evidence has led Paletz and Entman to conclude that "drama is a defining characteristic of news. An event is particularly newsworthy if it has some elements of a dramatic narrative....American officials held hostage in the far-off but journalistically accessible land of Iran provide a particularly strident example."[20] Indeed, the hostage crisis is a good example of an event that was the object of sustained news coverage because it contained so many dramatic angles, almost all of which involved personalized themes and plots.

Dramatized news fits neatly with the tendency toward personalized information discussed above. Drama, after all, is the quintessential medium for representing human conflict. Promising psychological release and resolution, drama satisfies emotional concerns aroused in the development of characters and plots. Although there are occasional "walk-on" roles for ordinary people, the majority of news plots revolve around a cast of familiar officials who become "star" actors. There is a clear selection mechanism at work when it comes to who "makes" the news on a regular basis and who doesn't.

The main principle involved with casting newsmakers in their nightly roles has more to do with their potential as dramatic actors than with any natural preeminence they may have in the political scheme of things. The president is the dramatic actor *par excellence*: There is only one of him, he is easy to keep track of, he can be typecast (e.g., as national "father figure" or as staunch defender of freedom against the Communist enemy), and he is easy to bring onto the scene on almost any political pretext. It is also helpful that presidents are usually willing to feed journalists as many dramatic "moments" as the latter are willing to broadcast and print. The justices of the Supreme Court, by contrast, make poor dramatic material largely because they are reluctant to walk onstage and play for the audience. The small number of articulate, often eccentric, justices would otherwise make wonderful dramatic characters. And there is no shortage of available information about court proceedings—it is just that the business of the Court, while important, doesn't fit the news bias toward personalized, dramatic coverage. If the media adopted another information format, the Court might share the front pages with the president—a place in the news more in keeping with the Court's place in the Constitutional scheme of things.

The House and Senate offer two more examples of political institutions with equal standing under the Constitution, but with grossly unequal coverage in the media. A handful of glamorous members of the Senate receive the lion's share of coverage, while the House remains largely a jumbled assembly of nameless seat holders. Washington press observer Stephen Hess has noted that

> the national press corps always has paid more attention to the Senate than to the House of Representatives. This is true even during periods . . . when the House of Representatives is the body in opposition to the president. (Richard Fenno, the eminent congressional scholar, has claimed that such attention is a manifestation of an "all-encompassing pro-senator bias on the part of the media.") The Senate has the constitutional right to reject a president's treaties and a president's nominees, appealing prospects to a press corps that loves controversy. The Senate is also the incubator of presidential candidates who are then automatically newsworthy. But most important, there are almost four-and-a-half times as many House members as there are senators. As philosopher David Sidorsky notes, the goal of journalists is to transpose "an inherently ambiguous and complex event into a short narrative that can be simply told, have a central plot, and retain the interest of the reader or viewer." It is easier and faster to build a coherent story with a smaller cast of characters. The House of Representatives is too much like *War and Peace*; the Senate is more on the scale of *Crime and Punishment*.[21]

These problems could, of course, be resolved if the media shifted their information focus from personalities to institutions and from melodrama to political analysis. We will explore such alternatives in later chapters, but for now the fact remains that journalists are locked into a reporting format that personalizes and dramatizes reality on its way from the "news scene" to the home audience. *Even when the chosen cast of characters fails to provide a suitable dramatic script, the journalist can choose from a stock of plot formulas that are used so often they become unconscious models for transforming ongoing life into "news reality."*

Robert Darnton, formerly a top reporter for the *New York Times*, told of his early problems as a journalist before he had learned to parse the dramatic highlights from the dull details of most stories. On one of his early assignments on the city desk of a small town, he wrote a story of a bicycle stolen from a paperboy. The story was rejected by his editor. A colleague suggested a much more dramatic version involving the boy's love for the bike, his trauma following the theft, and his Horatio Alger–like scheme to pay for a new one. Upon checking the new plot against the facts, Darnton decided that reality was close enough to the dramatized version to write the story—a story that was published in his paper.[22]

Lewis Lapham tells of similar experiences in his early days as a reporter. He notes how he marveled at the ease with which the senior reporter in the city room "wrote the accounts of routine catastrophe."[23] Finally, the old reporter's secret came out:

> In the drawer, with a bottle of bourbon and the manuscript of the epic poem he had been writing for twenty years, he kept a looseleaf notebook filled with stock versions of maybe fifty or sixty common newspaper texts. These were arranged in alphabetical order (fires, homicides, ship collisions, etc.) and then further divided into subcategories (fires—one-, two-, and three-alarm; warehouse; apartment building; etc.). The reporter had left blank spaces for the relevant names, deaths, numbers, and street addresses. As follows: "A ——— alarm fire swept through ——— at ——— St. yesterday afternoon, killing ——— people and causing ——— in property damage."[24]

This preoccupation with drama makes it hard to draw the line between journalists as reporters of fact and as creators of fiction. After making the observation that drama is a requirement for a major news story, Paletz and Entman go on to observe that some stories deficient in their own "high drama" may "have drama grafted on." "Journalists have been known to highlight if not concoct conflict and to find characters to symbolize its different sides. One reason: to attract an audience that is thought to have little patience for the abstract, the technical, the ambiguous, the un-controversial."[25]

We shall see later on that the public is not as simpleminded as the news experts assume. But this is beside the point. Nowhere in journalism texts is news defined as "whatever the audience wants, no matter how contrived or irrelevant." News, at least in theory, is supposed to inform people, not merely entertain them. The trend toward ever more dramatic and entertaining news may mean that a new form of mass communication is emerging. This evolving communication form may still go by the term "news," but it would be a serious mistake to assume that the traditional meanings of that term still apply.

Its unique blend of egocentrism and dramaturgy sets American journalism apart from other news systems, while setting Americans apart from the world they live in. Fiction writer Don DeLillo has captured the intense "psychodrama" aspect of foreign affairs coverage:

> I think it's only in a crisis that Americans see other people. It has to be an American crisis, of course. If two countries fight that do not supply the Americans with some precious commodity, then the education of the public does not take place. But when the dictator falls, when the oil is threatened, then you turn on the television and they tell you where the country is, what the language is, how to pronounce the names of the leaders, what the religion is all about, and maybe you can cut out recipes in the newspaper of Persian dishes. I will tell you. The whole world takes an interest in this curious way Americans educate themselves. TV. Look, this is Iran, this is Iraq. Let us pronounce the word correctly. E-ron. E-ronians. This is a Sunni, this is a Shi'ite. Very good. Next year we do the Philippine Islands, okay?[26]

The dramatization of events on the local scene has also gained increasing acceptance with the advent of "news doctors" who have promoted successfully the "action news" format. Virtually every major media market now has a news program called "Action News" or "Eyewitness News." Part of the action format calls for changes in the pace, delivery, scenery, and casting of the program. The action focus also makes direct inroads into story content and presentation. Consider, for example, the multitude of ways in which a routine event like a murder can be covered. At one extreme, a murder can be reported analytically in order to show how various aspects of the crime reflect social problems known to be linked with violent crime (problems such as poverty, family violence, unemployment, alcoholism, social instability, or prison system failures). Such reporting angles are seldom used in action news programs because they contradict the action philosophy of the news doctors. TV and radio stations in competitive media markets tend to follow the costly advice of news consultants like Frank Magid, who is reported to endorse the example of a murder story built around the dramatic effects of the camera retracing the route of the killer as he stalked his victim. Such reporting, according to Magid, has the virtue of making you feel "as if you were really there."[27]

As the preoccupation with action news grows, dramatization becomes a routine practice. For example, many stations have purchased expensive helicopters, airplanes, and remote transmission equipment to enhance their action news image. Such equipment usually becomes a visible feature of the station's news coverage, both to justify its expense and to ensure that the news program lives up to its action news advertising. As a result of this built-in bias in favor of action reporting, a new breed of news stories has begun to appear: stories that have less to do with the importance or meaning of an event than with the capacity to use costly equipment and convey images of drama and action.[28]

A case in point involves a big-city TV station that had consistently placed last in the local news-ratings battles. After hiring one of the news-doctor firms, the station adopted the action news format, complete with a new title, music, cast, set, helicopter, and an advertising campaign featuring, of course, dramatic shots of Channel 7's new "Chopper 7" going after the hottest news. The station quickly won first place in the ratings war but may have lost its chance to win any serious news game. Following the switch to action news, a typical evening's newscast began with the report that a U.S. Navy jet from a local base had crashed on a training flight across the country. Prior to the advent of action news, the story would never have opened a newscast (for a variety of reasons, among them that the crash involved no fatalities, it occurred on the other side of the country, the plane's base was some sixty miles from the city, and there had been no official Navy reaction to the crash). However, the incident created an opportunity to fly to the air base in Chopper 7 and transmit a live report from the runway where the plane had taken off earlier in the day. The report consisted of little more than meaningless but very dramatic shots of other planes taking off from the same airstrip. Despite the virtual absence of meaning in the story, the image created was a dramatic one, and the advertised promise of "action news" was once again fulfilled by having the lead story of the nightly news captioned with "Live Report from Chopper 7."

Pressures to win the "ratings wars" in local television markets flow from corporate offices to newsroom staffs. Even the most respected broadcast organizations may yield to temptations to increase audience and profits by dramatizing the news. Such dramatization blurs the distinction between news and entertainment while drawing reporters dangerously close to becoming actors in news events. TV journalists talk to us from high-tech choppers and sleek vans while rushing to news scenes where they may become the most animated actors present.

The dangers of a "make-it-dramatic" news policy are illustrated by coverage of a kidnapping in a small Pacific Northwest city. The largest and most respected broadcast news organization in the region assigned a crew from Seattle (about 80 miles away) to cover the incident. After days of dramatic plot development involving a distraught family, a helpless child victim, and a police manhunt, the climax occurred: The news crew intercepted a police broadcast suggesting that the money drop and victim release were in progress. The brightly marked news van raced to the scene, lights on and camera rolling. The intrusive television presence foiled the release of the child, and it was several days before another plan could be worked out with the kidnapper. The police and the victim's family were outraged by the journalists' bold entry into the scene of action. Questions were raised by the police about interference with police work, and the victim's family charged the news crew with disregard for the safety of the child. The news organization refused to address the issues of its coverage policies and, instead, fired the reporter and the assignment editor involved—a move that raised questions in the local journalistic community about whether company policy or employees should have been held responsible for the incident. One thing is clear from this example: The "Action News" imperative to put the viewer in the center of developing news drama brings journalists to the brink of becoming newsmakers.

As the preceding examples indicate, dramatized news is more melodrama than serious theater, more soap opera than Shakespeare. One does not leave the theater after watching *Hamlet* with the feeling that the poor guy was a real "loser." *If journalists pursued more serious dramatic techniques, the results might be less objectionable—and it certainly would not require the talents of a Shakespeare to make a big difference in the way the news selects and represents "reality." In legitimate drama, including many movies and popular novels, one is made aware of the role played by history, institutions, power, conflict, hidden interests, and accident in human affairs.* These and other factors are usually missed in news melodramas that locate human action in timeless webs of motive and intrigue. *The use of more serious dramatic techniques to introduce an occasional bit of analysis would constitute a major change in the news formula.* But as long as the journalistic imperative is to "capture the moment," simple melodrama will do.

The Political Effects of Dramatized News. The most obvious effect of dramatization is to trivialize news content. In place of unswerving attention to major events and problems, there is an increasing tendency to substitute manufactured drama. *Even when the drama may reflect an actual feature of the situation, as in the case of a congressional vote, the preoccupation with drama often distracts attention from any broad or enduring political significance the event may have had.* As Tuchman has observed so cogently, the action imperative feeds on events that have some rapidly developing action to report. As a result, chronic social problems and long-standing political issues often go unreported because they develop too slowly.[29] In these respects, dramatization compounds many of the same effects of personalization.

In addition to magnifying the pitfalls of personalization, dramatized news also creates a difficulty of its own. Because dramas are simple, easy to grasp, and offer a semblance of insight into the individual motives behind an action, they may give people a misguided sense of understanding the politics of a situation. People may think they understand an issue when, in fact, their understanding is based on a mixture of fantasy, fiction, and myth. Under these circumstances, according to Lapham, the political world becomes sheer abstraction, and

> we exhaust ourselves in passionate arguments about things that few of us have ever seen. We talk about the third world as if it were a real place rather than a convenient symbol, about the gears of the national economy as if it were as intelligible as the gears on a bicycle. People become lifelong enemies because they disagree about the military strategy of the Soviet Union; on further investigation it generally turns out that neither antagonist speaks Russian or has been to Russia.[30]

And so the old political conflicts that divide us are reinforced time and again by the formula dramas in the news. For example, when the Soviet nuclear power plant at Chernobyl suffered a major failure, there was a two-day period of chaos and confusion during which the Soviet government remained silent about the incident. There were many ways in which the media could have filled the silence. The early reports might have pointed out that a similar official silence occurred a few years before when a U.S. plant at Three Mile Island, Pennsylvania, leaked a radioactive cloud into the atmosphere. The "caution" in the American case was justified (by U.S. officials, of course) as a sensible response to a confusing situation that was difficult to assess in the first days. Responsible authorities said they wished to avoid a panic among the local population.

The "responsible authority" theme has a place in standard news scripts about the United States, but not about the USSR. The Soviet silence could not be presented as a reasonable period of fact-gathering in a difficult situation unless the media chose to break its old dramatic mold. True to predictable melodramatic form, the news was filled with American academic "experts" on Soviet behavior who explained that Soviet leaders routinely keep secrets from their own people. (What is gained from using the same stereotype to explain everything that another country does?) At the same time, the Soviet stereotype made it easy for people so disposed to breathe a sigh of relief that at least "we" don't live in a country like that. Since the parallels to the earlier U.S. incident were at odds with the emerging news drama, there were few references to Three Mile Island, except those made by U.S. officials who seized the opportunity to claim that the Three Mile Island "incident" was minor compared with the Soviet "disaster."

Once the door to the dramatic imagination was opened, the story continued to build to major proportions based on almost no documented facts. Soon, interviews with panicky U.S. citizens on the scene were augmented by the guesswork of an unnamed but "reliable" Kiev resident who placed the death toll at 2,000 or more. Early Soviet claims of only a handful of deaths were discounted under the stereotype of Russian deception. Yet, when the chaos began to be sorted out and U.S. medical personnel arrived on the scene to help out, it became clear that original Soviet death estimates were correct. Also confirmed was the possibility that the early situation was chaotic, and that Soviet officials, like U.S. authorities earlier, were ill prepared for it and wished to avoid panic. But by then the most dramatic days of the episode had been dominated by negative Soviet stereotypes. Moreover, the momentum of the anti-Russian melodrama carried throughout the remaining coverage; any signs of reasonable Soviet behavior were overshadowed by continuing negative speculation about things ranging from whether Soviet officials gave neighboring European countries adequate warning to whether precautions had been taken to keep contaminated milk off the market.

To return to the earlier question, what was gained from such dramatization? Very little, beyond giving the impression that the incident was a serious one—an impression that could have been created in other, more useful ways. For the rest, the information in the news served little purpose but to reinforce already negative impressions of the Soviets, an easy and unnecessary accomplishment. The most important question here is: "What was lost in presenting the information this way?" The answer to this question reveals what may be the most significant effect of news dramaturgy: the loss of useful information about important problems and, consequently, the loss of opportunities to see the world differently and more constructively. Lost in coverage of Chernobyl was the awareness of common, universal problems inherent in nuclear energy: the costs and risks of accidents, governmental preparedness, the benefits of civilian evacuation weighed against the likelihood of panic, and, perhaps above all, the importance of being able to share information and admit mistakes in a world atmosphere of sympathetic understanding, not stifling recrimination. The net effect of this news melodrama was to invite a sense of self-righteous condemnation of an enemy and its problems, while evoking equally complacent reassurance that we were somehow different. Under such circumstances, the next U.S. disaster will surely come as a surprise and fall quickly into another pattern of gripping but unhelpful melodrama. *This, ultimately, is what is wrong with the false sense of understanding conveyed by melodramatic news: It leaves us unprepared to deal effectively with problems.* The human capacity for planning, compromise, and sensitive analysis dissolves in the face of crisis, confrontation, and simplistic images.

In a world where political events are already far removed from the immediate experience of the average person, news dramas may push political consciousness permanently into the realm of fiction. This principle applies equally to coverage of foreign affairs and to issues seemingly much closer to home, like crime. For example, a big-city television station produced an expensive and much advertised documentary special on violent crime. The newspaper and television ads were dominated by the horror-movie use of the word "FEAR" that seared the page and dripped from the TV screen. True to its advertising, the program presented numerous examples of particularly violent crimes and showed how local people reacted to them. When the news adopts the images of popular drama and literature, it is little wonder that people begin to confuse reality and fantasy. As the following personal statement of a newspaper columnist indicates, our own lives become dramatized:

> Is it possible for a woman to walk alone, footsteps echoing through the night city, without feeling as if she's performing in a Brian DePalma movie? I can't. I've been conditioned into DePalma-style reflexes: twitches and eye rolls, in response to any unlikely sight or sound. What is that shape moving shadowlike in the alley? Is that a garbage bag or a man hunkered down in the service doorway? If I venture out alone after midnight, I enter an atmosphere as different from the everyday world as if I've gone under water. I can hear my own breathing, the hammering of my heart, the clickety-clack of my heels on the pavement. Unescorted, I am accompanied by fear, chaperoned by phantoms of my own imagination. Why has that man changed direction, just as I've turned the corner? Is that he now walking behind me?[31]

There is no doubt that crime is a fearful prospect when it strikes, but so are things like lung cancer, poverty, hunger, unemployment, homelessness, war, and many other social "disasters." *The news audience is exposed to more fearful images of some of these things than others—not because they are inherently more or less fearful, but because the conditions conducive to media melodrama come together more coherently around some issues than others.* Crime is an issue tailor-made for hyper-dramatism: Almost everyone agrees it is a problem and should be eliminated; almost everyone agrees that criminals are bad and have no excuse for their behavior; politicians get a lot of mileage from talking about an issue that is guaranteed to produce a supportive response from a scared public; and the media appear to be performing a useful public service by running cautionary stories on the issue. *The result of this open license to dramatize the issue, however, is that the popular fear of crime is way out of proportion to the chances of ever being affected by it.*

By contrast, media attempts to educate the public about the dangers of cigarette smoking have not succeeded in raising even realistic fear levels among the millions of continuing smokers who have more to fear from their addiction to cigarettes than from crime. While journalists dramatize the effects of smoking from time to time, cigarette companies are given equal opportunity to run counter information in the news. And the government is reluctant to fully dramatize the issue due to the heavy pressure applied in Washington by the cigarette lobby. Surely the predatory cigarette industry could be represented in as fearsome and sinister a way as lurking muggers and pickpockets, yet the political conditions for hyper-dramatism are just not present on the cigarette issue (at least by comparison to the alignment of politicians and journalists on matters like crime and the activities of the Soviet Union). And so, public fear is built up about some things and diffused on others.

Even when fears are aroused, the personalized melodrama fails to provide the sort of understanding that gets to the root of a problem, resulting in continuing treatment of the symptoms. Since crime is dramatized in terms of evil or sick individuals preying on innocent law-abiding citizens, it is not surprising that the pat resolution of crime dramas is for politicians to call for more arrests, bigger police budgets, new jails, and tougher judges. Unfortunately, none of these dramatic remedies seems to have any effect on crime, since the causes have more to do with poverty, social environment, and restricted opportunity for economic success via other careers. Thus, the crime issue is put to rest time and again with irrelevant but dramatically conclusive actions. And just as drama-tically, the issue will return again to capture the news spotlight in the future. Impossible to get at the root causes of problems like crime, you say? Look at the international crime statistics that show most other liberal capitalist democracies ranking far below the United States in the rates of virtually every category of violent crime.

Perhaps the news, and the personalities who dominate it, have simply put us out of touch with our own reality and how to deal with it effectively. This, then, is the sequence of effects flowing from dramatized news: 1) distraction from potentially important causes of problems, 2) creation of a false sense of understanding rooted in individualistic explanations, and 3) the promotion of dramatically satisfying but practically unworkable so-lutions.

Fragmented News

Lifting actors out of political context and surrounding their actions with titillating but irrelevant "fantasy themes" make it very hard to put together a coherent picture of the world.[32] *Events in fragmented news exist in self-contained dramatic capsules, isolated from each other in time and space. The impression given off by the news is that of a jigsaw puzzle that is out of focus and missing many pieces. When focus is provided it is on the individual pieces, not on how they fit the surrounding picture.* When information is delivered in such fragments, people are invited all the more to project their own interpretations onto the world. Thus, in place of a picture of the world that is held accountable to detailed new information about situations, new information is either cast adrift or assimilated into old plot formulas. In either case, the world is reduced time and again to a myriad of encapsulated "happenings," each with its own emotional coherence, but each isolated and mysteriously unrelated to the others. And so the world appears fragmented and confusing even though each of its parts is coherent and dramatically whole. *With respect to information fragmentation, the news defies the old adage that the whole is greater than the sum of its parts. In news reality, the whole is decidedly less than the sum of its parts.* Columnist Russell Baker once parodied the typical newscast in the following terms:

> Meanwhile, in Washington, the Carter Administration was reported today as firemen still sifted through the ruins of a six-alarm blaze in Brooklyn that left two Congressmen, who were said to have accepted cash contributions from Korean agents, despite their fifth defeat in a row at the hands of the Boston Celtics....
>
> Seventeen were dead and scores injured by the testimony that two Senators, whom he declined to name, rioted in the streets of Cairo following her son's expulsion from school for shooting a teacher who had referred to him in the easy-going style of the Carter White House, as exemplified by the dispute over the B-1 bomber.[33]

Sometimes, even the internal coherence of a single news report is lost. In their occasional attempts to achieve "analysis," journalists may abandon normal dramatic, narrative forms. Resulting reports not only display the usual disconnection from other issues and events but often fail to make sense on their own. *Lacking real guidelines for analysis and criticism, media efforts to be analytical or critical frequently border on nonsense.* Edwin Diamond tells the story of a network news producer who visited a seminar at MIT devoted to television news. The producer proudly showed a videotape of a recent "analytical" report on the economy. Diamond describes the report and his students' reaction:

> There was the anchor wishing us good evening; cut to the Washington reporter with the latest inflation bad news; then quickly three consumer reports from around the country; then a U.S. map with graphics showing cost-of-living rates; back to the anchor and then the Washington reporter, followed by tape and sound "bites"—15-second quotes—from congressional leaders and cabinet officers. Finally, a Wall Street reaction ...and then break for commercial. In all, no more than three minutes had elapsed.
>
> As the various tape, sound, and graphics parts in the economics package gave way to each other, the producer snapped her fingers and whispered "hit it..." right in time with each element. She was proud of the network handiwork, but students in the classroom shot up their hands. What was that all about? What did it mean? What were you trying to tell us about the economy?...When we all watched the videotape once again from the point of view of the audience—people who know little about the effort that goes into the smooth mingling of tape and sound videofonts and slides, and care even less—we had to admit that it

was difficult to grasp, sort out and understand the news somewhere underneath all the production.[34]

As this example illustrates, action news often tries to imitate "analysis" by trading in the story format for news collages, called "clusters" in radio and television, which contain many images with few coherent connections.[35] Similar fragmentation effects are achieved in newspapers that jump back and forth between interviews, actors, scenes, factual information, and plots. Recall, for example, how the newspaper article on the elimination of the government job program required the reader to make the leap from the isolated personal case of a San Francisco street sweeper to the broad economic implications involved.

Despite occasional internal breakdowns resulting from unguided attempts at analysis, isolation between stories is the more common form of information fragmentation, and, therefore, the one we will concentrate on here. *Most news stories, as currently conceived, refract the everyday real world into free-floating particles of dubious meaning. In this refraction process, events resulting from the same political or economic forces are often treated as though they were independent. Long-term trends and historical patterns are seldom made part of the news because they are hard to tell as simple stories. Events spring full-blown, from out of nowhere, into the headlines. In place of seeing a coherent world anchored in clear historical, economic, and political tendencies, the public is exposed to a world driven into chaos by seemingly arbitrary and mysterious forces.*

An excellent case in point is media coverage of events in Central America—those five bang-bang, shoot-'em-up, strife-torn, ungovernable little "Banana Republics." Beginning with coverage of the Nicaraguan revolution in 1978, the news alerted the American people that revolutions were "breaking out" in the region traditionally regarded by U.S. policy-makers as "our backyard." Continuing strife in Nicaragua, Guatemala, and El Salvador gained a prominent place in the news of the 1980s.

Where did these revolutions come from? Out of thin air, according to media coverage. A study by Emile G. McAnany of television news stories on Central America revealed a stark break in coverage of the region before and after the media "discovered" the Nicaraguan revolution in 1978. For the six years prior to the media declaration of turmoil, Central America, though fraught with problems, was practically unheard-of in the news, receiving less than a one-tenth-of-one-percent share of the nightly television news on the three networks during the period 1972–1977. Beginning in 1978, however, coverage of the region shot up over six-fold and increased steadily into the 1980s. McAnany concludes from the data that television failed to cover the build-up to the Central American crisis and "did not cover it until it had become a full-blown 'event' for the media."[36]

What better way to displace meaningful understanding of problems in the region while reinforcing stereotypes of unstable, ungovernable Banana Republics? Leave it to the media. What little coverage there was in the six years before the media announced the existence of a problem in the region was devoted almost entirely to stories of a stereotypical nature. Over half the "pre-revolution" coverage was devoted to natural disasters, like hurricanes and earthquakes, while another sizable chunk dealt with government corruption and military coups. And when coverage escalated after 1978, a full 88 percent of all stories fell into the "war-terrorism" category. McAnany concludes: "If one can take these categories as indicative of what the American public knows about Central America through television over the last decade, it is that this is a crisis-ridden area with either hurricanes, earthquakes, or wars plaguing its people."[37]

As the U.S. government stepped into this seemingly chaotic void in the 1980s to straighten the region out, timeless, rootless, fragmented news made it easy to graft new themes onto news coverage. The new themes, like the originals they supplemented, depended more for their credibility on American fear, fantasy, and stereotype than on local circumstances. Hence, Central America was given renewed meaning and purpose toward the mid- to late-1980s as the news told how the United States was restoring democracy to the region while combating the encroachment of the evil Soviet empire in America's backyard. These new images, like the Banana Republic stereotype that came before them, were easy to communicate in stories that had no past, no future, and no economic or political analysis—stories that only conveyed an image of the present media moment, unrooted in local circumstances.

Indeed, it might be argued that image, illusion, and stereotype are the only messages that can be communicated by fragmented news. After all, fragmented news has a life and a reality of its own. Story plots are self-contained and incorporate broader social context only at the peril of overloading the simple melodrama of the moment. A shred of credibility is added to the mix by documenting that at least most of what is reported actually happened—never mind that much more of what actually happened went unreported, and never mind that some of what was reported may have been staged for those very purposes. In the case of Central America,

no preparation was given to the public for seemingly "sudden" civil wars in Nicaragua and El Salvador and little background explanation even after the fact was provided. Once engaged, the wars and especially the U.S. foreign policy position regarding the origin [i.e., communism] and solution [i.e., democracy] of the civil wars seem to take the spotlight, keeping the public focused on official positions and explanations rather than on important historic shifts in social and political relationships in the region.[38]

And so goes news coverage of most of the world beyond our borders.[39] Unfortunately, so goes most domestic coverage as well. As was the case with personalization and dramatization, fragmented news coverage applies to most news subjects, both foreign and domestic. A good example of fragmented domestic coverage is the media treatment of the Reagan administration's extensive program of social "reforms." Beginning in his first months in office, Ronald Reagan built a coalition that successfully dismantled nearly forty years of government social protection programs. The cuts in every social service and public protection area were awesome. Yet there were no headlines proclaiming: "Reagan Coalition Dismantles Forty Years of Government Reforms." Instead, the dismantling of each program was announced separately, often days apart, and frequently was dwarfed by the ongoing crises of state and economy. In looking at the *Wall Street Journal* coverage of just five of the dozens of Reagan dismantling efforts, we find that only two received front-page coverage (Social Security cuts and the termination of the CETA job training program). A proposal to close the Consumer Product Safety Commission was given about four inches on page 5 in one issue, and a longer article on page 48 in another. A plan to shut off welfare to families of strikers was relegated to page 6. The decision to stop tracing the ownership transfers of firearms was covered on page 31. The impact and linkages among these issues were further diminished by the fact that the stories were spread over a period of two months.[40] What stopped journalists from announcing these and other actions as a major and significant trend once the pattern became evident? Trends do not conform to the narrow definition of daily news unless, of course, they are in the interest of governments or interest groups to announce. More important, trends seldom contain the dramatic elements of a good story. Headlining trends and linkages would require placing information in analytically useful forms, a function that the news is ill-equipped to perform.

The Political Effects of Fragmentation. There are, of course, numerous "good reasons" for such bad reporting. Journalism's hallowed prohibitions against commentary and interpretation seem to justify the isolated representation of separate events, no matter how interrelated they may be. Moreover, press releases from official news sources seldom take pains to point out inconsistencies, complex relations, or other "big-picture" aspects of events. These strategies of propagandists are rewarded by the journalistic preoccupation with "daily news," which means that the news slate is wiped clean each day. News update sections are relegated to the back of the newspaper and saved for "slow news days" in radio and television broadcasts. The imperatives for drama and action further separate stories from one another. Since dramatic formats contain their own plot and resolution elements, linkages between these "news capsules" can reduce their impact and confuse their plots. In fact, connections between news stories can raise the unsettling idea that nothing should be taken at face value, that behind every story there is a still larger story.[41] It is an unfortunate by-product of using stories as the basic units of news reporting that linkages evoke unpleasant images of political conspiracies or journalistic attempts to obfuscate simple issues. By contrast, other forms of presenting information such as ideologies and theories use such connections to simplify explanations and enhance meaning.

Whatever the organizational reasons for news fragmentation, the troublesome result is that events spring on the public full-blown, from nowhere, and with little analytical context. *This gives political insiders a tremendous lead in formulating policy solutions, with the result that the public is repeatedly left out of the important political discussions of their time.* Before people can grasp the situation, a high-level solution is slapped on, and off we go to the next one. Most issues are gone again before public opinion has time to catch up with, much less get ahead of, them. *Only on enduring and volatile matters does public opinion figure into the political process, and most often the policy question is not how to "follow" the will of the people but how to shape it in support of the wishes of high-level policy makers who have already decided what must be done.* The news is the only chance the majority have to keep ahead of the policy game, but the fragmentation problem assures that the people will be left well behind on most issues. Consider McAnany's overview of foreign crises in the news:

There is a sudden and "inexplicable" upheaval in a remote and unknown land (read Vietnam or Iran as well as Nicaragua and El Salvador).

The U.S. reaction is crisis-oriented policy to support the status quo.

The public witnesses the action played out on the evening news in two- or three-minute minidramas.

The current administration asks the public to support its foreign policy as being in the national interest and presents the policy as the only alternative.[42]

It is no wonder that public opinion studies have shown that most people have trouble thinking in abstract, logically integrated ways about political issues. An inventory of findings from public opinion research sounds like a list of the effects of news fragmentation. The average person has trouble stating clear positions on issues; most people tend to remember few facts about important issues; the majority of people see few connections between issues; and many people change their opinions easily about issues.[43] The parallels between news fragmentation and public opinion characteristics suggest that the public's true failing may have been to follow the news and take it seriously.

Public confusion may be symptomatic of an even deeper effect of news fragmentation: a diminished sense of our own history as a nation. True, most Americans are "proud" to "stand tall" for their country, but how many can explain what exactly they are proud of or what in particular they are standing tall for? Answers to these questions come out in the form of illusory words like "freedom" and "democracy"—the sorts of emotionally satisfying but poorly anchored and defined images sustained by fragmented news.

When it comes to articulating a sense of national history—who we are as a people, what we have done, and where we are going—most people are stopped short. It is dangerous for any nation, much less a major empire, to have such a diminished sense of its world role and therefore such a dim grasp of the historic choices before it. Historic events, like the latest U.S. interventions in Central America and the ones a generation before, just seem to "happen." Any "mistakes" along the way, like supporting dictatorships in Guatemala, Nicaragua, and El Salvador before the "trouble" began, are noticed too late, if at all. History marches on, while the American people follow behind in confusion, bearing the responsibility for making the best of it.

Perhaps in simpler, more traditional times, people could trust wise leaders and elites to understand the course of history, but in the modern, mass media age, we increasingly share one consciousness as a people: mass consciousness. McAnany describes the problem like this:

> What sense of history a nation has of itself often comes from the scholars who write for an elite audience. In the present age of mass communications, however, the majority of a nation, often including its elites, learn less from books than from the mass media, especially electronic journalism. Television has become in the U.S., for example, the single largest and most trusted source of daily news for the majority of its people. And it is from this source that the public derives its perceptions of itself and of other countries.[44]

Despite the responsibility attached to the role of "contemporary historian," the media seem unsure what to do and unwilling to tamper with their profitable, if irrelevant, news format. And so, when the few critics in Congress ceased to ask the administration about the analogy between Central America and Vietnam, the media stopped asking, too. Nor did it occur to most news organizations to explore thoroughly what the Vietnam analogy really meant in the first place. Thus, the past grows dimmer. And when Latin American countries organized their own peace-making efforts for Central America in the 1980s, there was virtually no exploration of why these countries would break with U.S. policy. Nor was there discussion of what reason the government in Washington had for thinking it knew better than the countries involved how to manage their internal and international affairs. Similarly, when U.S. planes conducted an air attack against Libya, little was made of the fact that no European government except England endorsed the action, even to the extent of allowing the American planes to fly over their countries. Indeed, the concern in the media seemed to be that the refusal to permit overflight meant a trickier mid-air refueling operation and greater discomfort for the pilots due to the longer flight.[45] Left also to future historians to figure out is what it means for one of the wealthiest and allegedly most democratic nations in world history to have thousands of homeless people roaming the land and millions more existing, neglected, in bitter poverty. These and other issues will be purely academic concerns when they are assigned meaning by future generations of scholars. But who, in the meantime, is engaging the public in the critical task of understanding the significance of events and choices inherent in today's reality? Not the news media, who cling to a fragmented format for announcing "That's the Way It Is," despite the fact that little sense, other than the most illusory, can be made of "It."

Normalized News

Consider the picture so far: Each day the news consumer is bombarded by dozens, or hundreds if she is conscientious, of compartmentalized, unrelated dramatic capsules. Some emotional satisfaction can be derived from forming strong identifications with or against the actors who star in these minidramas. But what about facts? What about knowledge and practical information? Recalling facts from the news resembles a trivia game played alone. Most people cannot remember one-fourth of the stories in a TV news broadcast immediately after watching it, and information recall about the remembered quarter is sketchy at best.[46] It is no wonder that details like why there were revolutions in Nicaragua and El Salvador, why the NATO allies objected to certain U.S. policies, or why there are millions of Americans living in poverty, get lost in the news.

The chaos of the news picture is reduced psychologically not by bringing in new, more detailed information, but by driving it out. In place of grappling with the puzzling circumstances and moral dilemmas of situations, the news overlays situations as quickly as possible with familiar images (both moral and empirical) of a normal world. The potential for confusion and disorientation inherent in personalized, dramatized, and fragmented news leaves people vulnerable to old, familiar, reassuring images of how the world works—images that drive bothersome details out of mind. It seems somehow "normal" for there to be political upheavals in ungovernable little Banana Republics, just as it seems normal for the United States to step in and help restore order before our enemies do. The problem of poverty in America becomes a familiar, tolerable, "normal" problem once we hear from one side that people are poor because they don't want to work, and the other side chimes in that there aren't enough jobs and the government has abandoned the poor. Neither pronouncement changes the fact of poverty, but both of them combine to make the problem blend into the normal scheme of things.

The backdrop for the whole drift of news imagery toward the familiar and normal is the daily search for dramatic closure to the news story. Will our world be OK? Will the problem be solved? More important than a close look at what the problem is, or whether the solution really makes sense, is the reassuring pronouncement by an official or an authority that things will work out and life will return to "normal" soon. *Thus, the fourth major information bias in the news is the tendency to filter new information through traditional values, beliefs, and images of society and to deliver the filtered information through the reassuring pronouncements of authorities charged with returning things to normal.* The basic job description for public officials might read: WANTED: ATTRACTIVE MEDIA PER-SONALITY WITH GOOD DELIVERY OF MIDDLE AMERICAN BELIEFS. MUST BE ADEPT AT PUBLIC REASSURANCE.

Journalists can, of course, conjure up normalizing images on their own, but the gatekeeper role of the media seems less obtrusive when reporters remain behind the scenes, editing the remarks of others as though the news was written by someone other than the journalist. Moreover, the normalizing themes of news stories seem more objective, not to mention dramatic, when pronounced from the mouths of actors on the world stage. And, most of the time, political actors are only too happy to join journalists in their normalizing work. As a result of this community of interest shared by journalists and powerful authorities, official sources usually get the last word in a news story. In fact, most news stories reserve for official sources the first, the last, and many of the words in between. Much of the daily news is devoted to official actions and reactions. It is convenient that there is a never-ending supply of official news because news organizations need a huge volume of news every day. The public relations branches of government, interest groups, and industry are dedicated to filling up this daily "news hole."

There are, of course, many reports of the activities of socially and politically deviant actors such as strikers, protest groups, or splinter parties. However, virtually all reports of such actors tend to fall into one or more of the following categories:

1. *Reports of lawbreaking, violence, or distasteful behavior that tend to discredit the actors involved.* For example, environmental groups may publicize their opposition to nuclear power plants by dis-rupting work or occupying the grounds. News reports that associate the group with illegal tactics, arrests, and criminal prosecution may damage the credibility of the group and its cause.

2. *Reports that balance a deviant perspective with an official reaction in*

opposition. For example, many political organizations during the 1960s claimed that the FBI had attempted to sabotage their organizations and harass their members. These charges were always accompanied by denials from the FBI, the Department of Justice, the president, and other authoritative sources. It was not until years later that FBI officials admitted to congressional investigators that they had engaged in illegal activities against political groups. By that time the issue was dead.

3. *Reports on the positive activities of a group that quickly fade from the news, implying that the group and its goals were of little consequence.* For example, many grass-roots groups receive initial press coverage when they announce their intentions to tackle a political problem. However, such groups usually lack the money and public relations skills required to keep their concerns before the public over the long haul.[47]

Journalism tends to present a simple world where Middle Americans and their authorities are on one side holding the line of normalcy, decency, and the American way of life against a host of deviant actors, ranging from political "extremists," Communists, and terrorists, to criminals, minorities, and the impatient poor, all of whom threaten to change the normal accepted status quo. If the news audience rooting for those holding the line understood what motivated the groups on the other side, it is doubtful that there would be as much resistance to or fear of change as there is. However, the issues at stake are filtered through stereotypes or prior images, and so, to paraphrase the words of one of our greatest image-makers, what Americans really fear is fear itself. (It is doubtful that the structural changes required to make real headway against social problems could be any more fearsome than the amount of strife and turmoil generated by holding the imaginary line of normalcy against the groups on the other side.)

Okay, but what about those times when the media expose official corruption and duplicity? What of those occasions when journalists look critically on old policies and social attitudes? Occasional instances of press criticism do stand out against the familiar pattern of official reporting. Even though these moments of judgmental journalism seem to suggest an independent press, they are, in fact, the exceptions that prove the rule of normalized news. *Most news reports that seem critical of authority reflect one or more of the following properties:*

1. *They are rare.* The comparatively small number of critical reports convey the impression that official positions are credible in the vast majority of cases.
2. *They tend to be personalized.* The bulk of news criticism is directed at personal flaws and failings rather than enduring, "normal"

institutional arrangements. Thus, politicians may come and go, creating an occasional sense of "change," while institutions slip farther from comprehension and the grasp of popular reform. Most of the time even politicians escape press criticism unless they commit a grievous sin against the law or middle-class sensibilities. Certainly, excessive traditionalism or the failure to grasp new situations is no grounds for criticizing leaders. It is no wonder that the classic newsmaking strategy for leaders is to wrap themselves in the flag, recite "apple pie" values, and cloak any innovative idea in the language of tradition (while declaring undeniably old solutions to be revolutionary).

3. *They are ritualized.* Far from being an ever-vigilant and critical policy watchdog, the press attacks politicians at measured intervals as if motivated more by the desire to appear critical than out of consistent concern about whether the government is advancing public well-being. C. Jack Orr's study of reporters' questions at presidential press conferences showed that criticial questions tend to come at measured intervals and have little to do with the substantive details of policies. Moreover, press conferences contain roughly the same percentage of hostile questions no matter who the president is or what the pressing issues of the day may be.[48] These are the ritualized behaviors of a press more concerned about its public image as critical watchdog than about developing practical guidelines for being a serious watchdog on a daily basis. The public, not surprisingly, are not entirely convinced by the ritual, with a majority believing that news organizations are "often influenced by powerful people and organizations" like the federal government, business corporations, advertisers, unions, and the parties.[49] Moreover, many people see the personal element in press attacks in a negative light, as somehow "picking on" the poor public figure.[50] Perhaps the press would be surprised at the favorable public response if it gave up normalized news with its ritualistic criticisms in favor of genuinely critical news based on clear guidelines of journalistic adversarialism.

4. *They nearly always return the situation to normal by the end of the story or the series of stories.* The underlying assumption in almost all mass media criticism is that the basic political system and its values are unquestionable. Problems in the system and its component institutions must be due to individuals and human failure. The classic closing line to news dramas set in motion by this normalizing assumption is "The System Worked!" Below are three cases that illustrate these four reasons why the exceptional cases of "critical" journalism prove the rule of normalized news.

Watergate: The System Worked! The Watergate scandal is often cited as a classic example of a real watchdog press in action. True, Watergate involved nearly two years of intensive press scrutiny of President Richard Nixon and his aides. The issue at stake was whether the White House illegally spied on the Democratic party during an election campaign and whether the president knew about it and subsequently tried to cover it up (another illegal activity). Although the situation was full of major questions about the potential for official misuse of the huge national security system that has evolved since World War II, the press deflected these issues in favor of asking whether Nixon had personally remained pure and uncorrupt in his use of the state security apparatus. Curiously absent from the barrage of coverage was the simple question of whether anyone should be expected to remain pure when given the chance to wield such great power with so little public accountability. In short, little attention was paid to the institutional flaws that might tempt a president to use CIA personnel to spy on his domestic opposition and then obstruct subsequent FBI investigation of those illegal activities. When, over a dozen years later, even more shocking institutional angles were opened up, the press was uninterested in pursuing them. Evidence from mysteriously "sealed" FBI files pointed to the possibility that the CIA may have abused its own institutional cover of legal secrecy by running a double-agent operation, spying on both the Republicans and the Democrats![51] This important lead raised the additional possibility that the mysterious leaks from the anonymous informant "Deep Throat" who fed the "investigative" reporters key information were the result of this CIA operation. This, in turn, signals the important possibility of institutional power struggles between the CIA and the president—power struggles that would never be revealed to the American people in the absence of media scrutiny.

Whatever the various institutional angles, the press avoided all of them in favor of reporting the steady stream of leaks from "Deep Throat" and the various investigative bodies at work on the case. This brand of "investigative reporting" deflected questions about institutional problems or abnormalities in favor of dramatizing the personal culpability of the most publicly visible actors involved.[52] Whereas all institutional paths led to questions of change and reform (questions the press chose largely to avoid), the personal drama held out the promise of returning the political system to normal as soon as the individuals were accused, charged, and removed from office. True to the chosen normalizing plot, when Nixon resigned from office NBC correspondent Roger Mudd led the nation in the cheer "The System Worked!"

The melodramatic resolution—a tearful Nixon saying goodbye to the White House staff, and an upbeat ending of good news for the system—

seemed to make sense at the time. But in retrospect it seems that the news exonerated a "system" containing the institutional weaknesses that permitted the abuses of power to occur in the first place. Even at the level of personal melodrama, "The System Works" seems an ironic ending. After all, the "system" pardoned the worst offender, gave light sentences to most of the others, and turned almost all of the criminals into millionaires and media celebrities in the process.

Picking on the President: Ronald Reagan and the Teflon Presidency.

When a conference of prominent media executives and journalists convened midway through the Reagan presidency, they lamented the fact that their best efforts to be critical were unappreciated by the public.[53] Instead of being perceived as noble crusaders, the press was seen as a pack of dogs barking questions over the din of helicopter blades at a president who seemed perplexed at the journalistic clamor, smiled bemusedly at the pack, waved, and climbed aboard his helicopter. The press seemed rude and was foiled time and again in its unsuccessful efforts to get a rise out of the man they came to regard as the "Great Communicator"—the figure who appeared immune to criticism, encased behind some sort of "Teflon presidency."

Perhaps what the media executives and journalists failed to consider is that it was the nature of their own criticism, not the act of being critical in and of itself, that rankled the public and played into the image of an already popular president. Although the press find it hard to imagine any other sort of criticism than the ritualized, personalized attacks they engage in, Reagan and his media advisors figured out very quickly the special rules of the press criticism game. Rather than becoming hurt or angered by press attacks, as other presidents have, Reagan learned to smile benevolently, wave at the camera, nod knowingly to the home audience, and then simply ignore the attack. The result was that the press always seemed to be agitated about something, but it was hard to figure out what it was. And when it was clear what the journalists were riled up about, it seemed that they were being rude and disrespectful to the president. Although this sort of critical stance is unlikely to win much favor with the public (other than those who don't like the personality under attack), the press seem paralyzed and unable to engage in any other sort of criticism.

This sort of news criticism is ineffectual and therefore normalizing. Consider the example of one of the first "hard looks" the media took at the Reagan presidency—an example that might have taught the press some lessons, but became instead the model for ritualistic sniping for the next seven years. With much fanfare, NBC aired a special news report and analysis of Ronald Reagan's first year in the White House.[54] Following the first characteristic of critical news mentioned above, the special was a *rare* moment of criticism following a long period of uncritical reporting of

Reagan's activities. Also typical of the ritualized nature of most press criticism was the "hard-nosed" posturing of the reporter, and the focus was on the person rather than the issues. The *personal attack* created the illusion of critical reporting, without risking the introduction of much political substance or detailed analysis. Despite the use of such standard news formulas, it was hard not to get caught up in the dramatic illusion that there was really something important going on. Reporters on the program charged that Reagan might not have understood the nature of the presidency in some of his dealings with Congress. The host of the program interviewed the president and asked him, point-blank, to "comment" on reports from his own staff that he was not really aware of the details of most issues—in fact, some said he did not even understand most issues. Was it true, the interviewer asked audaciously, that the White House staff tried to prevent unrehearsed encounters between the president and the press because they often resulted in embarrassing statements?

Despite the sense of an almost ruthless attack, there was something missing: a serious look at Reagan's policies. In addition to violating the canons of the news format, such an approach would have raised the un-comfortable question, "Where was the press with these criticisms when these same policies were being debated before Congress and the public?" Instead, the safe but impressive strategy adopted was to frame the program around questions of Reagan's "personal rating" and his "score as president."

The moral to this story is that appearances can be deceiving in news reporting. Although the NBC "White Paper" discussed above seemed to take issue with the establishment, it really did nothing of the kind. By avoiding a serious and timely criticism of specific policies, the report did little to disrupt "normal" images of society and its problems. Even if the program had raised criticisms of specific issues, the formula for news criticism would have introduced them in the form of equally "normal" views held by members of the opposition party in Congress. In the end, press attacks on officials and their views are of little consequence, since both officials and mainstream views seem to be infinitely replaceable in American politics.

"Irangate": A Chip in the Teflon?. As this edition of *News* went to press, Ronald Reagan was surrounded by the greatest controversy of his presidency. Several of his closest advisors were implicated in a plot to sell weapons to Iran in exchange for U.S. hostages being held by alleged terrorist factions in the Middle East. The profits from the arms sales were allegedly laundered through Swiss bank accounts and then diverted to "Contra" leaders in charge of the U.S. proxy war against the government of Nicaragua. Not only had the president violated his own solemn pledge never to negotiate with terrorists, but his staff were deeply implicated in

what appeared to be illegal activities in violation of a congressional prohibition on United States assistance to the Contras. High crimes on the doorstep of the Oval Office! Shades of Watergate!

Unlike Watergate, however, the Democrats decided not to launch a frontal attack on the inhabitant of the Oval Office. Reagan was, after all, still popular, a formidable television actor, and a lame duck. Many respected members of Congress from both sides of the aisle urged the president to apologize to the American people and get on with the business of government. The press, having no assault by Congress to report, vowed to exercise moderation in an effort to avoid repeating its apparent overly zealous personal attack on Richard Nixon more than a dozen years earlier. The result? The personal melodrama in the news centered around the somewhat tedious question of whether the president would say he was sorry—an overture to contrition that for months he steadfastly refused to make. In his 1987 State of the Union message, Reagan borrowed a line from the Richard Nixon Watergate script, and said that as Chief Executive he would accept the responsibility for the mistakes of his staff, but no wrong had been done, and, therefore, no apology was necessary.

It seemed that the Teflon was still working and that the former screen actor still had some of his old audience appeal. Although his popularity dipped slightly below 50 percent for a brief period, he soon rebounded above the magic 50 percent level—even though nearly 70 percent of the public actually believed that he was lying to them! But the point of this story really shouldn't have been whether the president was lying, or how much he personally knew about illegal activities, or even why the public might endorse a leader who lies to them. The point, lost again in the personalized, dramatized, fragmented news coverage, was whether there were fundamental institutional problems in the relations between the presidency and Congress in the area of foreign policy. The question neglected in the news was whether things were no longer working "as normal" in the system of checks and balances mandated by the Constitution for making foreign policy. It is hard to report possible abnormalities when the overriding journalistic bias is to restore normalcy to the system by the end of the story. The most tempting news formula for scandal coverage leads to the dramatic conclusion that "The System Works" whenever wrongdoers are found out and punished. Never mind the plot complication that something about the system may have invited the wrongdoing in the first place. The storybook version of life in the American Camelot still tells of the nearly perfect system and its nearly perfect people.

True, it was reported that members of Congress were upset—even alarmed—about White House disregard for congressional advice and consent in making foreign policy. Yet detailed discussions of key institutional problems like the following were all but lost in the "Irangate" melodrama: Has the president's National Security Council become a private State Department, operating from the White House basement? Has the potential for abusing the powers of the Central Intelligence Agency become too tempting for White House staff to resist? Does the screen of secrecy laws surrounding the executive branch invite a disregard for public accountability? Is the congressional oversight process in need of serious reform? Is it relatively easy for the president to use the powers and vagaries of a huge budget and a labyrinthine bureaucracy to circumvent the will of Congress? Have the checks and balances of the Constitution become, in foreign policy, little more than flowery ink scratchings on a yellowing document? Such questions seem more important than whether the president will say he is "sorry." It could also be argued that such questions are even more dramatic than the saga of presidential contrition. The trouble is that these questions are part of the wrong drama—they just don't fit the news script of national normalcy.

We can expect "Irangate" and the scandals of the future to go the way of Watergate and the scandals of the past. Wrongdoers will be punished by the law or by public disapproval, or both. And as news reality dissolves into book contracts and movie deals, the press can close another chapter of that never-ending news saga, "The System Works!" And, don't forget, COMING SOON TO A THEATER NEAR YOU: Sylvester Stallone starring as Lieutenant Colonel Oliver North in RAMBO XIV: WINNING THE BIG ONE FOR THE GIPPER. Watch as the president's favorite American Hero and most trusted assistant flies a secret mission deep into terrorist territory. Cheer as hostages are released! Gasp as he takes the law into his own hands! Enter the world of Swiss banks, freedom fighters, jungle wars...DON'T MISS IT!

How to Normalize the World When Officials Aren't on the Scene. The standard journalistic treatment (whether critical or reassuring) of officials and their positions is just one way in which the news presents the world in "normalized" terms. As mentioned earlier, when officials are not around, journalists draw many of their story plots from the numerous subconscious dramatic themes of the culture—themes that clearly delimit good and bad, right and wrong, desirable and undesirable, normal and abnormal, the thinkable and the unthinkable. Such themes leave their marks on the news:

- A teacher's strike is reported as a traditional wage dispute, thereby ignoring more pertinent issues of racism in the schools and political control of educational policy.[55]
- Extensive coverage of Poland's internal political struggle in the 1980s made little effort to point out the profound differences

between Polish and American workers, thereby creating false grounds for the American audience to become involved with the situation.[56]

- A report on China after Mao used American stereotypes of progress and development to describe a "typical" Chinese family: "They chatter in eager, sometimes mirthful, manner about the improvements in their lives since Mr. Deng has been in power. Their sofa, TV, a coat of blue paint on the walls and partitions separating the living room from the eating area are all post-Mao additions."[57] From reports like this many Americans received the misguided impression that China is "going capitalist."

In short, the news takes us on a daily tour of the world-as-it-ought-to-be: a world filled with mainstream American values and comforting images of authority and security. Even many technological failures that underlie human tragedies such as earthquakes, floods, and droughts are displaced from the news picture by the normalizing "act-of-God" theme. A major study using computer models, satellite photos, and high-level policy interviews conducted on five continents concluded that the widespread destruction commonly dismissed in the news as an "act of God" is "more properly attributable to such acts of man as poor land-use planning, unrestrained population growth, shoddy construction, and unattended warnings."[58]

As if to affirm that nothing serious lies beyond these boundaries of normalized news, daily journalistic fare also contains a sampling of the truly bizarre: the wrecking crew that demolished the wrong building, the eccentric millionaire who left his entire estate to his cat, the confusion that resulted when a gang of robbers dressed as cops encountered a squad of cops dressed as robbers, or the travails of people who have adopted dolls as children and must find sensitive babysitters when they go on vacation.

The Political Effects of Normalized News. *The main effect of normalized news is obvious: it narrows the range of acceptable, even "thinkable," models for political action.* Noam Chomsky recounts the story of a Soviet newscaster who was yanked off the air and sent out for "rehabilitation" after he described the Soviet intervention in Afghanistan as an "invasion." Popular American stereotypes of life in Russia are confirmed by this story showing that it is "unthinkable" for journalists there to say anything contrary to the propaganda line of the government. But Chomsky draws a different, less normalizing moral from the story. Arguing that American journalists are better socialized than their Russian counterparts, Chomsky suggests that direct U.S. government meddling in the news is simply unnecessary because no mass media American newscaster would ever think to call a similar U.S. military action an invasion![59]

Is it impossible that the United States would ever invade a small, weak country with which it was not at war, or is it just impossible for Middle Americans to think such a thing? This is an important question; in its answer lies the key to evaluating the quality of the U.S. public information system and, consequently, the degree to which policy makers are accountable to the people and to the values of the Republic. In recent years the government has intervened militarily (either directly or by proxy) in places like Grenada, Lebanon, Libya, Angola, Cambodia, Afghanistan, El Salvador, and Nicaragua. In no case was there a cry from the mainstream press that these actions might have been ill considered (in light of political alternatives) or even illegal (in light of treaties and U.S. laws forbidding the attack or overthrow of sovereign states). In these contexts there was no mention of U.S. invasion. Nor did the press attempt to put in context the concerns of allies, both in the affected regions and in Europe, that American military policies were unwarranted, dangerous, and an affront to international law.

To the contrary, critical suggestions that the United States may have "invaded" other countries came not from public officials or from journalists but from the mouths and placards of "left-wing" protesters who raised their concerns in the streets. From the more decorous halls of government came the more reasoned voices of the loyal opposition— voices careful not to step across the boundaries of the "thinkable" for fear the news would unleash the scathing attacks of more powerful and popular actors against them. Thus, unlike the Soviet Union, there is always an opposition voice somewhere in American news, but like the Soviet Union, there is a clear line drawn between legitimate (i.e., "thinkable") views and illegitimate (i.e., "unthinkable") ones. What, Chomsky asks, is the real difference between Soviet-style and U.S.-style propaganda? (Pardon the outrageous question, but where else could it be asked except in a discussion of the "unthinkable"?)

Given this distinction between legitimate and illegitimate opposition, there is little incentive for public officials ever to say anything startling, thought-provoking, or otherwise at odds with "the thinkable." Indeed, talking in stereotypes probably helps journalists and news audiences identify positions as "official." The result is that whether the "official" opposition comes from conservatives or liberals, one thing is almost certain: We will know the lines by heart. Mainstream political groups may disagree with one another bitterly, but no matter how aggressive their posturing, they suffer the common fate of being trapped by their signature stereotypes.

A news system that keeps thinking the thinkable, while pushing the unthinkable off the legitimate public record, not only hinders the evaluation and creative change of policy but results in the representation of a narrow range of interests in a system often idealized as being broadly representative.

However, since these narrow interests are portrayed as "legitimate" by the news, they may loom much broader and all-representative in the minds of Middle Americans who would like to think that everybody is (or ought to be) just like them and that the whole world is (or ought to be) their world. Remember, "The system works!"

To say the least, the daily news falls short of its reputed function of presenting unvarnished political facts so that people can draw informed conclusions from them. It is closer to the mark to conclude that the news helps people confirm their favorite political truths because those truths form the implicit guidelines for selecting and writing news stories. As one critic observed, both the public and journalists are involved more in a process of creating convenient fictions than discovering convincing facts: "We are all engaged in the same enterprise, all of us caught up in the making of analogies and metaphors, all of us seeking evocations and representations of what we can recognize as appropriately human. Stories move from truths to fact, not the other way around...."[60]

In this process of legitimizing a narrow range of political values (and the actors who endorse them) the news accomplishes another important end: It legitimizes itself. As mentioned earlier, claims about "objective" reporting rest on very shaky foundations. For every story angle highlighted, another goes unreported. For every source included, another is excluded. With each tightening of the plot line, meaningful connections to other issues and events become weakened. Every familiar theme or metaphor used in writing about an event obscures a potentially unique feature of the event. Even though it is impossible for the news to be objective, it is important that it seem objective or, in the terms of the trade, "believable." The appearance of objectivity or believability depends heavily on the use of official sources and normalizing themes. The routine acceptance of official views helps to legitimize them, which in turn helps make the news seem objective. According to Tuchman:

> Challenging the legitimacy of offices holding centralized information dismantles the news net. If all of officialdom is corrupt, all its facts and occurrences must be viewed as alleged facts and alleged occurrences....
> For example, if the institutions of everyday life are delegitimated, the facts tendered by the Bureau of Marriage Licenses would be suspect. One could no longer call that bureau to learn whether Robert Jones and Fay Smith had married. In sum, amassing mutually self-validating facts simultaneously accomplishes the doing of newswork and reconstitutes the everyday world of offices and factories, of politics and bureaucrats, of bus schedules and class rosters as historically given.[61]

The news is worth studying, as Tuchman suggests, because it plays a major part in creating the reality in which we live. Even though the news may be illusory, the world it helps legitimize is not. War is an ever-present possibility. Oppression is a fact of political life. Capricious economic cycles dictate the quality of existence. Many people accept these aspects of reality as inescapable tragedies of the human condition. A review of the effects of mass media news suggests that the "inevitability" of our existence is more a product of how that existence is communicated to us than the result of tragic human nature. The news world simply does not contain a vision of human alternatives; it presents, instead, a picture of an inescapable status quo.

SUMMARY

Setting limits on the imaginable and the politically possible; arriving too late (and doing too little) to educate people and get them involved in policy making—these are among the effects of mass media news in American politics. These effects speak to a serious bias in our information system. It is not an ideological bias of the Republican-Democrat sort that most people seem to worry about. It is a more fundamental bias about the very nature of politics. A clear set of transformations happens to political events as they pass through the journalistic gate. In order to become newsworthy, an event must be "coded" in the most personalized and melodramatic terms possible. Such representations fragment the resulting picture of politics into ambiguous information particles free of institutions and free of history—particles that are not of much use to anyone but the propagandist. The painful confusion and disorientation that would result from trying to make sense of this journalistic version of political reality is eased somewhat by grafting onto the news familiar, normalizing themes from American culture and political folklore along with the reassurances of trusted authorities.

    Far from encouraging people to grasp other points of view or other realities, or to "think the unthinkable," the news invites us to turn away from the world to an inner reality of egocentric and ethnocentric concerns: How does this effect me? Is my country still Number One? The news is no mirror on the world. It is more like a finely tuned probe into the psyche of the stereotypical Middle American—a mirror of the American mind. Despite the unrepresentative quality of news reality, it seems objective. News is highly believable for those whose beliefs are engaged by it. And yet who are these people, these Middle Americans, who so freely project their news reality (and the politics that go along with it) onto the rest of humanity? How do politicians feed the right information so consistently to the media? And how do journalists mediate so effortlessly between the people and the politicians? How do journalists transform the raw material of politics into a vision that seems so believable that it is widely accepted as "The Way It Is"?

Understanding the production of the U.S. public information system is the task of the remainder of the book. We are not going to probe the surfaces of some dark conspiracy. Rather, we will find that the workings of the system are in full view; all that is required is to put the pieces together in a sensible way. Fortunately, most of the pieces to the news puzzle are right in front of us. For all of its defects, the news continues to be largely a public production, with government press offices, media organizations, and popular tastes all available for inspection. The openness of the system may be its saving grace when we turn to questions of reform later in the book. First, however, it is important to understand how the system works. The next three chapters explore how the different interests of politicians, the press, and the public converge to create the system of political information we know as the daily news.

NOTES

1. Gallup-Times Mirror, *The People & the Press* (Los Angeles: Times Mirror, 1986), pp. 28–29; see also Robert P. Vallone, Lee Ross, and Mark R. Lepper, "The Hostile Media Phenomenon: Biased Perceptions and Perceptions of Media Bias in Coverage of the Beirut Massacre," *Journal of Personality and Social Psychology* 49, no. 3 (1985): 577–85.
2. See, for example: David L. Altheide, *Media Power* (Beverly Hills: Sage, 1985); Michael Parenti, *Inventing Reality: The Politics of the Mass Media* (New York: St. Martins, 1986); Edward Jay Epstein, *News from Nowhere* (New York: Random House, 1973); Herbert Gans, *Deciding What's News* (New York: Vintage, 1979); Timothy Crouse, *The Boys on the Bus* (New York: Free Press, 1978); Robert Darnton, "Writing News and Telling Stories," *Daedalus* 104 (Spring 1975): 175–97; Mark Fishman, *Manufacturing the News* (Austin: University of Texas Press, 1980); Todd Gitlin, *The Whole World Is Watching* (Berkeley: University of California Press, 1980); Harvey Molotch and Marilyn Lester, "News as Purposive Behavior," *American Sociological Review* 39 (1974): 101–12; Harvey Molotch and Marilyn Lester, "Accidental News: The Great Oil Spill," *American Journal of Sociology* 81 (1975): 235–60; Leon V. Sigal, *Reporters and Officials: The Organization and Politics of Newsmaking* (Lexington, Mass.: Heath, 1973); David L. Paletz and Robert M. Entman, *Media Power Politics* (New York: Free Press, 1981).
3. Reported in Paletz and Entman, *Media Power Politics*, p. 17.
4. Quoted in Edward W. Barrett, "Folksy TV News," *Columbia Journalism Review*, November/December 1973, p. 19.
5. *Wall Street Journal*, 17 June 1981, p. 1.
6. Paletz and Entman, *Media Power Politics*, pp. 16–17.
7. Osnos's observations were aired in an interview on the National Public Radio news program "Morning Edition," 21 September 1981.
8. KIRO-TV, 11 P.M. news, Seattle, Wash., 28 October 1981.
9. NBC television network news update, 9 P.M. Pacific time, 28 October 1981.

10. ABC "Nightline," 11:30 P.M. Pacific time, 28 October 1981.
11. "President Wins AWACS," *Seattle Post-Intelligencer*, 29 October 1981, p. 1.
12. "Is This Any Way to Make Foreign Policy?" *Newsweek*, 7 July 1986, p. 34.
13. *Ibid.*, p. 33.
14. Michael Massing, "CBS: Sauterizing the News," *Columbia Journalism Review*, March/April 1986, p. 37.
15. *Ibid.*
16. *Ibid.*, p. 32.
17. *Ibid.*, p. 30.
18. Paletz and Entman, *Media Power Politics*, p. 17.
19. Reported in Epstein, *News from Nowhere*, pp. 4–5. The existence of such a conscious statement of a defining characteristic of news is all the more remarkable considering the trouble that most journalists have in clearly defining their professional product.
20. Paletz and Entman, *Media Power Politics*, p. 17.
21. Stephen Hess, "Covering the Senate: Where Power Gets the Play," *Washington Journalism Review*, June 1986, pp. 41–42.
22. Darnton, "Writing News and Telling Stories," p. 190.
23. Lewis H. Lapham, "Gilding the News," *Harper's*, July 1981, p. 34.
24. *Ibid.*, p. 35.
25. Paletz and Entman, *Media Power Politics*, p. 16.
26. Don DeLillo, *The Names* (New York: Vintage, 1982), p. 58.
27. Reported in Barrett, "Folksy TV News," p. 19.
28. I am indebted to Liz McHale for bringing this phenomenon to my attention.
29. Gaye Tuchman, *Making News: A Study in the Construction of Reality* (New York: Free Press, 1978), chap. 1.
30. Lapham, *Gilding the News*, p. 35.
31. Opening paragraph of a column by Laura Cunningham, *New York Times*, 3 September 1981, Home section, p. 16.
32. Dan Nimmo and James E. Coombs, *Mediated Political Realities* (New York: Longman), 1983.
33. Russell Baker, "Meanwhile, in Zanzibar...," *New York Times Magazine*, 6 February 1977, p. 12.
34. Edwin Diamond, "Disco News," in *Watching American Politics*, ed. Dan Nimmo and William L. Rivers (New York: Longman, 1981), p. 250.
35. Paletz and Entman, *Media Power Politics*, p. 23.
36. Emile G. McAnany, "Television and Crisis: Ten Years of Network News Coverage of Central America, 1972–1981," *Media, Culture and Society* 5 (1983): 202.
37. *Ibid.*, p. 203.
38. *Ibid.*, p. 204.
39. See, among others: Richard L. Barton and Richard B. Gregg, "Middle East Conflict as a TV News Scenario: A Formal Analysis," *Journal of Communication*, Spring 1982, pp. 172–85; and James F. Larson, *Television Window on the World: International Affairs Coverage on U.S. Networks* (Norwood, N.J.: Ablex), 1984.
40. See *Wall Street Journal*, 30 April, 5 May, 11 May, 3 June, and 17 June 1981.
41. See, for example, Edward Jay Epstein's fascinating suggestion that there may

have been a much larger scandal behind Watergate than the one revealed in the story of *All the President's Men*, by Carl Bernstein and Bob Woodward (New York: Warner Books, 1979). The dramatic plot helped confine the story to the White House. Moreover, any suggestion of larger conspiracies would have overburdened the already complex plot and undermined the credibility of the neatly contained White House story. See Epstein, "The Grand Coverup," *Wall Street Journal*, 19 April 1976, p. 10.

42. McAnany, "Television and Crisis," p. 199.
43. For detailed discussions of these findings, see W. Lance Bennett, *The Political Mind and the Political Environment: An Investigation of Public Opinion and Political Consciousness* (Lexington, Mass.: Heath, 1975); and Bennett, *Public Opinion in American Politics* (New York: Harcourt Brace Jovanovich, 1980).
44. McAnany, "Television and Crisis," p. 199.
45. See, for example, *Washington Post*, 15 April 1986, p. 1, and 16 April 1986, p. A25.
46. David H. Weaver and Judith M. Buddenbaum, "Newspapers and Television: A Review of Research on Uses and Effects," Washington, American Newspaper Publishers Association Research Center, Report No. 19, 1979; John Stauffer, Richard Frost, and William Rybolt, "The Attention Factor in Recalling Network Television News," *Journal of Communication*, Winter 1983, pp. 29–37.
47. For further evidence and analysis of these patterns in reporting, see Edie Goldenberg, *Making the Papers* (Lexington, Mass.: Heath-Lexington Books, 1975); and Gitlin, *The Whole World Is Watching*.
48. C. Jack Orr, "Reporters Confront the President: Sustaining a Counterpoised Situation," *Quarterly Journal of Speech* 66 (February 1980): 17–32.
49. Gallup-Times Mirror, *The People & the Press*, pp. 30–31.
50. Don Fry, ed., *Believing the News* (St. Petersburg, Fla.: The Poynter Institute, 1985).
51. See, for example, Phil Stanford, "Watergate Revisited: Did the Press—and the Courts—Really Get to the Bottom of History's Most Famous Burglary?" *Columbia Journalism Review*, March/April 1986, pp. 46–49.
52. For a more detailed analysis of the spoon-fed aspects of Watergate "investigative" reporting, see Gladys Engel Lang and Kurt Lang, *The Battle for Public Opinion: The President, the Press, and the Polls during Watergate* (New York: Columbia University Press, 1983). The Langs also provide extensive documentation on the overwhelming emphasis, both in the White House and among the press, on Nixon's personal image and popularity during the Watergate saga.
53. Fry, ed., *Believing the News*.
54. NBC News "White Paper" on the Reagan presidency, 10 P.M. Pacific time, 30 December 1981.
55. A case described by Epstein in *News from Nowhere*.
56. See virtually any mass media news story from 1981 to the present on the topic of the Polish labor movement.
57. Margaret Yao, "Under Deng's Regime, Urban Chinese Families Feather Their Nests," *Wall Street Journal*, 8 September 1981, p. 18.
58. Reported in *Columbia Journalism Review*, March/April 1986, p. 25.

59. Noam Chomsky, "The Bounds of Thinkable Thought," *The Progressive*, October 1985, pp. 28–31.
60. Lapham, "Gilding the News," p. 33.
61. Tuchman, *Making News*, p. 87.

CHAPTER 3

How Politicians Make the News

> ...when information which properly belongs to the public is withheld by those in power, the people soon become ignorant of their own affairs, distrustful of those who manage them, and—eventually—incapable of determining their own destinies.
>
> —*Richard Nixon*

At the close of World War II, the victorious Allied powers met to divide Europe into spheres of influence. These meetings—between Churchill and Stalin at Moscow in 1944 and between Roosevelt, Churchill, and Stalin at Yalta in 1945—were proclaimed in public to be reasoned deliberations that would ensure peace, stability, and freedom in the world for all time. Following Yalta, Roosevelt pointed to the Soviet promise of free elections in Poland as an example of the commitment to democracy that prevailed at the meeting. Stalin echoed Roosevelt's claim with the public assurance that "Poland must be free, independent, and powerful."

In contrast to these lofty images of the meetings and their results, another reality prevailed behind the closed doors of Moscow and Yalta. The agreement at Yalta excluded the Polish government in exile from a serious role in forming the new government. With this agreement, the three heads of state knew that there would be no real "freedom" in the elections that would be held two years later. In fact, their decision paved the way for the tradition of Soviet domination in Poland that persists to this day.

Churchill's own account of the Moscow session revealed that an atmosphere of brute political bargaining guided the division of the Balkan states. A half sheet of paper was used to jot down the amounts of "influence" the victors would exert in the territories in question: Romania, 90 percent Russian influence; Greece, 90 percent British; Yugoslavia and Hungary, a 50–50 split; Bulgaria, 75 percent Russian influence. Following

69

the bargaining, Churchill gave the paper to Stalin for his approval. According to Churchill's own account, Stalin simply "took his blue pencil and made a large tick upon it." Whereupon Churchill asked: "Might it not be thought rather cynical if it seemed we had disposed of these issues, so fateful to millions of people, in such an off-hand manner?" He proposed burning the paper, but Stalin insisted that Churchill keep it.[1]

There are two realities in the above story. One involves the actual political behaviors and concerns of powerful actors. The other involves the cosmetic presentation of a newsworthy version of the event, a version inspired by concerns about how the actual circumstances might seem to the public. Political actors are confronted constantly with concerns about how the actual politics of an event might seem and whether a more "seemly" image can be created and used to some political advantage.

Leaders who disillusion their followers live shorter political lives than leaders who learn to re-present situations to their best political advantage. It is hardly surprising, therefore, that the news is filled with self-interested, timeworn, romanticized, and often irrelevant versions of events. It is often argued (usually by retired politicians) that the practice of deception is the only recourse, given the unpleasant realities of politics. Despite this common lament of the "poor politician," one suspects that the realities of politics would not be so unpleasant if leaders were more serious about representing the interests and ideas of their followers. It is unfortunate that the selfless representation of others' interests is so seldom the stuff of which power is made or places in history won. Even more unfortunate, for those of us who watch world events from the outside, is the fact that it is almost never possible to know how closely the public version of an event conforms to the actual political circumstances involved. Indeed, the mark of skill in the political trade is the ability to make the public version of a situation convincing, no matter how far removed from actuality it may be. As former Secretary of State Dean Acheson once said, the task of public officers seeking support for their policies is to make their points "clearer than truth."[2]

On occasion, the contrived aspects of news stories are exposed as a result of slips, blunders, leaks, miscalculations, or defections of former insiders. For example, when Gerald Ford pardoned Richard Nixon for his Watergate crimes, Ford lost favor with many Americans who began to suspect that his earlier, "altruistic" proposal of amnesty for Vietnam draft resisters was an attempt to "buy" the sympathy of liberals hostile to Nixon.[3] When the U.S.-backed attempt to overthrow the Castro regime in Cuba ended in a military disaster at the Bay of Pigs in 1961, the Kennedy administration could no longer use the planned cover story that the invasion force of Cuban exiles (with its captured American equipment) had acted independently of the U.S. government.[4] President Eisenhower's repeated denials of U.S. spy flights over the Soviet Union became embarrassingly transparent with the Russian capture of a U-2 spy plane on the eve of a major summit conference.[5] Ronald Reagan's economic explanations lost some of their luster when David Stockman, budget director and chief interpreter of "Reaganomics," disclosed that economic figures had been "adjusted" to fit Reagan's "supply side" economic models.[6]

Perhaps because it occurs so rarely, it is exciting, dramatic, and somehow satisfying when a political cover drops to reveal a darker reality of corruption, power, and deceit. However, history suggests that for every revelation on the order of a Watergate or a Bay of Pigs, many more lie undetected until long after their political effects have been recorded. History tells us, for example, that Lyndon Johnson's justification for large-scale American involvement in Vietnam was based on a largely fabricated account of "unprovoked" attacks on U.S. ships in the Gulf of Tonkin.[7] Johnson, like Roosevelt twenty-five years before him, had searched for an "incident" that would justify entry into a war. Perhaps it was cruel fate that history made a hero of Roosevelt by providing him an immaculate justification in the form of the Japanese attack on Pearl Harbor, while Johnson was forced to resort to the tawdry business of fabricating his own incident. History also tells us of the major role of the U.S. Central Intelligence Agency in the 1973 overthrow of the government of Chile. We even learned, many years after the fact, that the Kennedy administration authorized the overthrow of the South Vietnamese government in the early days of U.S. involvement in Vietnam. This revelation took a rather perverse path to historical disclosure. Feeling that he was both misunderstood and victimized by history, Lyndon Johnson resented being blamed for the "credibility gap" that undermined public support for his policies in Vietnam. Perhaps in an effort to show that even the glorified Kennedy administration was guilty of a credibility gap, Johnson leaked to a reporter copies of diplomatic cables linking President Kennedy to the assassination of President Diem and the overthrow of his regime.[8]

As these and other examples indicate, many cases of political deception are eventually brought to our attention through historical research, government investigation, or the release of secret documents. However, *even if all past cases of news distortion were revealed after the fact (and this surely is not the case), such disclosure would not alter the political effects of lying and deception prior to their discovery. The problem with political deception passing as news is that as long as it goes undetected and unchallenged, it "is" the political reality under which people live. As Walter Lippmann observed sixty years ago in his classic work on public opinion, "the only feeling that anyone can have about an event he does not experience is the feeling aroused by his mental image of that event."[9] There is very little check on the kinds of images that can be created for political situations when the information received by the masses of people on the "outside" is controlled by a few people on the inside. As Secretary of State Acheson reminded us, the effective public official does not attempt to educate or convey "objective" images; the official's goal is to represent issues and events in ways that gain support, shape action, and influence outcomes.*[10]

The fact that political actors make a practice of creating images for political situations does not mean that the news is filled with wild, diverse, and highly imaginative political stories. Unusual stories tend to appear when, as in the rare case of Watergate, the actual details of an event become known. To the contrary, most political images are based on familiar symbols, formula plots, standard slogans, and tired rhetoric.[11] As pointed out in chapter 2, the world of political images is built from predictable symbolic transformations: the new into the old, the startling into the familiar, the self-interested into the public-spirited. Even threats and crises come presented in stereotypes of "Soviet aggression," "American firmness," "peace through strength," "productive and serious discussions," and so on.

There are those who argue that the news bias in favor of official, normalized political messages is not a bias at all: Mainstream views should receive a lion's share of news attention precisely because they represent the center of political thinking in America. This argument clearly fails to consider the role of the news in creating and legitimizing "official" or "normal" politics in the first place. Even more important, the failure to regard normalized news as politically biased ignores the possibility that many official pronouncements are inaccurate and inadequate descriptions of real events. The lessons of history tell us that it is precisely through the repeated use of normalized political images that the greatest political deception and distortion occurs. Thus, a hidden problem with reporting "official positions" as the main news of the day is the resulting likelihood of communicating a considerable amount of deception, lying, and political fabrication disguised as fact.

There is, therefore, a profound irony in newsmaking. *The credibility of a political image lies not in some independent check on its accuracy but in its past success as a news formula.* In this world of media reality, newsworthiness becomes a subsititute for validity, and credibility becomes reduced to a formula of who applies what images to which events under what circumstances. Ordinary logic tells us that the more standardized an image, the less valid and meaningful is its application to unique, real-world situations. Media logic, on the other hand, tells us that reality "is" the image applied to it. The more "official" the position, the more likely it is to be reported; the more it is reported, the more credibility it gains; and the more credibility it gains, the more "official" it becomes. It is obvious why common sense fares poorly in direct competition with media logic. Like any successful logic, media logic is functional; it enables both news and politics to operate on a routine, symbiotic basis. Common sense, by comparison, is of little use in unraveling the news web of political secrecy, double talk, and untestable abstraction.

If the images contained in official political positions were mere entertainment fare floating about in the electronic ether, there might be less cause for concern (other than for the low quality of the plots that politicians foist upon their audiences). As long as the images in the news are treated as real, however, people may be inclined to respond to them. Even, and perhaps especially, those images with the most dubious links to reality can generate actions in the real world, actions that have real effects: the election of corrupt leaders, the acceptance of oppressive laws or ideas, the labeling of social groups, support for wars, or tolerance of chronic social and economic problems. Thus the news images of the political world can be tragically self-fulfilling. Dominant political images can create a world in their own image—even when such a world did not exist to begin with.

THE GOALS OF IMAGE MAKING

In view of their political uses, it is not surprising that images are of great concern to politicians. Failure to control the news is often equated with political failure. As the campaign manager for a presidential candidate put it, "the media 'is' the campaign."[12] Or, as a key presidential adviser explained, there is no political reality apart from news reality. That assessment came from one of Ronald Reagan's top aides, James Baker, who was asked by an NBC correspondent why the president seemed so unwilling to compromise on a tough budget proposal he submitted to Congress. Baker said that any show of compromise or weakness was undesirable because, in the media, "everything is cast in terms of winning or losing."[13] Thus the president could not back down no matter how unrealistic his position. To be seen as unrealistic was preferable to being perceived as a loser, because being perceived as a loser would make him a loser.

It is clear that controlling political images in the news is a primary goal of politics, and, as such, it is important to understand what this entails. Most public relations experts agree that successful image making involves three things:

1. Composing a simple theme or message for the audience to use in thinking about the matter at hand. Call this *message composition*.
2. Saturating communications channels with this message so that it will become more salient than competing messages. Call this *message salience*.

3. Surrounding the message with the trappings of credibility so that, if it reaches people, it will be accepted. Call this *message credibility*.

Although these three components of political image making work together in actual political communication, it is useful to consider them separately in order to see what each one contributes to the audience's perception of a political situation.

Message Composition

The content of a political message is usually simple, familiar, and idealistic. Political messages generally begin with a key phrase, idea, or theme that creates a convenient way for people to think about a political object—be it an issue, an event, or even a person. For example, Franklin Roosevelt appealed to the hopes of the masses by using the simple term "the New Deal" to refer to his complex patchwork of untried economic programs. Borrowing these characteristics of simplicity and idealism, John Kennedy added the power of familiarity when he presented his programs to the people under the title of "the New Frontier." Ronald Reagan showed how far political connotations can be stretched by giving the simple, familiar, and idealistic name "the New Federalism" to his efforts to dismantle Roosevelt's "New Deal," Kennedy's "New Frontier," and Johnson's "Great Society."

Political themes and slogans can get an image started by encouraging people to imagine things about a situation. As the name implies, *an image is not some concrete entity that exists "out there" in the world; it is the product of human imagination shaped by the suggestive symbolism of political messages. The symbolic component of an image is so simplistic, abstract, and free of detail that the only way it can make sense is for people to add their own interpretations, fantasies, and concerns. Thus an image is an impression of something that is anchored partly in symbolic suggestion and partly in the feelings and assumptions that people have in response to that suggestion.* When people begin to supply the facts and feelings necessary to complete an image, the symbolic "message" component of political communication seems increasingly real and convincing; hence the irony that from some of the most simplistic and insubstantial ideas emerge some of the most heartfelt understandings.

When Richard Nixon's campaign strategists assessed his presidential prospects in 1968, they concluded that the biggest problem was the widespread perception that he was a "loser." In response to this problem the campaign was launched with the symbolic suggestion that there was a "new Nixon." Such an idea was every bit as illusory as the careful scripting of Nixon's new character. As with many effective political themes, however, the "new Nixon" became a much-discussed term that created for many people a seemingly concrete and legitimate reference for new political actions that otherwise might have been seen as ambiguous or deceitful.[14]

Message Salience

Creating an image requires more than inventing a catchy theme or slogan. Images come into being only when the symbolic component, or message, becomes a frequent point of departure for the popular imagination. Lots of catchy messages elude popular imagination because they fail to capture widespread attention. The need for a message to capture attention explains why the second goal of image-making is to saturate communication channels with the message. If a message becomes more prominent than competing messages, it stands a greater chance of shaping public thought and action. The goal of message salience explains why advertisers spend billions of dollars to chant their simple jingles and slogans over and over again in the media. The same goal explains why politicians spend considerable energy trying to get their simplistic messages incorporated in the plots of news stories.

It is not always easy for political actors to make their messages salient. Even though the salient messages in most news stories come from official sources, there is no guarantee that any particular official source can get its message across at will. In fact, recent political history suggests that many powerful figures end up the victims of the same news media that helped create them in the first place. Journalists can exercise many reporting options that may undermine the salience of a political message. The most obvious option is that reporters can simply stop covering an actor who, in their estimation, is no longer able to present a message in dramatic or effective ways. Alternatively, reporters can reduce the strength of an actor's political "signal" by boosting the coverage given to opponents' messages. In some rare cases, reporters may even undermine message salience by exposing a politicians's claims for what they really are, namely, transparent symbols with little real substance. These last two reporting options are particularly nasty because they damage credibility at the same time that they reduce salience. Such are the perils of life in the symbol business; today's truth may become tomorrow's travesty.

Boosting the salience of a message that is on the upswing makes the news media seem to be harbingers of new and creative ideas, while undermining the salience of stale messages makes journalists appear to be defenders of truth and political competition. However, it is worth recognizing that most of the messages eventually undermined by the media were promoted by them in the first place. Moreover, a message that loses salience in the news generally does so because another equally illusory symbolic creation takes its place. Perhaps most important, the real political effects of messages during their periods of news salience may be irreversible by the time they become deemphasized.

Although media decisions about what to emphasize and deemphasize in the news often seem arbitrary or capricious, there do appear to be patterns involved. For example, Paletz and Entman discovered three conditions surrounding the presidency that seem to affect whether the media will pass along a president's messages without commentary or whether they will dilute message salience with critical commentary or opposing views.[15] The first condition involves the "media status" of the president. If he is early in his term and effective in projecting a strong media image, the news is more likely to give strong emphasis to his chosen messages. Second, the more solemn the occasion or the more important the issue, the more undivided attention his messages will receive. Finally, the greater the perceived elite and public support the president has, the more salient his messages will be. Or, as Paletz and Entman put this last point, "the greater the opposition is believed to be, the more emboldened network correspondents are in their analysis."[16]

Paletz and Entman illustrate these conditions with the example of a news conference held by Richard Nixon during the darkest days of his Watergate crisis. Understanding the requirements of symbolic composition, Nixon chose a setting, an audience, and a set of carefully prepared messages designed to convey the impressions that he was far removed from Watergate and that the Watergate affair paled in significance when compared to his other accomplishments in office. Following the conference, however, was an "instant analysis" session in which CBS news correspondent Roger Mudd said: "I cannot see an awful lot of news in tonight's broadcast...."[17] Mudd and his colleagues then went on to remark about the handpicked audience and the political motives behind the messages that Nixon took such pains to deliver during the conference. Did such commentary have an effect on the salience of Nixon's messages? In order to assess this question, Paletz and Entman showed a tape of the news conference without the followup analysis to a group of people who had not witnessed the original performance. A tape of the conference plus the instant analysis was shown to another group in the experiment. The group who did not see the instant analysis emerged much more supportive of the president and his views.[18]

In view of the above findings, it is not hard to understand why politicians are so concerned with their images. In a sense, they are right in thinking that image is everything. Images feed on each other. To the extent that politicians can create appealing leadership images, salience is more likely to be conferred on their specific political pronouncements. To the extent that issues can be made to seem important by calling them "crises" or associating them with high symbols of state, opposing voices are more likely to be drowned out. To the extent that public favor can be won, future messages will receive less criticism, thereby escalating the spiral of popularity, thereby increasing future message salience, and so on.

Politicians who create such networks of reinforcing images are likely to be more successful in attaining the goal of message salience.

Message Credibility

Even a public bombarded with salient political messages cannot always be relied on to accept them. Only people in the advanced stages of becoming media zombies can be expected to believe everything they hear. Salient political messages are more likely to be supported when they are accompanied by some measure of their validity. Common sense tells us that arguments are more credible when they include sound logic, solid evidence, or reference to authorities. Most political images make some use of logic, evidence, or authoritative endorsement.

Unfortunately, common sense may fail us in our efforts to distinguish reliable trappings of credibility from unreliable or irrelevant ones. For example, when the Defense Department defends its budget requests every year, it plays a game requiring considerable symbolic skill. On the one hand, the testimony must reassure Congress and the people that the huge amounts spent on defense in the past have paid off in terms of American strength and preparedness. This calls for the introduction of facts and expert testimony to support an image of strength. On the other hand, the Defense Department must show that without continued and even greater expenditures, the United States will fall hopelessly behind in the arms race. This calls for impressive charts and graphs showing impending losses in weapon strength and technological sophistication. Enter an image of weakness.

If this image game is played well, the supporting evidence presented by the nation's most credible experts will lead to a logical conclusion every time: If the government will only fund the new arms programs proposed this year, the gap between the frightening image of weakness and the reassuring image of strength can be closed—at least until next year, when the statistics are brought out anew, the experts appear again, defense logic fills the hearing rooms, and as if by magic, the image of America as a cowering helpless giant once again appears in the minds of Americans.

It is impossible to know, of course, whether the experts and their figures are right because we have not had the chance to test their logic in a real nuclear war. But the trappings of credibility need not have anything to do with reality. They are instrumental in creating an image. The image is so terrifying that we are led to hope that by giving the defense officials what they want it will go away. And as if by magic, it does go away every year. In the process, we reinforce the very trappings of credibility that will bring it back again next year. How? By granting expenditures for arms programs in order to make the image of weakness disappear, we legitimize the use of the same "logic," "evidence," and "authorities" the next time that the image of weakness is released, like a genie, from the generals' briefcases.

THE TECHNIQUES OF IMAGE MAKING

The goals of image making are fairly straightforward: Select a theme or message to spark the imagination; make sure that the chosen message dominates communication about the matter at hand; and surround the message with the trappings of credibility. Simple though they may appear, these goals are not easy to attain. Effective image making requires sophisticated understanding and use of various communication techniques. There is, of course, no lack of time, energy, resources, or personnel devoted to the deployment of image techniques. For example, it has been estimated that anywhere from 30 to 50 percent of the large and well-paid White House staff is involved with media relations in some form.[19] It has been argued that the major preoccupation of the average member of the House of Representatives is running for the next election.[20] The Defense Department spends billions of dollars annually from its huge budget on public relations of one sort or another.[21] The U.S. Army even runs a special school to train its corps of public relations officers.[22] In view of these efforts, one observer has concluded that "the vast, interlocking federal information machine has one primary purpose: the selling of the government."[23] What do the public relations experts do? To put it simply, they use symbols in ways calculated to best satisfy the goals of image making.

Symbols

Symbols are the basic units of most human communication. Words are symbols that stand for objects and ideas. Flags, emblems, and uniforms are symbols of nationalism, group, or authority. Specific people can even symbolize general human attributes like heroism, patriotism, beauty, or greed. As these examples suggest, *symbols stand for, or represent, things (objects, places, ideas, etc.) for purposes of communication about those things*. Because of the existence of symbols, it is possible to communicate about something without having the object of communication immediately present. Thus, the word "tree" is a symbol that permits communication about trees whether or not a tree is present in the situation. The term *nuclear war* permits communication about something that does not exist anywhere except in the human imagination.

Symbols permit the recounting and vicarious sharing of experiences with people who did not participate in those experiences firsthand. Because of symbols, complex ideas and messages can be transmitted simply—as when the appearance of a uniformed police officer conveys a large set of understandings to people at the scene of a crime. Much of the routine business of life (including, unfortunately, subjects in the news) can be reduced to symbolic formulas for purposes of efficient communication. Symbols even permit our imaginations to work in concert to create and share ideas about things that have never existed (a unicorn) and things that may one day exist (a genetically engineered unicorn clone).

Since a major preoccupation of politicians is how to represent actual situations in the most favorable terms possible, it is obvious why symbols are so important in politics. Through the skillful use of symbols, actual political circumstances can be redefined and, for all practical purposes, replaced with a wide range of alternatives. In short, symbols offer politicians strategic choices about how to engage the popular imagination in any political situation.

In order to understand how symbols are used and what makes them effective or ineffective, it is useful to know something about their psychological effects. *Every symbol has at least two effects on us. One effect engages our thinking processes. This "cognitive" effect is responsible for the basic meaning of a symbolic message. The second effect engages our emotions, or "affect," by triggering a feeling about the message. The cognitive effect involves the possible meanings for any symbol, which can be narrow and specific or broad and numerous. For example, the term "freedom" has multiple associations for nearly everyone. In contrast, the term "congressional delegation" has a narrow, specific meaning. On the affective side, a symbol may elicit little emotional response or may evoke great outpourings of feeling. For example, the term "freedom" can be used in highly emotional ways, while "congressional delegation" provokes relatively little emotion from most people under most circumstances. Symbols that convey narrow meaning with little emotion are called "referential symbols." Symbols that evoke broad categories of meaning accompanied by strong emotions are called "condensational symbols."*[24] We have even invented symbols to help us talk about symbols!

The kind of image created for a political situation depends on what the key actors want the public to do in the situation. A faction interested in broadening the scope and intensity of public involvement may picture a situation in condensational symbols, while a faction interested in narrowing the scope and intensity of public concern can be expected to use referential terms. For example, groups that opposed U.S. actions in Vietnam represented the bombing of North Vietnam in condensational terms emphasizing savage destruction, government lying, and dangerous expansion of the war. The government, on the other hand, sought to minimize public concern with the details of the war. Public relations officers in the White House and the Pentagon invented an entire vocabulary of referential symbols to blunt the meanings and feelings attached to military actions. Thus, bombing raids on North Vietnam were referred to as "protective reaction strikes"—a term so narrow and bloodless that only its creators understood precisely what it implied.

Whether a particular symbol has referential or condensational effects depends partly on the symbol and partly on how it is used. In the right context, even the most innocuous referential term can be transformed into a powerful condensational symbol. For example, in the early days of the Vietnam war the Pentagon used the term "missing in action" (MIA for short) to refer to the troops missing and unaccounted for in combat. For years, this symbol was a descriptive term with a specific meaning and little emotional charge. Over the years, however, the number of MIAs grew, and many Americans became increasingly upset about the failure of anyone to account for these sons, friends, husbands, and lovers. Also during this time, the country became polarized into pro- and anti-war factions, making for a highly charged emotional atmosphere. Caught in the middle of this situation, Richard Nixon searched for some effective way of justifying his continued war policies despite broad opposition to them. Suddenly Nixon had his issue. He explained to the public that the breakdowns in his peace negotiations had been due largely to the refusal of the North Vietnamese to promise an accounting of prisoners of war and MIAs. He told the public that he could not end the war and turn his back on those brave soldiers. Seemingly from out of nowhere came demonstrations and endorsement of his position. Bumper stickers proclaiming the plight of the MIAs appeared everywhere. In the space of a few months the symbol had acquired a new way of being used, and the change of usage transformed it from an obscure referential term to a powerful condensational symbol. The lesson is important: *Symbols are not static; their communicational effects (both meanings and emotional impact) depend in large part on how they are used in specific contexts.*

This dynamic quality of symbolism helps explain why the narrow, redundant messages of "officialized" politics do not become intolerable to people. Since there are numerous ways to refer to almost anything, and since the real world constantly provides new contexts in which to place messages, there is a constant potential for subtle variation in the form or style of political communication. Cross-cultural studies of art, music, humor, literature, drama, architecture, folk tales, and, increasingly, political communication support the observation that human (and most other) intelligence is programmed to respond to variations on familiar patterns. People are attracted both cognitively and affectively to new twists on, or new contexts for, old themes.

From Reality to Symbol:
Turning the Ridiculous into the Sublime

In the case of politics, unfortunately, the old themes to which people respond are often poor representations of reality. To some extent, the poverty of political representation is disguised by the distance of political events from people's lives, combined with the intimacy and immediacy with which those events are represented by symbols in the news. Moreover, since people are creatures that seek meaning in their lives, the domination of political communication by a narrow range of political meaning encourages many people to accept official messages rather than settle for the doubt, anxiety, and social disapproval associated with the search for meaning outside mainstream channels of information.

The news, of course, magnifies all the factors affecting the acceptance of normalized political messages. First, by emphasizing style over content, the news exaggerates the drama and distinctiveness of old messages when such messages are presented with new scripts or new contexts. Second, by reporting dramatized and stylized political performances as though they represented the real motives and issues at stake in political situations, the news promotes the acceptance of often distorted symbolic versions of events. Finally, by implicitly endorsing official views and closing off the presentation of alternative information, the news enhances the psychological appeal of official meaning while undermining the appeal of alternative perspectives.

The flexibility of symbols is a great resource for politicians bent on transforming the real world of politics into a world of "realistic" political images. So great are the possible gaps between symbol and reality that actors sometimes propose truly absurd or transparent definitions of situations. *The frequent absence of feedback or commentary in the news can make the ridiculous appear to be acceptable, if not sublime.* For example, a local police department's increase in radar patrol activity triggered angry citizen protests against that spine-chilling condensational symbol "speed trap." The department launched a public relations effort to cool off the citizens with the reassurance that the radar activities were no more than "accident prevention patrols" and that worried motorists could call a special number to find out where these patrols were located each day (presumably so that the motorists would be sure to avoid having accidents in those areas).[25] In another case, the owners of a nuclear power plant that leaked radioactive gas were determined not to let the incident become a major news story like the one that haunted the nuclear power industry following the 1979 leak at Three Mile Island, Pennsylvania. The leak at the Louisa, Virginia, plant was followed by an eleven-hour communication blackout during which time press briefings were scripted for simultaneous delivery at the plant site and at the Nuclear Regulatory Commission headquarters in Washington, D.C. The opening announcement stated that the plant "burped" a small amount of radioactive gas into the atmosphere. To clarify this idea, the company spokesperson said, "It wasn't a leak, it was more like a burp."[26] The choice of a ridiculous metaphor evidently worked as the story died quickly.

Many political problems cannot be dismissed simply by turning speed traps into accident prevention patrols or nuclear gas leaks into burps. Some problems have widely recognized names, and the challenge for the public official becomes more a matter of avoiding their use than inventing a transparent substitute. For example, when unemployment goes up and productivity and profits go down, and the pattern persists, most people agree that the country is in a "recession." This condensational symbol strikes fear in the hearts of everyone—brokers, bankers, investors, workers, and, above all, presidents, who (being the great condensation symbols of American politics) are blamed for the situation. Most presidents faced with recessions engage in an amusing dance to avoid the use of the term, even when the situation is clearly defined. In one of the more blatant efforts to dodge the recession symbol, a Nixon administration press secretary fielded the following reporter's question at a time when the country had experienced several months of the dreaded word:

Q: How long do you expect the recession to last?

A: Well, it won't last long at all because we don't consider it a recession.

Q: How's that?

A: Well, we don't want to view the current economic situation as a recession. Therefore, it can't last very long.

Q: But what do you call the current situation?

A: It is from our standpoint a perfectly normal fluctuation in the economic cycle. You see, the term recession is very political. Our opposition would love to pin it on us, and we, of course, would rather not be stuck with it. So, unless something really disastrous happens, we won't talk about recession.[27]

Some years later, Ronald Reagan confronted another recession, one that he had promised to prevent if elected president. After first denying it and then avoiding it, he finally acknowledged the situation in the most casual possible way. As he was leaving the White House on his way to meet a visiting dignitary, Reagan casually remarked to a reporter: "I think there's a slight and I hope a short recession. I think everyone agrees on that."[28] Following this early bout with recession, Reagan's economic staff went to work on the problem. In place of the new, "revolutionary" programs promised by the administration, the approach taken looked much like traditional, stop-gap measures: massive government spending, tax cuts, incentive programs for business, and huge deficit financing of the government to pay for it all. Reagan, of course, did not take pains to point out that he acted much like all of the irresponsible presidents of the past against whom he had railed during his campaign. Rather, he continued pronouncing his programs "revolutionary" and pointed to the recovery of the economy as his proof.

There are two morals to the above story. First, a moral about poli-

ticians: insofar as complex, ambiguous, or unpopular realities can be hidden behind simple, clear, and pleasing symbols, they probably will be. Second, a moral about the press: blurring reality behind a haze of symbols is easier and more convincing when the news fails to take issue with the resulting "credibility gap."

Easily intimidated by Reagan's popularity, the news media took little issue with the gap between Reagan's rhetoric of economic revolution and his actual resort to unprecedented levels of traditional economic measures —measures that were widely known at the time to have long-term negative effects on the economy. The tacit acceptance of Reagan's pleasing symbols by the press played into the president's popularity, and the high level of popularity (and media passivity) in turn invited the president to take great liberties with the use of symbols. And so reality goes. . . .

From Symbol to News:
Bridging the Reality Gap

When a simple message is used as a caption for a complex issue or event, the first step has been taken toward creating an image. As suggested earlier, simply throwing symbols at a situation does not guarantee that the popular imagination will be engaged by them. Even more important than the symbols is their presentation to the news media. The salience, credibility, and image effects of political symbols depend on how those symbols are reported as news.

In some cases there is very little that a political actor can do to turn a political message into a widely reported news story. For example, when Jimmy Carter urged the country to "wage the moral equivalent of war" against its energy problems, the phrase was reported more widely as a sign of Carter's desperation than as a valid description of the magnitude of the energy problem. Carter had violated the three canons of journalistic respect: He was a faltering president, with low popular and elite support, speaking on an issue that at the time was not regarded as serious by a majority of the public.

When conditions are better suited to journalistic cooperation, public officials often succeed in dictating the content of news stories. Most "newsmakers" have the resources to produce highly professional media performances: writers, media directors, costume consultants, readily available dramatic settings, and an attentive press corps ready to cover official announcements and events. Through the careful preparation of messages, public officials often succeed in controlling the information pertaining to all the key elements of the news story: the "scene" (where), the status of the "actor" (who), the motives or "ends" the political action is to serve (why), the "means" through which the action will accomplish its ends (how), and the significance of the political "action" itself (what). The goal, of course, is to control information pertaining to all the components of the unfolding "real-life political drama" and thereby control the content of the news stories written about the situation. However, some situations are too spontaneous, and some actors too poor in skills or resources, to control all news information about an event. Thus, attempts at the political manipulation of the news run along a continuum from fully controlled news events at one end, to partially controlled news events in the middle, to uncontrolled events at the other extreme.

Fully Controlled News

Fully controlled media presentations are often called "pseudo-events."[29] Pseudo-events disguise actual political circumstances with "realistic" representations designed to create politically useful images. A pseudo-event uses careful stage setting, scripting, and acting to create convincing images that often have little to do with the underlying reality of the situation. By incorporating fragments of an actual situation into a dramatized presentation, a pseudo-event tempts the imagination to "fill in the blanks" and build a complete understanding out of fragmentary facts. In a well-fashioned pseudo-event, the script, the action, and the setting make enough reference to known properties of the situation to cause difficulty in distinguishing between what is real and what is merely "realistic."

The distinction between real and realistic is illustrated by a pseudo-event used by Richard Nixon to shape public reaction to a disastrous oil spill in the Santa Barbara Channel in 1969. Nixon intervened in the situation when the environmental issues were embraced by a volatile antigovernment student movement. Nixon's political motive was to "contain" the political movement, not the oil spill. Using his status and popularity as a newly elected president, Nixon quickly intervened in the situation to create the impression that the oil spill was no longer a major problem and that the damage had been repaired. After announcing that the situation had been serious but was now under control, Nixon completed the pseudo-event by conducting an "inspection tour" of a sparkling clean Santa Barbara beach. This walk on the beach would have been less convincing had he (or the press) announced that the chosen stretch of beach had been cleaned especially for the event, while miles of beach to the north and south "remained hopelessly blackened."[30]

The Nixon walk on the beach displayed the defining properties of most of the pseudo-events that dominate the daily news. According to Boorstin's definition, a pseudo-event has four characteristics:

1. It is not spontaneous, but comes about because someone has planned, planted, or incited it.
2. It is planted primarily for the immediate purpose of being reported.

3. Its relation to the underlying reality of the situation is ambiguous.
4. It is intended to be self-fulfilling.[31]

Both the trip to Santa Barbara and the walk on a prepared beach were planned for purposes of being reported as news (points 1 and 2 above). Indeed, the event contained the makings of a great news story: A new president visits the visually interesting scene of a dramatic disaster to show his concern for the problem. The relation between the news story and the underlying reality of the situation was ambiguous (point 3) in the sense that the image of reassurance and concern disguised a reality of devastation and cynical lack of care. In other words, the public was shown a real beach but it was not shown the real problem. Finally, the event was self-fulfilling (point 4), meaning that the news created the image that the problem had been solved because the media showed a scene in which the problem seemed to be solved. In the world of politics, it is understandably easier to create the appearance that a problem has been solved than to solve it.

How effective are pseudo-events in shaping the news? A well-conceived event has such strong story lines that it becomes hard for reporters to find alternative news angles. Even when truly significant spontaneous occurrences find their way by accident into a carefully staged performance, the overall theme of the performance is often strong enough to downplay the spontaneous elements in the plots of resulting news stories. In 1970, for example, Richard Nixon shared his Thanksgiving dinner with a group of wounded Vietnam veterans. The event served the dual purpose of counteracting his image as a "cold" person and promoting support for his new interest in the human side of the war (i.e., the fates of missing, captured, and wounded troops). Even though many of the invited soldiers decided to spend the day with families, the empty places in the White House dining room were filled with staff members from the local naval hospital. On cue, the press was ushered in for a brief picture session. After the dinner, an enterprising reporter decided to interview the soldiers who sat at Nixon's table. During these interviews the reporter discovered the bombshell news that Nixon had mentioned a daring attempt to rescue American prisoners from a North Vietnamese POW camp. This disclosure was big news on several accounts. First, the raid involved an offensive mission into North Vietnam, risking a possible escalation of the war during a period of intense peace efforts. Second, the secretary of defense and other officers of the administration had lied repeatedly under oath during congressional testimony, claiming that no such raids had taken place. Finally, the raid had been a failure, indicating possible breakdowns in U.S. intelligence and special forces capabilities. Despite the importance of these factors, the reporter and his editors at the *Washington Post* decided to base the headline story on the "President spends Thanksgiving with the troops" angle. Nixon's disclosures were buried in later paragraphs of that article.[32]

Partially Controlled News

Some political situations are not as easy to control as Thanksgiving dinner with the troops or a walk on a beach. Many public settings have an element of spontaneity in them. For example, press conferences can be controlled insofar as choice of time, place, and opening remarks, but they always contain some risk of unexpected or hostile questions from the press. In other cases, an official may be surprised by an issue and asked to comment, even though he or she is unprepared to do so. When the comforting script of a pseudo-event is unavailable, political actors must resort to other means of protecting desired images.

A common means of handling partially controlled situations is to anticipate and prevent possible moments of spontaneity in advance. For example, press conferences are often structured tightly to promote desired messages and prevent spontaneous distractions. In a press conference, opening remarks can be written in newsworthy style, reporters can be called on or ignored, time limits can be imposed, and stage settings can be manipulated. Some officials grant interviews only if certain "ground rules" are agreed to by reporters. Some sensitive remarks may be branded as "off the record" and thereby censored from reporters' stories. Some actors limit their public appearances to avoid spontaneous settings, particularly those with reporters present.

In short, the struggle over partially controlled political turf is ongoing, with the victories generally going to high-status officials who can use prestige, power, and other resources (e.g., busy official schedules) to define their relations with the press. When those rare moments of spontaneous exchange do occur, the news most often records only those patented political avoidance terms like "no comment" or those windy bursts of political rhetoric that seem to have nothing to do with the issue at hand.

Sometimes the most effective means of operating in an uncontrolled situation is to hide in the background and release information via an anonymous news "leak." Leaks are useful for delivering messages in many unstable situations. In some cases an official may favor a policy but not know how the public will react. An anonymous leak describing the policy gives the official a chance to change course if the opposition is too strong. In other cases the information leaked is privileged or secret, thereby presenting problems for any kind of formal public release. At times, the political message is not important enough to guarantee coverage if released through normal press channels or presented as a pseudo-event. If the right reporter is given a "scoop" based on the information, however, the chances are pretty good that the story will receive special attention. Strong emphasis given to a story by one news outlet may prompt others to cover it the next day. This use of leaks was acknowledged humorously when Ronald Reagan opened a press conference by saying that he did not have an opening remark because his planned statement was so important that he decided to leak it instead, thereby boosting the chance that it would receive the media attention it deserved.

Sometimes leaks come in handy for repairing images damaged by news reports of opposing views. During the election of 1980, for example, Jimmy Carter pursued a "Rose Garden" campaign strategy. He staged numerous pseudo-events at the White House designed to show off the trappings of incumbency along with his deep involvement in solving the nation's problems. Since Carter was blessed with none of the conditions for favorable news coverage and since the news formulas pertaining to elections emphasize opposition attacks, Carter's desired image was taking a beating in the news. In response, the Carter staff leaked a memo from the president to his chief advisers explaining why the demands of office prevented his participation in the first of the televised debates between the candidates.[33] Such leaks can provide touches of "independent documentation" for faltering pseudo-events.

Leaks also offer control over one of the most important variables in partially controlled situations: timing. The timing of a leak or a press release is crucial. For example, it is common wisdom that bad news is best released on weekends when reporters are off duty, news programs are scarce, and the public is distracted from worldly concerns. In other cases, the issue of timing means getting the jump on opponents who may attempt to plant their own images about a situation. A well-timed leak may accomplish these and other goals of "timed release" information while disguising the motives of the actors involved. Such was the case with the Reagan administration's presentation of the 1983 budget. The proposed budget was a political disaster. There were huge deficits where Reagan had promised a balanced budget. There were painful cuts in already weakened social programs. To top it all off, the country was in serious economic trouble. The political task was to soften the blow of more bad news.

Normally the budget is delivered to the press on a Friday with a strict embargo not to publish any stories about it until after the president has delivered his budget message to Congress and the nation on Monday. The early release allows reporters to digest the huge mass of information in order to write stories around the president's message. The embargo ensures that the president's message will be the salient news theme at the start of the week. The Reagan media staff evidently decided that the budget was such a gross departure from Reagan's earlier promises that the news on Monday would be both salient and negative. To prevent this, the budget director leaked the budget on Friday by "forgetting" his prepared materials in a congressional hearing room following a high-level congressional briefing. In a few hours the budget was in the hands of news people without the usual embargo. Since a summary of the president's message was included in the briefing materials, the story that would have dominated

Monday's headlines was, instead, scattered across the less visible weekend news channels. By Monday, the news concentrated more on other angles than on damaging comparisons between what Reagan promised and what he delivered. When asked about the apparent leak, White House communication director David Gergen denied it and explained that the embargo stamp had been omitted "accidentally" from the budget books taken to the briefing.[34]

Uncontrolled News

Few things strike more fear in the heart of a politician than a news story that has gotten out of control. Sometimes control of a story is lost because the underlying reality of a situation is simply too big to hide, as was the case with Lyndon Johnson's increasingly empty assurances that the United States was winning the war in Vietnam. In some cases, former insiders "blow the cover" on a story, as happened when John Dean delivered his damaging Watergate testimony against Richard Nixon, or when former war strategist Daniel Ellsberg leaked secret government documents about Vietnam. In many instances, a story gets out of control when a politician fails to handle the pressures of a partially controlled situation. A classic case in point was Gerald Ford's blunder during a presidential debate when he claimed there was no Soviet domination in Eastern Europe.

Whatever the reason for loss of control, the political imperative is to once again contain reality behind a screen of politically advantageous images. For example, Ronald Reagan dominated the news for over a year with his promise that "supply side" economics would cure the nation's economic ills and balance the national budget. When Reagan submitted a budget with a $150 billion deficit at the height of a serious recession, the news became much more critical of his economic pronouncements. True to his "Great Communicator" billing, Reagan scrambled (along with his staff of media strategists, of course) to regain control over journalistic treatment of his economic policies. A great symbolic show was made of budget cuts proposed by the White House. Although the proposed cuts were insufficient to offset proposed increases in defense spending, much less solve the deficit problem, the press dutifully put Congress on the hot seat as it reviewed the "president's budget." Since members of Congress could not have faced their constituents had they made the called-for cuts in social programs, the severe cuts were not made in full, giving Reagan an opportunity to "blame" Congress for the budget ills. A second symbolic diversion was offered by Congressional consideration and passage of the Gramm-Rudman balanced budget legislation. The president supported the bill and proclaimed that it would pave the way for a balanced budget (even if not in his political lifetime). These two symbolic gestures, combined with the short-term economic satisfaction of the middle classes, took the journalistic heat off administration economic policies. The Great Communicator was back in control of his news imagery. As for economic reality? Well, it lay somewhere beyond the political illusion, a forgotten victim of journalistic neglect.

Press Relations: From Cooperation to Intimidation

Beyond the choice of symbols and the staging of news events, the daily working relations between reporters and newsmakers can play a major part in the willingness of reporters to transmit all the news that politicians deem fit to print. *Most newsmakers strive to maintain cooperative relations with the press by scheduling press conferences and issuing releases at times convenient for making deadlines; offering scoops and exclusive interviews to "friendly" reporters; and even wining and dining a press corps eager to bask in the limelight of the famous and powerful.*

Such simple courtesies often pay big dividends in terms of controlling the timing, content, and amount of coverage. For example, shortly after Ronald Reagan became president, he attended a major "North-South" economic summit conference held in Mexico. The conference was sure to receive a great deal of press coverage because it was Reagan's first major diplomatic venture outside the country and because it was an important forum for defining the nature of the economic debt crisis that threatened all the countries in the hemisphere. The key administration concern was how press coverage would go: Would the media focus on Reagan's positions and postures as a new leader, or would his image suffer from Latin American concerns about the debt crisis and his perceived insensitivity toward the plight of neighbors to the south?

Although a huge press entourage accompanied Reagan on his trip, few of those reporters ventured beyond the comfortable American compound to find out how other countries viewed their own problems. As one observer put it:

> ...Reagan brought an enormous White House press corps. If the spokesmen for the poorer countries thought that meant access to the American media, which rarely discuss the issues of development, they were in for a surprise. "We'll try to feed you as often as possible," Secretary of State Alexander Haig promised at an early briefing in the makeshift White House press room, situated in the basement of the hotel where most of the American reporters stayed. The Reagan administration did feed the media, and many American journalists' accounts of what happened at [the conference] came straight from that official source. Some members of the White House press spent an entire week without meeting a single foreign delegate.[35]

Cooperation with the media extends beyond the care and feeding of reporters to the scheduling of major news events so they don't conflict with entertainment programming that generates ratings and revenues for the networks. Times have changed since the golden days of broadcasting when a political broadcast gave prestige to a network and saved the production costs of live programs. According to an analysis by Foote,

> Herebert Hoover went on radio ninety-five times during his presidency, and Franklin Roosevelt at least twenty times. During 1934, the year Congress was writing the Federal Communications Act, the two networks managed to find free time for 350 speeches by Congressmen and Senators, an average of nearly one program a day.... These political broadcasts substituted in many ways for news programs that were just then coming into their own and demonstrated the networks' commitment to public service.[36]

Now the problem of media access is a much more delicate economic matter resolved for the most part by running political messages into the regularly allocated news slots on the broadcast networks. Attempts to communicate with the American people at other times can cost the networks upward of $200,000 for every thirty-second commercial spot lost during a political preemption of entertainment programming. Failure to cooperate with these corporate economic realities could cool political relations with the media, as noted by former White House communications director David Gergen:

> I would never call and say we're going to do a speech on Tuesday night at 8 o'clock without first asking what's on the air that night. Our television guy would look it up and determine how much of a problem it was going to be with the network. It was idiotic, if they've got "Dynasty" on, to try to schedule something. That has to be a matter of discretion [otherwise] you heard from them. They would tell you very informally that this is a problem for us. "And this is part of the score card we have with you guys." I was aware at all times what our relative standing was with the network—whether we were in good standing, bad standing. You could take too much. You could go out and try to gouge them, play them as the enemy, etc. I felt there was a different way to play. If you do it very professionally, you'll get more out of them.[37]

Against this backdrop of cooperation, the press strategists who work for newsmakers feed the messages of the day to the press. The art of "message management" was never carried to a higher form than during the Reagan years in the White House. Having established a largely coopera- tive relationship with the press, the administration concentrated on the content, salience, and credibility of its messages. *The daily goal of the political staff was to produce a single dominant news story that all members of the administration would be disciplined enough to stand behind. The presence of an agreed-upon "story of the day" made the journalistic task of deciding what to cover an easy, even trivial, one while maximizing political control of news images flowing from the executive branch. The "united front" of administration officials generally thwarted journalistic attempts to develop other stories or to find newsworthy disagreements in the ranks.*[38] And the overall cordial atmosphere of administration-press relations worked against any incentive to avoid the course of least resistance: running the carefully produced story of the day.

Even in the most cooperative and harmonious press relations, however, some clouds will surely appear. At times, the most gracious political hosts may have to play rough with the media. *When cooperation fails, intimidation of the press is the next best strategy for news control.* On several occasions, for example, the Reagan administration chose to intimidate the media, and it paid off. One incident involved a speech by the president on the subject of U.S.-Soviet relations and national defense. The speech was the kick-off for the annual administration propaganda campaign to increase the already sizable national military budget. Support for such increases during a time of budget crisis and international instability required generating fearful images of a hostile Soviet enemy. Such images are routinely delivered without comment by the press to the American people. On the evening of February 26, 1986, however, ABC broke with tradition and did something different. Following the president's speech and a reply from the Democrats, ABC host David Brinkley was left with more time than originally scheduled for a brief interview with Vladimir Posner, a correspondent for Radio Moscow. A short question-and-answer session with the personable Russian might have gone unnoticed, but an early finish to Reagan's speech left ABC with eight long minutes to fill before the start of "Dynasty" (the news event had, of course, been scheduled to fit within the programming priorities of the networks). Brinkley let Posner fill the time with Soviet positions on the arms race and reactions to Reagan military policies.

It may have seemed to ABC at the time that the American people would benefit from hearing the "enemy" speak directly, but the network had another reaction entirely from the White House. The next morning, ABC News received a scathing letter from White House director of communications Patrick J. Buchanan, who compared ABC's decision with putting a Nazi on the BBC following a Churchill speech. Buchanan said on behalf of the White House: "We were rather astonished...to see ABC gave this Soviet propagandist a standing he does not merit, a legitimacy he does not deserve....The debate over what America requires is a debate for Americans to conduct."[39] Within a few hours, ABC News executive Richard Wald issued a statement admitting that the network had made a mistake, and ABC News president Roone Arledge sent President Reagan a telegram of personal apology.

The interplay of intimidation and cooperation strategies can be quite

sophisticated, as indicated by another example from the media management lore of the Reagan years. When the war in El Salvador become
dramatic enough to warrant regular news coverage, the venerable *New
York Times* hired a bright young reporter named Ray Bonner to cover it.
Unfortunately, Bonner was inexperienced in the fine points of press-
government cooperation and had the audacity to develop contacts among
rebel leaders fighting the U.S.-backed government. Some of Bonner's
early stories suggested that the rebels had considerable popular support,
while the regime proclaimed "democratic" by U.S. officials had engaged
repeatedly in terrorism, torture, intimidation, and massacre of its own
people. Such intrusive realities contradicting the daily line of the White
House became too much for the administration to bear. Not only was
Bonner snubbed repeatedly at the U.S. embassy in San Salvador (a serious
problem for a journalist dependent on official reactions to all stories), but
Times executive editor Abe Rosenthal paid a visit to San Salvador where
he held a meeting with U.S. ambassador Deane Hinton. According to a
"well-placed" reporter on the *Times*, Ambassador Hinton "became
hysterical" about Bonner's critical reporting and flagrant disregard for the
daily news images preferred by the administration. Although Rosenthal
denied being influenced by the embassy, he recalled Bonner from El
Salvador.[40]

Replacing Bonner in El Salvador was a reporter with no experience
(or contacts) in the region. No sooner had the *Times* made the change than
the embassy changed its press strategy to one of cooperation and opened
its arms, doors, and reception rooms once again to the news-hungry press
corps. A new press officer was appointed and daily briefings on the war
were resumed. The briefings were warm, witty, and filled with newsworthy quotes. The result of a new era of cooperation? *Times* coverage
swung clearly toward the official definition of the situation with the "story
of the day" making the headlines of the day. Coverage of grass-roots issues
and popular sentiments in El Salvador all but disappeared in the new era of
cooperative relations.

The successful attack on an organization as prestigious as the *New
York Times* sent shock waves through the rest of the media. According to a
reporter for another paper, Bonner's transfer "left us all aware that the
embassy is quite capable of playing hard ball," and as a result, "people
treat it carefully. If they can kick out the *Times* correspondent, you've got
to be careful."[41]

At the same time that cooperation had been restored among reporters
and newsmakers on the beat, President Reagan himself applied the final
pressure toward the new media consensus by delivering a nationally
reported speech at a Veterans of Foreign Wars convention. The speech
derided the "hype and hoopla" of media coverage on Central America:
"You wouldn't know from some of the coverage that the greatest portion

of our aid to Central America is humanitarian and economic assistance. You wouldn't know democracy is taking root there."[42]

This speech was the last element in a successful administration intimidation campaign. By the time it was delivered, the content of the news had already turned around and was heading safely back toward the administration fold. As news critic Michael Massing observed, the president would have been more truthful had he opened his speech by saying:

> You wouldn't believe how easy it is for me to shape press coverage of a foreign policy issue like Central America. We had some problems at the start of my term, but recently we've managed to overcome them. I must say lately the stories in the press have been very supportive of our efforts to halt communism down there.[43]

Although the Reagan administration alternation of cooperation and intimidation strategies stands as an exemplar of news control, most political actors monitor the news closely and many succumb to temptations to apply pressure when necessary. Stuart Loory, a reporter for the *Los Angeles Times*, recounted an incident of intimidation that occurred when he was a member of the press corps accompanying President Nixon on a European trip. Loory noted that the pope gave Nixon a greeting at the Vatican that was uncharacteristically political in content. The pope hinted at criticisms of U.S. policies in the Middle East and Vietnam. Loory noted that the tone was unusual in a public greeting and wrote of the pope's "polite coolness" toward Nixon. The very next day, when the tour reached Yugoslavia, top presidential aide H. R. Haldeman confronted Loory and demanded an accounting of the previous day's Italy article. Loory noted that "Haldeman had a report back on my story twenty-four hours later," even though the story "had travelled from Rome to Los Angeles, from there to Washington, and then back across the Atlantic to Belgrade."[44]

In another incident from the Nixon White House, *Newsday* correspondent Martin Schramm found himself the victim of intimidation following the publication of an article critical of the shady dealings of Nixon's close friend Bebe Rebozo. After the story appeared, Schramm was denied access to White House communication director Ron Ziegler. He was also excluded from the press corps that accompanied Nixon on his historic trip to China. Despite its status as a major national paper, *Newsday*'s harassment from the White House lasted for nearly a year until Ziegler proposed to let bygones be bygones on the eve of the 1972 election.[45]

Sometimes intimidation takes the form of challenging the patriotism or the political neutrality of the media, as when Dean Rusk, secretary of state under Lyndon Johnson, challenged the media to defend their coverage of a successful enemy military campaign in Vietnam with this remark: "There gets to be a point when the question is whose side are you on. I'm the Secretary of State, and I'm on our side."[46] Even Thomas Jefferson, the staunchest defender of the press in early America, turned against the papers after he became president.

Measured doses of intimidation provide the perfect counterpoint to the normal routine of press-government cooperation. Intimidation creates an atmosphere in which every reporter knows that writing an unfavorable story may jeopardize the access to newsmakers on which his or her career depends. As a result, subtle uses of intimidation (or the potential use of it) may grant powerful officials disproportionate news access with which to promote desired political images. One recalls here the words of former NBC president Julian Goodman in response to one of his reporters' complaints about Nixon's excessive use of the TV networks to deliver messages directly to the public. The reporter asked, "Julian, what is your attitude toward President Nixon's requests for television time?" Goodman replied, "Our attitude is the same as our attitude toward previous Presidents: he can have any goddamn thing he wants."[47]

THE EFFECTS OF NEWS CONTROL

There are several ways to think about the effects of politicians' efforts to control the news. For example, it would be useful to know what proportion of the daily news is directly attributable to official propaganda efforts. It also makes sense to think about the specific political effects of politically loaded versus more detailed, analytical news. Finally, it is worth considering the possible impact of simplistic, repetitive political images on the human capacity to think and reason about politics.

How Much News Is Politically Controlled?

Even a casual look at the daily paper or the nightly news suggests that the bulk of "important" news is devoted to the official actions of the government. The majority of these stories, in turn, seem to be simple condensations of what politicians say and do. In short, the news seems to consist mainly of stories in which at least one point of view is the "official" one. Many stories are framed by two familiar "official" angles—the "Republican" and the "Democratic," for example.

How accurate is this impression that the content of the news is dominated by prepared official messages? Leon Sigal addressed this question in his study of the news content of two of America's finest newspapers, the *New York Times* and the *Washington Post*. If any news outlets would be resistant to the pressures to publish the daily messages of the establishment, it would be these papers. Unlike television and smaller papers, the *Times* and *Post* tend to cover a broad range of national and international affairs in depth. Moreover, they have large reporting staffs, which should free them from dependence on press releases and wire service copy as the scripts for news stories. Finally, the *Times* and *Post* have images as critical, liberal papers that are not afraid of exposing government deception. These images are anchored in examples of journalistic independence such as the *Post*'s Watergate coverage and the *Times*'s publication of the Pentagon Papers. Alas, these images of independence are just that: images.

How did these bastions of journalism fare against the everyday pressures and temptations to report prepared political information? Not very well. Among Sigal's findings were the following:

Government officials (either domestic or foreign) were the sources of nearly three quarters of all news, and only one sixth of the news could be traced to sources outside the government. The breakdown of news sources looked like this:[48]

Sources	Percent
U.S. officials, agencies	46.5
Foreign, international officials, agencies	27.5
U.S., state, local government officials	4.1
Other news organizations	3.2
Nongovernmental Americans	14.4
Nongovernmental foreigners	2.1
Nonascertainable	2.4

Less than 1 percent of all news stories were based on the reporter's own analysis, while over *90 percent* were based on the calculated messages of the actors involved in the situation.[49]

The vast majority of news stories (from 70 to 90 percent, depending on how they are categorized) are drawn from situations over which newsmakers have either complete or substantial control. Here is the breakdown of the contexts from which the *Times* and *Post* drew their information:[50]

Context	Percent
Press conferences	24.5
Interviews	24.7
Press releases	17.5
Official proceedings	13.0
Background proceedings	7.9
Other nonspontaneous events	4.5
News commentary and editorials	4.0
Leaks	2.3
Nongovernmental proceedings	1.5
Spontaneous events	1.2
Reporter's own analysis	0.9

By any accounting, the conclusion is inescapable: Even the best journalism in the land is extremely dependent on the political messages of a small spectrum of "official" news sources. The *Times* and the *Post*, no doubt, include more detailed background information (not to mention more coverage of obscure events) than most news outlets, but the basic messages in their stories still represent official views. With respect to the substitution of images for information, there is little difference across news outlets. There may be fewer intellectual trappings attached to the images that pulse from the television nightly news, but it is not really clear what the highbrow trappings of the more intellectual print media really accomplish. One suspects that the highbrow media simply make the same messages more palatable to people with highbrow self-images.

The Political Effects of Controlled News

Perhaps the most obvious political effect of controlled news is the advantage it gives powerful people in getting their issues on the political agenda while defining those issues in ways likely to influence their resolution. Unofficial groups have much more difficulty influencing political outcomes because their perspectives are seldom given credibility via news coverage. As a study of grass-roots organizations by Goldenberg has shown, it is hard for unofficial actors to amass the credibility, resources, and information control necessary to dominate the news long enough to affect the outcome of issues.[51] When grass-roots groups do make the news, it is often in the context of negatively perceived events like demonstrations, sit-ins, and other protest activities that may offend the public and draw easy criticism from public officials.

The continuing preference given to narrow official perspectives has an even more serious effect than just influencing the outcomes of specific issues. The long-term effect of politically controlled news is to limit the range of problems, solutions, values, and ideas presented to the American people. The political world becomes a caricature drawn out of unrealistic stereotypes, predictable political postures, and superficial images. The same unworkable solutions are recycled in melodramatic efforts to "solve" chronic problems. People come to accept the existence of problems like poverty, crime, delinquency, war, and political apathy as facts of life rather than as the tragic results of the concentration of political power, the exploitative nature of economic relations, and the cynical uses of political communication. The failure of the news to inform the public about underlying causes of chronic problems creates a sense of helplessness and confusion on the part of those who view politics from the sidelines. The participation of the news media in promoting the official cover stories about these problems further undermines the chances for the kind of public understanding required for effective political action and real political change.

Even when public officials are caught in acts of blatant deception and misinformation, the result is more likely to create public confusion than to alter the rigid patterns of selecting, defining, and resolving public issues. Short of taking to the streets, people can only watch helplessly when the officials responsible for solving problems are shown to have cynical disregard for the public's need to know the facts and options surrounding those problems. Sometimes the frustrated public is reassured that cases of deception by public officials were justified in order to protect sensitive information for reasons of "national security." Lying, in short, is represented as essential to the public interest. Sometimes people are told that the truth would have been too complex to present to an apathetic and ignorant public. Never mind that apathy and ignorance are probably the results of official deception and neglect. Lying, in short, is represented as the only means of getting the people to grasp the truth. Even when an official becomes genuinely discredited, new images can be created so that his policies can be recycled by successors, as when Lyndon Johnson was driven from the presidency only to have his unpopular war policies dressed in new images and continued by his successor.

WHY IMAGES PREVAIL

If we add up all the above political effects of images in the news, an even more ominous problem begins to emerge. When people live in a world of images that remove them from reality, there may be enormous pressures to preserve the images at all costs. *It is even possible that disproving the facts and assumptions on which images have been built may not always shake the images themselves. In fact, there may be conditions under which discrediting an image may actually strengthen its acceptance.* Impossible? Remember the earlier discussion about the weak relationship between image and reality. The thing that makes an image compelling is not sound logic based in objective fact, but its appeal to hopes and fears based in self-fulfilling logic and self-serving fact. There are at least three conditions under which an image may persist in the face of seemingly contradictory evidence.

First, unless a discredited image is replaced with an easy-to-grasp alternative understanding of a situation, people may find it hard to give up the original image. When people are faced with the choice of replacing a meaningful understanding with nothing, it is hard to sacrifice meaning for meaninglessness. There is ample evidence that people confronted with the loss of meaning may cling even more strongly to their original, discredited beliefs. Similarly, political true-believers whose methods fail to solve the problem often call for more of the same remedy rather than change their thinking. Thus we have the paradox that solutions may end up worsening the problems they were intended to solve; witness the arms race, the frequent insanity of mental hospitals, the "crime school" atmosphere of prisons, the self-fulfilling nature of welfare, the increasing concentration of wealth following from "trickle down" economic theories, and on and on.

Unfortunately, the news almost never contains new understandings for people to use in replacing dubious images. At best, the news presents familiar recycled images offered by official opposition groups. Thus, people are faced with an empty choice: Rationalize the continued acceptance of a discredited image or shift to a formerly discredited image that now, by comparison, represents the only meaningful alternative way of understanding the situation. Thus, many disillusioned working-class Democrats voted for Ronald Reagan in 1980 in hopes that his "what's good for big business is good for working people" approach to the economy was viable. Less than a year later, this image was discredited by the factual evidence that many of its principles had failed when put in practice. These millions of people were confronted with the choice of rationalizing the failures of "Reaganomics" or returning to the familiar Democratic image of the "welfare state" economy that had been discredited in their minds only a year before. The result? Most of them either voted for Reagan again in 1984 or abstained entirely from the political process. Psychologists tell us that persistent adoption of nonfunctional understandings in our everyday lives produces at best neurosis and at worst schizophrenia, paranoia, and other psychoses. Perhaps it is a good thing that people are not encouraged to incorporate politics as a central part of their lives.

A second factor that might lead to the continued effectiveness of a seemingly discredited image is that discrediting often places people in the difficult position of not knowing which authority to believe. Should they accept the public official who denies having misled the public, or should they accept the news media's impartial reporting of the allegations of some other equally authoritative official? Since neither version of the truth brings the public any closer to the actual situation, the truth becomes hard to determine, if not downright irrelevant. For example, in the early stages of U.S. political and military involvement in El Salvador, the government publicized a State Department "white paper" titled "Communist Interference in El Salvador." The report laid the foundation for an image of Soviet-provoked revolution in El Salvador. The report contained many factual errors and unsupported claims, none of which prevented the State Department from releasing it as headline-making news. The *Wall Street Journal* (hardly a liberal mouthpiece) published an article pointing out the flaws in the report and noting an admission by the report's author that parts of the white paper were "misleading."[52] Following the article's publication, the State Department issued an attack on the *Wall Street Journal* denying that the author of the white paper had discredited his own report and calling the report "an accurate and honest description of Communist support for the Salvadoran insurgency."[53] At that point, the news story was closed. The *Journal* defended itself in an editorial, and the public was left with the choice of whom to believe: the U.S. Department of State or an authoritative newspaper's report.

The next phase of the government's efforts to build a case for its involvement in El Salvador continued to take advantage of the same "Who are you going to believe?" approach to maintaining an image contradicted by observable reality. U.S. military aid to El Salvador was tied by law to the Salvadoran government's observance of certain human rights standards. Therefore, it was not in the interest of the Reagan administration to admit that the Salvadorans had committed numerous atrocities that made a mockery of human rights concerns. For the two years prior to crucial congressional hearings on the question of military aid to El Salvador, there were numerous reports in the news of atrocities committed by the Salvadoran government against thousands of its own citizens: torture, mass murder, destruction of villages, rape, and other acts of terrorism. However, following the successful intimidation campaign (discussed earlier) against the media, American reporters were not present in the war zone, and neither the U.S. nor the Salvadoran government would admit that such atrocities had occurred. As a result, human rights incidents were labeled in the news as "unconfirmed reports" even by such "liberal" news outlets as National Public Radio.[54] Why? Because the U.S. government refused to "confirm" those reports (even though the subsequent congressional testimony indicated that the State Department had documentation of thousands of human rights violations). And the Salvadoran government defined the incidents in symbolic terms like "successful search and destroy missions against known terrorists."[55] Thus the favorable image of a corrupt political regime was kept alive by pitting the official positions of the governments against "unconfirmed reports" from unknown sources. The irony, of course, is that the news media looked to the governments to discredit their own images. Under these paradoxical conditions, what was the public to believe—uncertain facts, or familiar official statements like the State Department's dramatic claim that "The decisive battle for Central America is now under way in El Salvador. If, after Nicaragua, the government of El Salvador is captured by a violent minority, who in Latin America will live without fear?"[56]

A third condition that can lead to the continued effectiveness of an image in the face of evidence to the contrary is when the initial message on which the image was built remains more salient than subsequent disclosures of contradictory evidence. Since the media depend on cues from news sources to determine the "bigness" of stories, an initial story may receive intensive coverage simply because it was a well-constructed pseudo-event. Follow-up stories pointing out errors may be based on reporters' own initiatives that have less clear-cut claims to prominent coverage. Since facts generally take the back seat in the news to more abstract images, it is not always clear how factual contradictions ought to fit into a story. The most obvious exception, of course, is when the contradiction is pointed out by a political opponent, thereby providing a script for a standard news formula.

An example showing how documented factual errors can fail to receive as much coverage as the original story occurred in the aftermath of a Reagan press conference in which several key messages from the president were bolstered by erroneous evidence. Reporters had become annoyed at Reagan's use of dubious information to support his political messages. Several reporters set out to investigate the claims made at the press conference. It was later found that a statement about tithing (giving 10 percent of) his income to charities and worthy causes was untrue—he had contributed none of his income to charities. Also shown to be untrue was his claim that state-funded abortions in California had increased dramatically when women were allowed to use rape as an "excuse" for abortion. In fact, a sweeping reform in California assistance programs, not the admission of the "rape excuse," accounted for the California abortion increase. Reagan also cited the case of an Arizona welfare program that had increased its services and lowered its costs by turning to private sector support—claims that were denied by the director of the program.[57] By any measure, these corrections were given less prominent coverage than Reagan's original messages in which the statements in question appeared. More important, the facts were challenged through personalized news stories about Reagen rather than in stories aimed at the political images that the facts might have helped to inspire.

There was a postscript to the above story. As suggested earlier, politicians monitor the news closely in the daily battle to protect their images. Minor though the media criticisms might have been, they were not lost on Reagan. At his next press conference, a reporter began to question the source for one of Reagan's patented claims of factual proof. Anticipating such an incident, Reagan drew a folded sheet of paper from his coat pocket and said it contained proof of his earlier statements. He then admonished the press for questioning the statements from his last press conference. When asked by reporters to reveal that proof, he refused to do so. Reagan clearly understood that in the news, facts are incidental to images—even images about facts. Rather than introduce facts that might not have ended the matter (even if they existed), he simply invoked a condition favorable to maintaining an image about his facts. By holding up the mysterious sheet of paper, he in effect asked the audience, "Who do you want to believe here, your president or these reporters?" Thus, the conditions that bolster faltering images can operate together to prop up even the most dubious of images.

WHAT COMES FIRST: APATHY OR DISINFORMATION?

The cases of news management presented in this chapter offer a deeper understanding of some of the questions raised earlier about the nature of the American political system. Why, for example, are most people so apathetic politically? Why do people seem to change their political views so readily and then cling to them so strongly, only to change them again just as suddenly? Why do people seem unable to think clearly and critically about politics?

These and other related questions lie at the center of a puzzle surrounding American politics. If America is truly one of the world's strongest democracies, why do people take so little initiative in formulating problems and solving them? The easy answer is that people are by nature apathetic, fickle, and ignorant. Even if such untestable assertions were true, they would not contain adequate answers to the puzzle of American democracy. Why, for example, are people who are so fanatical about sports, entertainment, or religion so apathetic about politics? How can people with such well-developed views of religion or society be so confused about politics?

If in fact our main experience of the political world is created by political actors producing easily grasped images, and if these images are filtered through the medium of news before they reach us, then we may have the clues necessary to solve these mysteries. As mentioned earlier, people tend to become helpless when they encounter inconsistent, changing, and unworkable explanations for life's problems. In fact, helplessness becomes a learned survival skill in capricious environments. Have we, perhaps, confused the signs of learned political helplessness by calling it "apathy"? Similarly, when people are constantly presented with the choice between a familiar explanation of a situation and no explanation, they usually opt for the familiar, no matter how empty or irrelevant it may be. Meaning, even when it becomes perverse, is a hard thing to do without. Thus, when each failed approach to chronic problems is supplanted by equally failed but familiar past approaches, should people be expected to choose nothingness instead? This raises the question of whether people change their political minds readily, or do they, in effect, have their minds changed for them? Finally, when people are confronted with ideas that contain little in the way of intellectual challenge, thought-provoking logic, or credible opposition (except for other official sources promoting their own empty images), it is hardly surprising that the average person is not very articulate about politics. Ask a fan why her team lost the championship or ask a farmer about the effects of commodities markets on crop prices, and you will hear thoughtful replies. Ask a citizen about the economy, and you will probably hear the sixty seconds of pro or con rationalizations that have become the formulas for news stories on the subject. Sometimes, of course, you will not even hear simplistic formulas because when images really succeed, words, like facts, become incidental.

NOTES

1. From William Pfaff, "Yalta Only Symbol," *Seattle Post Intelligencer*, 26 January 1982, p. A11.
2. Dean Acheson, *Present at the Creation: My Years in the State Department* (New York: Norton, 1969), p. 375.
3. See W. Lance Bennett, Patricia Dempsey Harris, Janet K. Laskey, Alan H. Levitch, and Sarah E. Monrad, "Deep and Surface Images in the Construction of Political Issues: The Case of Amnesty," *Quarterly Journal of Speech* 62 (April 1976): 109–26.
4. See Bruce Miroff, *Pragmatic Illusions: The Presidential Politics of John F. Kennedy* (New York: Longman, 1976).
5. See David Wise, *The Politics of Lying* (New York: Vintage, 1973).
6. See William Greider, "The Education of David Stockman," *Atlantic Monthly*, December 1981, pp. 27–54.
7. See Richard Barnet, *Roots of War* (Baltimore: Penguin, 1972).
8. For a more detailed discussion of this incident, see Wise, *The Politics of Lying*, chap. 5.
9. Walter Lippmann, *Public Opinion* (New York: Free Press, 1922), p. 9.
10. Acheson, *Present at the Creation*, p. 375.
11. See Murray Edelman, *Political Language* (New York: Academic Press, 1977).
12. Quoted by F. Christopher Arterton, "Campaign Organizations Face the Mass Media in the 1976 Presidential Nomination Process" (Paper presented at the meeting of the American Political Science Association, Washington, D.C., September 1977), p. 4.
13. NBC News "White Paper" on the Reagan presidency, 30 December 1981.
14. For a detailed discussion of how this worked, see Joe McGinniss, *The Selling of the President* (New York: Pocket Books, 1969).
15. David L. Paletz and Robert M. Entman, *Media Power Politics* (New York: Free Press, 1981), pp. 69–70.
16. *Ibid.*, p. 70.
17. *Ibid.*, p. 66.
18. *Ibid.*, p. 66–68.
19. Wise, *The Politics of Lying*.
20. David R. Mayhew, *Congress: The Electoral Connection* (New Haven: Yale University Press, 1974).
21. See William J. Fulbright, *The Pentagon Propaganda Machine* (New York: Vintage, 1970); also Barnet, *Roots of War*.
22. Wise, *Politics of Lying*.
23. *Ibid.*, p. 273.
24. For the classic discussion of symbols in politics, see Murray Edelman, *The Symbolic Uses of Politics* (Champaign-Urbana: University of Illinois Press, 1964).
25. This incident involved the Bellevue, Washington, police department and was

reported on KIRO News Radio, Seattle, Wash., 16 February 1982.

26. UPI wire story, reported in the *Seattle Post-Intelligencer*, 26 September 1979, p. A2.
27. Reported over KNX News Radio, Los Angeles, Calif., date lost.
28. AP wire story reported in the *Seattle Post-Intelligencer*, 19 October 1981, p. 1.
29. Daniel Boorstin, *The Image: A Guide to Pseudo-Events in America* (New York: Atheneum, 1961).
30. Harvey Molotch and Marilyn Lester, "Accidents, Scandals, and Routines: Resources for Insurgent Methodology," in *The TV Establishment*, ed. Gaye Tuchman (Englewood Cliffs, N.J.: Prentice-Hall, 1974), p. 55.
31. Boorstin, *The Image*, pp. 11–12.
32. David Wise, *Politics of Lying*, pp. 3–16.
33. Reported in Paletz and Entman, *Media Power Politics*, p. 40.
34. AP wire story, *Seattle Times*, 8 February 1982, p. A3.
35. Sanford J. Ungar, "North and South at the Summit," *Atlantic*, January 1982, p. 7.
36. Joe Foote, "The Network Economic Imperative and Political Access," *Political Communication Review* 10 (1985): 2.
37. Quoted in *Ibid.*, p. 9.
38. For an excellent analysis of Reagan press strategies, see Steven R. Weisman, "The President and the Press: The Art of Controlled Access," *New York Times Magazine*, 14 October 1984, pp. 34–37, 71–83.
39. Quoted in *Columbia Journalism Review*, May/June 1986, p. 23.
40. Reported by Michael Massing, "About-Face on El Salvador," *Columbia Journalism Review*, November/December 1983, pp. 42–49. Quotes from p. 45.
41. *Ibid.*, p. 46.
42. *Ibid.*, p. 42.
43. *Ibid.*
44. From Wise, *Politics of Lying*, p. 348.
45. *Ibid.*, pp. 317–25.
46. *Ibid.*, p. 455.
47. *Ibid.*, p. 368.
48. Leon V. Sigal, *Reporters and Officials: The Organization and Politics of News Reporting* (Lexington, Mass.: Heath, 1973), p. 124. (Percentages total slightly over 100 due to rounding.)
49. *Ibid.*, p. 122.
50. *Ibid.*
51. Edie Goldenberg, *Making the Papers* (Lexington, Mass.: Heath-Lexington Books, 1975).
52. Jonathan Kwitney, "Apparent Errors Cloud U.S. 'White Paper' on Reds in El Salvador," *Wall Street Journal*, 8 June 1981, p. 1.
53. Frederick Taylor, "The El Salvador 'White Paper,'" *Wall Street Journal*, 21 August 1981, p. 22.
54. National Public Radio "Morning Edition," 1 February 1982.
55. Reported on "NBC Nightly News," 1 February 1982.
56. Statement by U.S. Undersecretary of State Thomas Enders on "NBC Nightly News," 1 February 1982.
57. These and other errors were reported by CBS anchor Diane Sawyer on the "CBS Morning News," 19 January 1982.

CHAPTER 4

Journalists and Political Reporting

> ...People may expect too much of journalism. Not only do they expect it to be entertaining, they expect it to be true.
> —*Lewis Lapham*

It is obvious why politicians attempt to control the news. It is less clear why journalists report so much politically loaded information. If the American news media were state-controlled or noncompetitive, it would be easy to excuse reporters for passing along without comment the political messages in news events. The emphasis given to official views in the news is less excusable when the American news media are proclaimed to be free agents operating in a political system that values free speech. How can we reconcile the official bias of the news with the common assumptions that the media are (or at least have the potential to be) objective, independent, professional, and even adversarial in their relations with news sources?

The problem of a "free press" dutifully reporting what officials dictate is so perplexing that a number of theories in communication, sociology, and political science have addressed the situation. Although each explanation proposes a different specific reason, they all seem to agree that the general answer has something to do with the routine newsgathering practices of reporters and their news organizations. It is increasingly clear that the everyday work routines of the media bias the news in favor of official views without really intending to do so. *Our first order of business, then, is to show how the everyday practices of journalists and their news organizations contribute to "normalized" (not to mention "personalized," "dramatized," and "fragmented") news.*

In addition to explaining how reporting practices bias the news, it is important to understand why these habits persist and why neither the press nor the public seems to grasp their true political effects. For example, many members of the press continue to defend their reporting habits as being largely consistent with the professional journalism norms of independence and objectivity. (These two standards have been combined in recent years into something journalists call "the fairness doctrine.") In light of this common defense of standard journalistic practices, it is worth taking a look at the real meaning of professional norms. Not all professional norms are in question here, as some professional ideals have served both the press and the public well. In a few celebrated cases, reporters and editors have even gone to jail in order to protect the confidentiality of sources or defend the principle of free speech. In many respects, however, the professional norms of independence and objectivity have backfired. In fact, it can be shown that journalists have become trapped within an unworkable set of professional standards, with the result that the more "objective" or "fair" reporters try to be, the more official bias they introduce into the news. *The second order of business, then, is to show how the professional code of the press perpetuates the problems it is supposed to prevent.*

HOW REPORTING PRACTICES CONTRIBUTE TO NEWS BIAS

Much like any job, reporting the news consists largely of a set of routine, standardized activities. Despite some obvious differences involving the nature of assignments and personal writing styles, reporters tend to cover news events in remarkably similar ways. The existence of standardized reporting behaviors and story formulas is not surprising when one considers the strong patterns of constraints that operate in the news environment. For example, the events staged by political actors tend to reflect the predictable political communication goals outlined in the last chapter. Moreover, most mass media news organizations tend to impose fairly similar constraints on reporters in terms of acceptable story angles, deadlines, and newsgathering resources. It is also the case that reporters are subjected to the standardizing influence of working in close quarters with one another, covering the same sorts of events under the same kinds of pressures. *In short, reporters confront three separate sources of pressure to standardize their reporting habits: pressures from news sources, pressures from news organizations, and pressures from fellow reporters. Each of these forces in the news environment contributes to the development of standardized reporting formulas that favor the incorporation of official political messages in the news and that lead reporters to write personalized, dramatized, and fragmented news stories.*

Reporters and Officials: Pressures to Cooperate
Most political events are so predictably scripted that reporters can condense them easily into formula plot outlines: who (which official) did

what (official action), where (in what official setting), for what (officially stated) purpose, and with what (officially proclaimed) result. For example:

> President ———— met at the White House today with President ———— of ———— to discuss mutual concerns about ————. Both leaders called the talks productive and said that important matters were resolved.

It does not take a careful reading to see that such a formula is virtually devoid of substance. The pseudo-events that provide the scripts for such news stories are generally designed to create useful political images, not to transmit substantive information about real political issues. Since such events are routine political occurrences, reporters quickly develop formulas for converting them into news whenever they occur. Compounding the temptation to report official versions of political events is the fact that reporters live in a world where "divide and conquer" is an ever-present part of life. Careers are advanced by receiving scoops and leaks; careers are damaged by being left out in the cold and excluded from official contact. Like it or not, reporters are dependent on the sources they cover. When those sources are powerful officials surrounded by an entourage of eager reporters clamoring for news, there is the constant possibility that those who report what officials want them to will be rewarded while those who fail to convert key political messages into news will be punished. Cooperation between reporters and officials is so routine that it is seldom necessary for officials to employ intimidation tactics of the sort described in chapter 3.

In view of the patterned nature of political events combined with the possibility of divide-and-conquer tactics from politicians, it is not surprising that the news seems to emerge from formulas that virtually write themselves.[1] Of course, knowing the formulas does not mean that reporters will always use them. However, in a workday world filled with short deadlines, demanding editors, and persuasive news sources, the formulas become the course of least resistance. Even when a formula is abandoned, there is seldom enough other information available in a typical political setting to construct another story. In the illusory world of political news, formulas describe "official" actions, and the seal of "official" approval becomes a substitute for truth and authenticity, which in turn makes the formulas seem legitimate.[2] Robert Scholes developed these ideas a bit further when he said:

> Perhaps the credulous believe that a reporter reports facts and that newspapers print all of them that are fit to print. But actually, newspapers print all of the "facts" that fit, period—that fit the journalistic conventions of what "a story" is (those tired formulas) and that fit the editorial policy of the paper....[3]

Anyone for changing that famous slogan to "ALL THE NEWS THAT FITS, WE PRINT"? *The point is that the formulas used to select and arrange facts in the news are produced largely through the mutual cooperation of reporters and newsmakers. These partners in "information symbiosis" may not share exactly the same goals or objectives, but together they create information that satisfies each other's needs.* It is all in a day's work.

In addition to developing work habits that favor official views, reporters are also human beings. Behind the occupational roles are people who sometimes identify with the newsmakers they cover. Regular contact under stressful conditions makes it easy to see officials as sympathetic characters faced with seemingly insurmountable obstacles in their efforts to do the right thing—not the least of those obstacles being a hostile pack of reporters. Of course, when officials go out of their way to antagonize the press, as the Nixon administration did during the early 1970s, it is more difficult for reporters to experience feelings of sympathy and identification. When officials court the favor and understanding of reporters, they are often paid back with sympathetic coverage that sticks close to the official's political line.[4] Such coverage is easily justified as an "objective" account of the official's public actions.

Adding yet another layer to the subtle working relations between reporters and officials is an even more painfully human factor: Journalists who cooperate with powerful officials often receive recognition and flattery and are taken into the confidence of those officials. In the intensely political environments that generate most of our news, nothing is valued as much as power. If one cannot possess power (and there always seems to be a shortage), then the next best thing is to be on the "inside" with the powerful—to be seen with them, to be consulted by them, to socialize with them, perhaps even to have them as friends. As Tom Bethell put it:

> To be on close terms with elite news sources is to be an "insider," which is what almost everyone in Washington wants to be. It is interesting to note how often this word appears on the dust jackets of memoirs by Washington journalists. But Nixon—his great weakness!—didn't like journalists and wouldn't let them be insiders.... Kissinger, on the other hand, was astute enough to cultivate the press, and he survived—not merely that, was lionized as "the wizard of shuttle diplomacy." (Is it not possible that the most awesome "lesson of Watergate"...will be a social lesson?)[5]

As the distinguished reporter Murray Kempton put it: "It is a fundamental fact about journalism, and might even be a rule if it had the attention it deserves, that it is next to impossible to judge any public figure with the proper detachment once you begin calling him by his first name."[6]

Reporters as Members of News Organizations: Pressures to Standardize

If their relations with officials set news formulas in motion, reporters' own news organizations reinforce the use of those formulas. Novice journalists experience constant pressures (subtle and otherwise) from editors about how to cover stories.[7] These pressures are effective because editors hold sway over what becomes news and which reporters advance in the organization. Over time, reporters tend to adjust their styles to fit harmoniously with the expectations of their organizations.

Why do editors, publishers, and TV news producers favor formula stories and "documentary" reporting of official events? In part, because standardized news is safe. *People in managerial posts in news organizations must constantly compare their product with the competition and defend "risky" departures from the reporting norm.* As Epstein observed in his study of television network news, even TV news assignment editors look to the conservative wire services for leads on stories and angles for reporting them.[8] *The wires establish a baseline for the day's news. Despite (or, as is more likely, because of) the fact that the wires cover the highest portion of planned official events and stick closest to official political scripts, they set the tone for each day's news. Following the daily lead of the wires becomes the most efficient and easiest-to-defend method of charting the day's reporting assignments.*

Although the conservatism of editors is the most obvious factor reinforcing reporters' use of news formulas, other organizational arrangements may have an even stronger influence on standardized reporting. Among the most powerful standardizing forces are daily news production routines. Newspapers and news programs require a minimum supply of news every day whether or not anything significant happens in the world. Perhaps you have seen a television news program on a "slow news day." In place of the usual stream of international crises, press conferences, congressional hearings, and proclamations by the mayor, the news may consist of a trip to the zoo to visit a new "baby," a canned report on acupuncture in China, a follow-up story on the survivor of an air crash, and a film spoof on the opening of baseball spring training in Florida. Slow news days occur during weekends, holidays, vacation periods, or recesses when governments are closed down. News organizations are ill-equipped to handle slow days because their daily routines are geared to reporting the official happenings from the news centers of the world.

In order for a news organization to function, it must fill up a minimum "news hole" every day. It must do this on schedule and in an efficient way. Producing a large amount of cheap, predictable news normally means assigning reporters to events and beats that are sure to produce enough acceptable stories to fill up the news hole by the day's deadline. During normal business periods, the public relations machinery of government and

business readily fills these organizational needs by producing events that are
cheap, easy to report, numerous, and predictable. Reporters, in short, are
given assignments based largely on the routine news requirements of their
organizations. The resulting patterns of contact between reporters and news
sources reinforce the use of standard reporting formulas.

Filling up the daily "news hole" on time means that news organizations must figure out how to make the spontaneous predictable. The obvious solution to this problem is to anticipate when and where the required
amount of news will happen every day. Since this task is made difficult by
the size of the world and the smallness of reporting staffs, the solution is
to adjust the definition of "news" (implicitly of course) so that things that
are known to happen on a regular basis become news. Reporters can be
assigned to cover those things and be assured (by definition) of gathering
news every day. As a result, the backbone of the news organization is the
network of "beats," ranging from the police station and the city council at
the local level to Congress, Court, and presidency at the national level.
These beats produce each day's familiar run of murders, robberies, fires,
accidents, public hearings, press conferences, and shots of the president
entering helicopters and leaving airplanes.

To break the daily routine, some reporters are given special
assignments to cover big stories like the Iranian hostage crisis or
spontaneous events like assassinations and floods. However, the expense
of special assignment coverage dictates that even the truly spontaneous
must be translated into familiar formulas. If an event is important enough
to justify special coverage, then it must be represented in dramatic terms.
Even assassinations and floods quickly become scripted. For example, an
assassination story will always include such basic dramatic ingredients as
elaborate scenic descriptions, information about who did it, a report on the
condition of the leader, a description of what happened to the assassin, and
speculation about who's in charge politically. A flood story also demands
dramatic pictures and detailed scenic descriptions accompanied by
accounts of the damage and human suffering, followed by a description of
relief efforts, and concluding with an assessment of when things will return
to normal.

In addition to beats and special-coverage assignments, many large
news organizations have developed a third newsgathering unit, the
geographically assigned crew. For example, television networks have news
crews (a correspondent and video and sound technicians) stationed in large
cities like Chicago, New York, Houston, Los Angeles, and Miami. The
assumption is that enough "news" will be generated from these areas to
warrant assigning personnel to them. The use of geographical assignments
reflects another way in which organizational routines have shaped the
definition of news into a convenient formula. Since national news cannot

all come from Washington, reporters must be assigned to other locations. But what other locations? Any location chosen suddenly becomes a defining center for "national news." As Epstein discovered in his study of television network news, almost all non-Washington news originates from the handful of cities where the networks station their crews.[9] One explanation for the choice of cities like Chicago and Houston for crew assignments is that these are major cities where important things happen. Another explanation for the way the networks (and to a lesser extent, the wire services) round out their national newsgathering is that communication and news production facilities are cheaper and more accessible in major centers of commerce than in more out-of-the-way cities. For example, it is more efficient to feed stories from Los Angeles to New York than from Seattle to New York. As a result, the news becomes still more standardized, with events in a few centers of politics and commerce given much more play than events elsewhere, regardless of their newsworthiness. Of course, if Seattle falls into the ocean, it will be covered as readily as when Los Angeles falls into the ocean, but a speech by the vice president or even the president in Seattle is less likely to be covered than the same speech delivered in Los Angeles, Chicago, New York, Houston, or Miami. Ever wonder why so many speeches are given in Los Angeles, Chicago, New York, Houston, and Miami?

The Paradox of Organizational Routines. The problem with routine newsgathering is that all the news starts looking pretty much the same. This would not be so bad from the standpoint of the profit-conscious organization if one news organization monopolized all the news, since the audience would not have consumer choices to make. However, there are many papers, radio programs, and television broadcasts from which to receive the daily news. It is hard to establish a competitive edge in the news market when efforts to make news production more efficient also make the news pretty much the same no matter which major paper one reads or which channel is tuned in. In short, routine reporting of news may be efficient, but it limits the share of the market that any media source can capture. For example, if all the news on television is pretty much the same, each network should capture an equal share of the audience, all other things being equal. Thus, efficiency may end up imposing an unintended ceiling on audience share, which limits the growth of profits in the news organization—and news is, after all, a big business.

The news industry has created a serious dilemma for itself. Changing news formulas in order to produce more distinctive, competitive news would end up costing more, thereby reducing efficiency and in turn reducing profits. Increasing the audience share is pointless if profits decrease in the process. As noted in chapter 1, this problem has led many other industries to "stabilize," each competing producer settling for a fixed market share because the methods required to expand the market would actually decrease profits. Examples of market stabilization abound in such industries as automobiles, steel, agriculture, and food products, just to name a few.

Another reason why breaking out of the news routine has not been attractive to news organizations is that it is not clear what the alternative would look like even if it were profitable to worry about it. Since news is largely the product of convenient conventions between politicians and journalists, it is not clear where to look for guidance in reforming the product. Any new format would surely draw criticism from politicians and other news organizations, and it might startle the public, risking the possible loss of audience share. As a result, tampering too much with the standard newsgathering routines is not something that the media like to think about. However, the media also find it hard to settle for fixed shares of such a lucrative market.

The economic dilemma of how to sell routine news has been resolved by the emergence of a growing industry of media consultant firms that advise radio and television stations and, increasingly, newspapers on how to expand the news audience and increase profits at the same time. "News doctors" like Frank Magid and Yankelovich, Skelly and White sell expensive audience analyses to news organizations much like marketing firms sell market analyses to the producers of toothpastes, deodorants, and hemorrhoid preparations.

Unfortunately for the news consumer, the entry of news doctors into the news business only increases the emphasis on formula news. As pointed out in chapter 1, most marketing advice involves the promotion of style over substance. Hence it is more likely that the major network news programs will refrain from altering their news content if there are changes that can be made in reporters, anchor personalities, theme music, or sets. Even when changes are made in news content, they are unlikely to alter the basic political messages that are locked into the news formula. For example, "CBS Evening News" introduced a special-feature report in its newscast. The only notable difference between those special reports and regular news stories was that the special segments were somewhat longer than typical news stories—a stylistic rather than substantive change. More time does not automatically translate into more distinctive or useful information, although journalists like to think so.

Instead of eliminating the formulas on which market efficiency and smooth news production depend, the news doctors specialize in "format cosmetics" such as dressing up formula reporting with different delivery styles, introducing new gimmicks into old formulas (e.g., "live helicopter coverage"), and determining what mix of formulas will work best in a particular market.[10] For example, Channel 5 in Metropolis, Illinois, might be encouraged to downplay dull coverage of city council hearings and run more crime stories because the news doctor's survey shows that people in town are particularly concerned about crime these days (and will surely be even more concerned after the number of crime stories increases). Meanwhile, Channel 4 in Pleasantville, New Mexico, is told that people are tired of crime stories but might be receptive to more news featuring local characters, scenes, and events. (The news doctor's survey shows that the people of Pleasantville have an unusual degree of civic pride, and a news program that tapped those attitudes would attract a larger and more loyal audience.) In East Egg, New York, the advice may be to buy a helicopter and expensive remote-transmission equipment so that Channel 3 can do more live stories. Even though very few meaningful things happen "live" at 6:00 P.M., the use of live action at the top of the news will distinguish Channel 3 in style, if not in substance, from its competition. Meanwhile, Channel 8 in Sprocket, Nebraska, is advised to add a 6:30 A.M. local newscast to its already lengthy news schedule. A survey has shown that people are "hungry" for news at that hour and no other TV station has tapped the market. In Capitol City, Georgia, Channel 2 is advised to rerun the 11:00 P.M. news at 2:00 A.M. because large numbers of swing-shift workers at local factories constitute an as-yet-untapped market for the news. The advice to Channel 11 in Nirvana, California, is to fire the aging and stodgy male anchor and hire an attractive but not too sexy younger female anchor.

And so it goes, a new face here, a new set there, here a format, there a helicopter, more crime, less city hall, more local color, more pictures, fewer talking heads, shorter stories, more weather (weather is becoming very big). And how about a hard-hitting political commentator to go with that new "action" image? When a news doctor enters the scene, the patient can receive anything from minor surgery to a complete program transplant, depending on how much the news organization can afford and how serious the problem is. A typical media consultant's services will include a survey of the tastes and habits of the news audience, some specific audience responses to the client's program or paper (usually through standard marketing techniques involving small "focus group" discussions), an assessment of the competition, an analysis of the current news organization, and a set of recommendations to company management about how to "enhance" the news product.

Such services are expensive, and the resulting advice is not easily dismissed. News organizations across the country are increasingly faced with the choice between buying a news prescription designed to keep them in sound financial health or losing the news image (and ratings) game to organizations that are more willing to buy helicopters, remote equipment, high-salaried reporters, attractive anchors, and news formulas geared to the tastes of the audience. Intense competition for audience share means that styles of news delivery are always changing, creating the illusion of consumer choice. The battle among news organizations never ends. No sooner had CBS recaptured its lead in the network ratings as discussed in chapters 1 and 2 than the other networks made format adjustments that closed the gap. And so CBS News president Van Gordon Sauter, who had steered the network successfully out of the "post-Cronkite" years, resigned to make way for the next facelift aimed at picking up a few precious points in the ratings game.

Even the newspaper, long the elite bastion of journalism standards, has succumbed to the formulas of the news doctors. One study found that between 1950 and 1970 the average American newspaper grew in length from 34 pages to 54 pages, while average hard news content dropped from 11.1 to 8.8 percent.[11] When the revered *New York Times* changed its format in 1976, a before-and-after comparison indicated that local and national coverage were down by 11 percent and 30 percent, respectively, while society and "women's" sections surged by 80 percent.[12] One newspaper revamped its entire format and called itself "The Newspaper for People Who Watch Television." In a typical edition of that tabloid, national and international news were boiled down to a column of "briefs" on page 2, while the front page featured a human-interest story about a recluse living without modern conveniences.[13]

It seems that the news doctors have produced two unfortunate results: the more effective deployment of standard political formulas and the general deemphasis of politics in favor of human-interest irrelevancies. There seems to be little resistance to these trends from the decision makers of news organizations. After receiving a survey of audience reading habits, the management of one major daily paper is reported to have issued a memo to reporters calling for more "fine examples" of rapes, robberies, and auto accidents on page 1.[14] Whether the news doctor's cure involves more human-interest stories or more stereotyped coverage of political heroes in action, the result is the same as far as political information goes: The news hinders rather than helps people understand the important events in their world.

The contribution of the news doctors to standardized news raises a number of important questions, including the following:

1. Is the news anything more than the collection of arbitrary (at best) or most-profitable (at worst) formula stories selected by news organizations to fill their daily quotas?
2. Should news be based on market considerations, or should it be based on some independent criteria of importance and newsworthiness?
3. Because people admit to watching or reading news about fires, murders,

accidents, and political heroes, does this necessarily mean that
a. they want more of it?
b. they think these things are important?
c. they think these things belong in the news?
d. they would not prefer alternative, nonformula news?
e. they would not be more engaged by news that actually *explains* human events?

Such questions are dodged by news doctors and media executives, who reply simplistically that they are interested only in making the news more relevant to people. *It is doubtful that current marketing surveys really measure popular demand at all.*[15] *For example, most media surveys are designed with the assumption that formula news is a given.* Audiences are not asked if they would prefer alternatives to formula news, they are simply asked which news formulas they like best. Market research that might turn up results damaging to product efficiency would defeat the purpose of the news doctors. *Thus, the standard excuse that the news reflects what the people want might be stated more properly as "the news reflects what people prefer among those choices that we find profitable and convenient to offer them." This is not the same thing as saying that the news is responsive to popular demand. Whether we look at standard organizational routines or the efforts of news organizations to "upgrade" their product, we find factors that reinforce the familiar trends toward more normalized news, more fragmented news, more dramatic news, and more personalized news.*

Reporters as a Pack: Pressures to Agree
As a result of the increasingly routine nature of newsgathering, reporters tend to move in packs. They are assigned together to the same events and the same beats. More than most workers, they share close social experiences on the job. Together they eat, sleep, travel, drink, and wait, and wait, and wait. As a result of such intimate social contact, reporters tend to develop a sense of solidarity. They learn to cope with shared pressures from news organizations and news sources. They come to accept news formulas as inevitable, even though they may express cynical complaints about them in between mad scrambles to meet deadlines. They respect one another as independent professionals but engage in the social courtesies of comparing notes and corroborating story angles.

This profile of the reporter's social world was called "pack journalism" by Timothy Crouse in his insightful description of press coverage during the 1972 election.[16] He concluded that reporters come into such close contact, under such sympathetic conditions, while covering such controlled events, that they do not have to collaborate formally in order to end up reporting things the same way. Once a reporter has been assigned to a routine event for which news formulas are well known, the temptation to produce a formula story is bound to be strong. Add to this temptation the presence of a tight deadline and an editor who will question significant departures from the formula used by other reporters, and the temptation to standardize becomes even stronger. Finally, put the reporter in a group of sympathetic human beings faced with the same temptations, and the use of formulas becomes easily rationalized and accepted with the social support of the group.

So strong are the pressures of the pack that they have been felt even by a trained sociologist who posed as a reporter in order to study newsgathering from an insider's perspective. While working as a reporter for a small daily paper, Mark Fishman was assigned to the city council beat. He quickly fit into the routine of writing formula stories that mirrored the council's careful efforts to create an image of democracy in action— complete with elaborate hearings, citizen input, serious deliberations, and formal votes. In a rare case when an issue before the council got out of control and turned into a hot political argument, the reporters at the press table reacted strangely. Instead of seizing the issue as the hottest news of the day, they ignored it. Ignoring a bit of news that did not fit the mold took some social prompting from various members of the "pack." As Fishman described it:

> The four members of the press (including Fishman) were showing increasing signs of impatience with the controversy. At first the reporters stopped taking notes; then they began showing their disapproval to each other; finally, they were making jokes about the foolishness of the debate. No evidence could be found in their comments that they considered the controversy anything other than a stupid debate over a trivial matter unworthy of the time and energy the council put into it.[17]

Fishman noted the strength of group pressure operating against independent news judgment: "Even though at the time of the incident I was sitting at the press table (as a reporter) making derisive comments about the foolishness of the council along with other journalists, it occurred to me later how this controversy could be seen as an important event in city hall."[18]

Just as Fishman succumbed to the pressures of the "pack" and still recognized them at a conscious level, most reporters are aware of group pressure but seem unable to escape it. In a study of the Washington journalism corps, the nation's reporting elite, Hess found that pack journalism was regarded by reporters as the most serious problem they faced.[19] As Hess noted, however, the social conditions of pack journalism will persist as long as news organizations establish their routines around the predictable actions of officials.

PROFESSIONAL JOURNALISM STANDARDS AND NEWS BIAS: WHY OBJECTIVE REPORTING IS NOT OBJECTIVE

The reporting routines described above are seldom regarded by journalists or the public as sources of political bias in the news. To the contrary, they are often taken as signs of an independent, professional American press. The existence of beats, special-assignment coverage, and regional news crews can be defended as the broadest possible "news net"—a net that assures coverage of virtually everything that happens. Story formulas can be represented as comprehensive documentary accounts of observable events. Competition among news orgainzations for increased market share is often billed as a healthy sign that news organizations are both independent and concerned with improving their news coverage. Rather than denigrating the press corps as a "pack," it is frequently claimed that individual reporters compete with one another for the freshest, most insightful angle on a story. Indeed, most of the defining characteristics of the professional press in America seem designed to reduce the chance that news bias will result from standard reporting practices. It is certainly worth asking the obvious question: "How is it possible that journalists consistently report such narrow political views when they are overwhelmingly committed to a professional code of independent, adversarial, objective reporting?" Any adequate explanation of political bias in the news must confront the problem of how such bias occurs in spite of strongly held professional values and practices that are widely regarded as insurance against it.

Not only do most reporters view the commitment to objective reporting as serious and credible,[20] but virtually every embattled politician since George Washington has accused the press of adversarial coverage. Even many members of the public seem convinced that the news, at worst, has a liberal, rather than an establishment, slant.[21] Nowhere in this popular scheme of things is there much room for the idea that the news marches in lockstep with powerful elites (both left and right) and non-threatening popular groups against the interests of large numbers of silenced Americans. Thus an adequate explanation of how the news comes by its status quo bias not only must explain the failure of professional norms to prevent such bias but also must account for the widespread belief of journalists, politicians, and the public that those professional safeguards have not failed.

The explanation proposed here confronts the paradox of objective journalism by showing that the news is not biased in spite of, but precisely because of, the professional journalism standards intended to prevent bias. The central idea is that the professional practices embodying journalism norms of independence and objectivity also create conditions that systematically favor the reporting of narrow, official perspectives. At the same time, the postures of independence and objectivity created by the use of these professional practices give off the impression that the resulting news is the best available representation of reality. In short, professional journalism standards introduce a distorted political perspective into the news yet legitimize that perspective as broad and realistic.

Fairness: The New Objectivity

In recent years journalists have increasingly adopted the term "fairness" in place of the once-popular claim of "objectivity." Fairness seems to be a more reasonable reporting goal in light of all the obstacles to objectivity: the values inherent in political events, the deceptions of newsmakers, the difficulty of achieving a wholly neutral point of view, the impossibility of covering all the sides and gathering all the facts, and the rush to meet unreasonably short deadlines. Because of these and other difficulties, the press is sure to come under fire for not being objective no matter how hard it tries to present "the facts." Thus, "fairness" sounds like a more reasonable and defensible goal: Reporters try to gather as much information as they can while giving "both sides" equal time to register their comments and interpretations.

The idea of fairness invites sympathy for journalists who are trying their best to be accurate under difficult circumstances. There is no doubt that reporting is not an easy business and that sympathy might be in order for the hard-working, under-appreciated professional. However, a sympathetic euphemism like "the fairness doctrine" might be more acceptable if it referred to real changes in underlying reporting practices that create news information biases. But the term "fairness" refers to much the same journalistic practices that originated and once passed under the cover of the lofty claim of "objectivity." And, in its own way, *fairness* still invites us to think that reporting is the best, most accurate possible. Since both fairness and objectivity conjure up images of accuracy, the new term, like the old, preys on deeply held public expectations that the news will be "true" and "believable." In this sense, fairness may be even more misleading than objectivity as a description of news content. At least objectivity stands in sharp contrast to the reality of personalized, dramatized, fragmented, and normalized news. Fairness, on the other hand, is a fuzzier term that implicitly invites us to rationalize away the information bias of news as being the best we can hope for given the limits under which well-meaning journalists operate.

But, you may say, isn't presenting both sides and giving them equal time about as close to accuracy as we can get? And isn't "fair" a better description of this approach than "objective"? Consider the number of dubious assumptions on which the newfound popularity of the term "fairness" rests. First, there is the problem of limiting complex, multisided issues to two sides. Then there is the question of which two sides to admit through the news gate. Almost invariably it is safer and therefore "fairer" to publicize the views of two familiar, predictable, and legitimate groups or actors. When an unexpected "side" is heard, cries of "unfair" can be heard from those sides who expect to control their share of the news. Thus, the two sides that appear in most stories are anything but a broad sample of possible viewpoints, and, therefore, fairness is a loaded term from the outset. For example, the ordinary assumption about "fairness" in reporting presidential addresses is that the opposition party will be given an opportunity to reply. Fair enough, right? But what if this is just a "knee-jerk" definition of fairness based on the poorly examined, common-sense notion that the two political parties are the two most legitimate "other sides" in American politics?—an assumption that is reinforced every time journalists build a story upon it. Yet attempts to break out of the "fairness ritual" are risky, as ABC found in the example from chapter 3 involving the presentation of a "third side" on the issue of arms control. Recall that even though ABC broadcast the obligatory response from the opposition to a presidential speech on arms control, the network clearly stepped beyond the bounds of "fairness" by inviting a response from a Soviet journalist. The point is not that the press has an obligation to be "fair" to the Russians, but it might be fair to the American people to at least let them hear what the other side has to say. However, the cries of foul from the White House provoked an apology from ABC, implying that it would not happen again. So much for the degree of substantive freedom surrounding the concept of fairness.

Beyond "two-sidedness," there is a second hallmark of fairness: "equal time." *Both sides, so the doctrine goes, should be given equal time to present their positions. The trouble is that equal time seldom translates into equal information, particularly in cases where an attempt is made to draw in a side that is seldom heard.* If one side, say the government or a party, fills its time with tired slogans and ideological precepts, a seldom-heard point of view will be hard to present as effectively in the same amount of time. *New ideas take more time and effort to communicate intelligibly than old, familiar ideas. Given equal time, the information edge goes to the official, stereotypical pronouncement in almost every case.* The press could, of course, devote the extra time and explanation necessary to make new ideas accessible to people, but that would seem unfair to the dominant actors and their supporters. It is safer to stick with an easy idea of fairness that involves granting equal time to the statements of the two most vocal sides.

Whether we talk about "fairness" or "objectivity," the important thing is to recognize that both terms are potentially empty euphemisms that disguise biases in news content. Since the contemporary "fairness doctrine" has its roots in the same practices that were originally called "objective reporting," the following discussion will use the term "objectivity" to point out the historical continuity of basic reporting practices.

If the reader perfers the term "fairness," feel free to substitute it, bearing in mind that *whether we call it fairness or objectivity, the words may change while underlying journalism practices remain much the same.*

Professional Journalism and Its Standard Defense

The popular defense of objective reporting is that it prevents, or at least minimizes, political bias and distortion in the news. The key practices that have fallen under the protective cover of "objective journalism" include the following:[22]

1. The professional journalist assumes *the role of a politically neutral adversary*, critically examining all sides of an issue and thereby assuring the impartial coverage of the broadest range of important issues.
2. The journalist resists the temptation to discuss the seamy sensationalistic side of the news by *observing prevailing social standards of decency and good taste*.
3. The truthfulness and factuality of the news is guaranteed by *the use of documentary reporting practices* that permit reporters to transmit to the public only what they can observe or support with physical evidence.
4. News objectivity is reinforced further by *the use of a common or standardized format for packaging the news: the story*. Stories serve as an implicit check on news content by requiring reporters to gather all the facts (who, what, when, where, how, etc.) needed to construct a consistent and plausible account of an incident. Since stories are also the most common means of everyday communication about events, they enable the public to judge the consistency and plausibility of news accounts. Moreover, since the use of stories is a standard reporting practice, the public can make systematic comparisons among the coverage given to events by different news organizations.
5. The use of standardized methodology and reporting formats enables any reporter to cover any kind of story, thus separating reporters from personal bias vis-a-vis the subject matter of the news. The *practice of training reporters as generalists* (as opposed to specialists) also helps to separate the desired documentary reporting function of journalism from undesirable pedantic or interpretive tendencies in news reporting.[23]
6. The above practices are regulated and enforced by the important practice of editorial review, which serves as a check against violations of the practices and norms of the profession.

When describing the major practices that comprise objective reporting, it is difficult not to mention their normative purposes in the same breath. As the above list indicates, practices and normative purposes are so closely connected in everyday usage that it is tempting to think that the practices were, in fact, designed to implement normative goals. Indeed it is difficult to imagine any other function for adversarial roles or documentary reporting or standards of good taste than the simple "objectification" of the news. It is also difficult to think that these practices do not help in some way to accomplish their stated purposes. Even if the press does not always succeed in its normative mission, the clear adherence to these news-gathering practices would seem to imply that the news must be as fair and objective as it can be, given the political pressures under which it is gathered.

The Shady Origins of Objective Journalism

Despite the appeal of the idea that professional journalism practices derive logically from the norm of objective journalism, there is considerable evidence that the practices preceded the norm. Most modern journalism practices can be traced to economic and social conditions affecting the success of mass market news around the middle of the nineteenth century.[24] *The objectivity norm did not emerge until the turn of the century when established news organizations began to legitimize their product and their status with claims about professionalism.*

In the early days of the American republic, the news was anything but objective. Most newspapers were either funded by, or otherwise sympathetic to, particular political parties, interest organizations, or ideologies. Reporting involved the political interpretation of events. People bought a newspaper knowing what its political perspective was and knowing that political events would be filtered through that perspective. In many respects, this is a sensible way to approach the news. If one knows the biases of a reporter, it is possible to control for them in interpreting the account of events. Moreover, if reporting is explicitly politically oriented, it becomes possible for different reporters to look at the same event from different points of view. Finally, since political events generally convey political messages, an overtly political reporting style is more likely to draw these messages out than to let them slide by unnoticed (with the risk that they might pass for broad, nonpartisan perspectives).

Their strong commitment to political analysis in news reporting notwithstanding, the early newspapers suffered economic limitations that made them unable to compete for large market shares as the nation and its communication system grew during the mid-1800s. The early papers were modest operations with small local readerships. As the country grew, a number of important changes affected the economics of the news business. For example, population began to shift to the cities, creating mass audiences for the news. The rapid expansion of the American territory during the nineteenth century created a need for the rapid and large-scale distribution of "national" news. Rapid breakthroughs in printing and communication technologies made possible the production of cheap mass media news that could be gathered in the morning on the East Coast and distributed by evening on the West Coast.

These and other patterns in the development of the nation produced dramatic changes in the news. By 1848, a group of newspapers made the first great step toward standardized news with the formation of the Associated Press.[25] The idea of pooling reporters and selling the same story to hundreds, and eventually thousands, of subscribing newspapers meant that the news had become a profitable mass market commodity. Of course, the broad marketability of the news meant that it had to be stripped of its overt political messages so that it would be appealing to news organizations of all political persuasions. In this fashion, "documentary reporting" was born. Moreover, the transmission of national news over the telegraph wires dictated a simplified, standardized reporting format— something that could convey a large amount of information in the most economical form. Thus the analytical essay rapidly gave way to the news story. The story was the perfect skeletal form for transmitting information over the "wires." The *who, what, where, when, why* of an event made for economical transmission and easy reconstruction and embellishment on the other end. As the market for mass media news grew, the demand for reporters grew along with it. Whereas writing a persuasive political essay required considerable skill in the art of argumentation and the science of political analysis, virtually anyone could compose a story. After all, stories are the basic media of communication about events in the everyday social world. The use of stories also guaranteed that the news would be intelligible to the growing mass news audience.

In this manner, the overlapping effects of communication technology, economic development, and social change gave rise to large-scale news-gathering and news marketing organizations. Along with these organizations came a standardized set of reporting practices. As mentioned above, news services like the AP ushered in the documentary report. The use of wire transmission, along with untrained reporters, promoted the shift to the story form. The discovery that drama sold newspapers promoted the first adversarial reporting. Early mass media reporters were rather like agents provocateurs, stirring up controversy and conflict in order to generate dramatic material for their stories. As papers began to compete in the marketplace they also competed for the "scoop" and the "big story," further stimulating competition and adversarialism among reporters. *As news bureaucracies grew in response to their economic success, editorial review practices emerged as expedient means of processing the huge flow of news. Standards of good taste guaranteed the inoffensiveness and mass marketability of the news product, particularly toward the turn of the century with the advent of a large, educated, middle-class news audience.*

Nowhere in this history of the development of modern journalism was there a guiding professional rationale for what was happening. *Even though we tend to think of the practices that emerged from this period as the hallmarks of "objective journalism," the concept of "objectivity" and its related professional rationale came much later. Journalism, like most professions, developed a set of business practices first, then endowed those practices with a set of impressive professional rationalizations, and finally proceeded to rewrite its history in ways that made the practices seem to emerge, as if through immaculate conception, from an inspiring set of professional ideals.*

In fact, the creation of a professional creed of "objective journalism" (and its use to describe existing reporting practices) can be attributed to a number of rather mundane causes. For example, successive generations of reporters began to regard their work as a skilled occupation that should demand higher status and better wages. The move toward a professional status both enhanced the social image of reporting and paved the way for higher wages by restricting the entry of newcomers "off the street" into the journalism ranks. Professionalism meant that formal training and screening could be required for skills that had been acquired formerly "on the job."[26] The image of professional reporting was advanced further by a group of big-city newspapers that sought to sell the news to the rapidly growing and untapped middle-class market at the turn of the centruy. Life in urban settings was becoming dominated by the affluent middle class of professional, clerical, and business people who sported formal educations along with intellectual pretensions. Representing the news as objective, nonpartisan, and tasteful became an effective marketing ploy geared to the life-style of this group. Consider, for example, the *New York Times*'s early slogans "All the News That's Fit to Print" and "It Will Not Soil the Breakfast Cloth."[27] Thus, existing practices became redefined around a professional image that dressed old news content in a new style. This emerging professional image of the mainstream mass media also became a convenient means of discrediting the muckrakers on the journalistic left and the sensationalistic "scandal sheets" on the political right.[28]

A final boost to the emerging code of objective journalism came in the form of a growing concern among intellectuals following World War I that democracy was in trouble and could be saved by a professional press dedicated to the mission of providing objective information to the public.[29] This noble purpose helped consolidate the existing pressures for professionalization. Led by persuasive spokesmen like Walter Lippmann,[30] journalists began to regard objective reporting as both a description of their existing work practices and as a high moral imperative. Perhaps the best capsule summary of this curious transition of journalism from a business into a profession is Lou Cannon's observation that what began "as a technique became a value."[31]

Professional Practices and News Distortion

Each of the defining elements of objective journalism makes a direct contribution to news bias. Professional claims of fairness and objectivity to the contrary, each component of news objectivity creates conditions favorable to the reporting of status quo news. This should not be surprising in view of the above capsule history of the news profession. *All the basic practices that later became known as "objective journalism" were developed as efficient means of selling mass social and political values to a mass audience. As diverse political perspectives gradually disappeared from the news or became discredited as not "objective," it became increasingly easy to convince people that the dominant mass media political perspective that remained was somehow objective. The logic of such a claim is simple: As one reality comes to dominate all others, it begins to seem that the dominant reality is objective.* The absence of credible competition supports an artificial claim of objectivity. Unfortunately, this illusion of objectivity has been created by a set of journalist practices that actively promote status quo political perspectives while drowning out competing views. The following discussion shows how each element of "objective journalism" actively promotes narrow political messages in the news.

The Adversarial Role of the Press. If the media were truly adversarial in their dealings with politicians, they would face a serious dilemma: The news could end up discrediting the institutions and values on which it depends for credibility. If officials and their positions were routinely attacked or held suspect by journalists, the media would have no source of "official acknowledgments." To a remarkable degree, the illusion of news objectivity is maintained through a combination of the narrow range of perspectives admitted into the news and the heavy reliance on official views to certify those perspectives as credible and valid. Recall, in this light, Tuchman's earlier claim that adopting a true adversarial position would "dismantle the news net":

> Challenging the legitimacy of offices holding centralized information dismantles the news net. If all of officialdom is corrupt, all its facts and occurrences must be viewed as alleged facts and alleged occurrences. Accordingly, to fill the news columns and air time of the news product, news organizations would have to find an alternative and economical method of locating occurrences and constituent facts acceptable as news. For example, if the institutions of everyday life are delegitimated, the facts tendered by the Bureau of Marriage Licenses would be suspect. One could no longer call the bureau to learn whether Robert Jones and Fay Smith had married. In sum, amassing mutually self-validating facts simultaneously accomplishes the doing of newswork and reconstitutes the everyday world of offices and factories, of politics and bureaucrats, of bus schedules and class rosters as historically given.[32]

It is equally true, of course, that the news would lose its image of objectivity if reporters openly catered to the propaganda interests of public officials and government institutions. If both genuine adversarialism and its complete absence would undermine the illusion of news objectivity, then there is an obvious implication: Any observable adversarial behavior on the part of the press should reveal itself more as a "posture" of antagonism than as a no-holds-barred approach to the content of the news. A ritualistic posture of antagonism between press and government creates the appearance of mutual independence without throwing open the content of the news to the serious coverage of a broad range of political perspectives. Such ritualistic posturing dramatizes the myths of a free press and an open government that have been important parts of the American image since the days of the Zenger trial and the fight over the Alien and Sedition acts. It is in the nature of ritual to evoke such myths or beliefs without challenging them.[33]

Let's begin this analysis of "empty adversarialism" with a review of some earlier points. If the adversarial relationship is a ritual that both mystifies and legitimizes the reporting of narrow political messages, then the following sorts of characteristics should be observed: (1) the incidence of criticism and confrontation should occur regularly, as a matter of everyday reporting orientation, as opposed to more sporadically, for example, when there is some demonstrable reason to believe that a serious political question is at stake; (2) challenges and charges will tend to be aired selectively both by the press, who, for example, favor inter-elite confrontations, and by politicians, who typically ignore the attacks of "fringe elements"; and (3) charges against officials will be restricted to them personally and clearly separated from their institutions and offices. Such characteristics should pertain equally to routine news coverage (e.g., events on a reporter's "beat") and nonroutine coverage (e.g., crises and scandals). In addition to these points from earlier chapters, recall Orr's seminal study of the presidential press conference.[34] Analyzing data from a sample of Kennedy, Johnson, and Nixon press conferences, Orr found that the proportion of hostile or critical questions was virtually constant across presidents, conferences, issue categories, and political contexts.[35] Not only did the incidence of confrontational questions fall into a routine pattern, but nearly all hostile questions were personal in nature. Many of those personal questions signaled clear deference to office and institution. Moreover, questions that could have been phrased as strong political attacks generally contained open invitations to redefine the issue or dismiss the entire question. Based on these patterns, Orr concluded that the adversarial postures of press and president create a dramatic image of journalistic aggressiveness while communicating a subtle message of institutional deference.

Similar ritualistic elements have been observed in the reporting of less "routine" events like scandals and crises. Such investigative reporting has been a hallmark of adversarial journalism. Despite the claims of journalists to the contrary, a number of observers have argued that crises and scandals have become routine news events, complete with standard reporting formulas.[36] For example, Altheide and Snow analyzed news coverage of the Carter administration's Bert Lance scandal.[37] They concluded that the scandal was cast quickly into standard reporting formulas. These formulas were not only instrumental in creating the scandal but also obscured indications of the actual political significance and magnitude of the incident. The coverage damaged Carter personally, while issues of office and state were assiduously avoided. The overall impression from the intense media investigation was one of dramatic confrontation between press and establishment, yet nothing was reported that might have jeopardized the overriding interests of either the press or the establishment.

In both routine and investigative reporting, the adversarial relationship is a ritual that creates an image of no-holds-barred reporting while circumscribing actual news content in the process. The ritualistic elements built into specific news stories are reinforced by more general adversarial postures that transcend specific stories. For example, one indicator of the commitment of the press to adversarial displays is the format of virtually every news interview and interview program, from the stage settings that place press and politicians in confrontational poses, to the "tag team" question-and-answer formats, to tone of voice and terms of address. Elites also contribute to this enduring antagonism by routinely attacking the press as liberal, biased, and hostile. Such attacks frequently appear in elite publications and occupy the agendas of business, government, and journalism symposia.[38] Occasionally such charges are dramatized through formal political attacks, such as the ones during the McCarthy era and the Nixon administration. One analyst found the Nixon-Agnew attacks on the press so ritualized that he interpreted them in terms of ethological concepts of animal aggression and territorial defense.[39]

It is important to recognize that this ritualistic conflict is limited further by the mutual acknowledgment of each side's political legitimacy. Antagonistic postures would serve neither press nor politicians if they succeeded in undermining the institutions of press or government. Thus, reporters are ever at the ready with pronouncements that "the system worked"—the dramatic endnote to the Watergate crisis. At the same time, the news never pronounces official judgments that "the system failed." Politicians, for their part, acknowledge the legitimacy of the press in numerous ways such as holding routine briefing and conferences, including journalists in all official state occasions, and treating the media as a partner in official attempts to communicate directly with the mass public (e.g., town meetings, phone-in programs, and fireside chats hosted by news reporters and anchors).

Simply because the press and public officials strike a careful balance between surface conflict and underlying value consensus does not mean that there is active collusion at work. As with most rituals, news reporting requires genuine involvement of actors in their roles. Both public officials and journalists are personally involved in the conflict over the presentation of daily news information. Both sides have enough to gain and lose on a personal level to make the displays of aggression genuine.[40] Nevertheless, each side also stands to undermine its own legitimacy by attacking the other on fundamental value questions. Hence a stable symbiotic relationship has emerged in which adversarialism seems genuine without presenting a risk of opening up news content.[41]

Standards of Decency and Good Taste. When viewed through their normative justifications, standards of decency and taste seem designed to keep the reporter's attention focused on important issues and away from the seamy, sensationalistic aspects of political life. Only in cases where questionable behavior reflects on leadership qualities or respect for law will the media turn its eye to moral questions, as happened, for example, with the extensive news coverage of the "Chappaquiddick scandal" involving Ted Kennedy. Despite the apparent justification for this restraint in raising moral questions, standards of decency and good taste help to create distorted news.

The practical application of standards of good taste creates two paradoxes for news content. First, standards of taste have a bias in favor of precisely those mainstream, status quo values that the bulk of political propaganda promotes.[42] Moreover, the avoidance of offensive ideas and values removes from the public awareness many undesirable but true aspects of the real world. As a result, the definitions of and the solutions for the problems in the news, however artificial, may appeal to the ideals of the middle-class public.

The second paradox of standards of taste results from the fact that they ignore a key feature of politics. Politics is the primary social activity through which widely divergent values and morals come together in struggles for dominance and legitimacy. The selective attention to preferred morals not only passively promotes the work of propagandists, as mentioned above, but it actively distorts the values and issues at stake in many situations. In this latter role, standards of taste may lead to overt censorship of some aspects of news events, thereby making journalists active agents in shaping the definitions of political situations.

The capacity of standards of taste to affect the definition of political events is illustrated by the news coverage surrounding a statement made by Agriculture Secretary Earl Butz during the 1976 presidential campaign. While flying between campaign appearances, Butz made a blatantly racist remark to a group of reporters. This remark was not only significant on its own merits, due to its appalling racist content, but it was also pertinent to the campaign because it was offered in response to a question about Republican election strategies. Although the statement contains offensive languge of the sort not often found in scholarly writing (not to mention news stories), its political magnitude can be conveyed only by quoting it directly. When asked about the efforts of the Republican party to mobilize the black vote, Butz remarked that it was pointless to worry about the black vote because blacks were unconcerned about politics. He then summarized his view of the concerns of blacks as follows: "I'll tell you what coloreds want. It's three things: first, a tight pussy; second, loose shoes; and third, a warm place to shit."[43]

It is arguably in the public interest to publicize a racist remark uttered by a U.S. cabinet officer while campaigning for the president who appointed him. However, the professional press regarded Butz's offense to good taste as a higher consideration than his offense to political sensibilities. The pervasive commitment to the decency code was reflected in a simple piece of data. Not one major news outlet ran the Butz remark at the time it was made. Only when the statement was quoted later at the end of a rambling article on the campaign in the underground newspaper *Rolling Stone* was it necessary for the respectable press to acknowlege that the incident had in fact happened. Even when major press and broadcast outlets ran the story, they did not use the verbatim language. Only one major daily paper (the Madison, Wisconsin, *Capitol Times*) and no commercial broadcast outlets used the actual words. In defense of their use of inoffensive euphemisms in place of the real language, editors and news producers pronounced the litany of the decency code. An editor at the *New York Times* put it this way: "...we recognized that if we used this series of filthy obscenities then we'll probably use the next." The editor of the *Des Moines Register* said he found the remark so offensive and so atrocious that "I couldn't bring myself to give it to people with their breakfast." The editor of the *Washington Post* produced a tortured chain of logic leading to the conclusion that only if the president himself had uttered the remarks would he have printed them, but lesser officials did not merit such a violation of the journalism code.[44]

The point is that the impact of the statement was lost when euphemisms were substituted for the actual language. As a result, the Ford campaign was spared the painful embarrassment of one of those rare moments when it lapsed from its agenda of carefully staged and scripted performances.[45] Such moments ought to be the focus of serious news coverage because they are as close as the public ever comes to witnessing natural political events. It is unfortunate that the sharp moral edges of these incidents are often sheathed by the press.[46]

The decency code is so entrenched that it applies to virtually everything, including coverage of important health and biological issues.

For example, it took over two years for the mainstream media to explain that one way in which the dread disease AIDS (Acquired Immune Deficiency Syndrome) is spread is through anal intercourse. The potential for a large-scale, life-threatening epidemic called for rapid delivery of as much explicit information as possible to the public. Yet in the early, panicky years of the disease, the decency code governed information content about AIDS. Early stories suggested that the disease was transmitted "not through casual contact," and through the "exchange of bodily fluids." As one editor put it, "We would make the reader guess what was going on rather than use the term 'anal intercourse'....We wouldn't spell it out." A television reporter recalls receiving pressure from her producer to refrain from using explicit language in response to a few phone calls from morally offended viewers. It took years for consensus to emerge in the media that informing the public about health risks was more important than censoring offensive language from the news.[47]

Documentary Reporting Practices. Objective reporting is based on the overriding principles that journalists do not embellish their stories, advocate particular interpretations of ambiguous events, or otherwise "make up" the news. The guarantee behind these principles is the practice of documentary reporting. *Reporters trained in the documentary method are disposed to report only the information that they have witnessed and only the facts that credible sources have confirmed. Although the goals of documentary reporting are hard to fault, the practice of the documentary method creates a trap for journalists confronted with staged political performances. Only in rare cases when performances are flawed, or when behind-the-scenes staging is revealed, can reporters document in good professional fashion what they know otherwise to be the case: The news event in question was staged for propaganda purposes.* Since, as Boorstin pointed out, pseudo-events contain their own self-supporting and self-fulfilling documentation, the documentary method highlights the very aspects of events that were designed to legitimize them and to blur the underlying reality of the situation.[48] *The paradox of the documentary method is clear: The more perfectly an event is staged, the more documentable and hence reportable it becomes.*

   In response to this dilemma, news organizations have begun to expose some of these planned "media events."[49] However, the proportion of stories exposing media events is minuscule in relation to the high percentage of news based on media events. The result of this imbalance between reported and actual occurrences of staged events may be similar to the distorting effects of adversarialism. By exposing only a fraction of the political manipulation in the news, journalists may reassure the public that they are monitoring such manipulation and alerting the public when it occurs.

The Use of Stories as Standardized News Formats. Although the origins of the story form were primarily economic in nature, stories quickly became justified in terms of the norm of objective journalism. *Stories can be represented as standardized and mechanical means of communicating information—a representation that gives journalists a claim to a universal methodology of objective reporting. The problem with this normative definition of the news story is that it is a very selective rendition of what storytelling is all about. As anyone who has ever told stories knows, the telling of a story requires choices to be made about what information to include, what words to assign to the included information, and how to tie together all the chosen symbols into a coherent whole.* These choices in turn depend on assessing the audience, the point that is to be made to that audience, and the plot techniques (flashbacks, sequencing, character development, climax, etc.) that will best make that point. In short, stories are not mirrors of events.[50] A well-constructed story may be plausible, but plausibility and truth in the world of storytelling have little connection.[51] An obvious implication of these features of storytelling is that they give reporters room to emphasize dramatic and narrative aspects of events.[52] Epstein suggests that the use of artistic (i.e., literary and dramatic) forms in news construction is encouraged by editors, one of whom even issued a memo containing formal instructions about how to incorporate dramatic structure into stories.[53] Gans notes the frequency with which reporters "restage" aspects of stories to heighten their dramatic qualities.[54]

Despite the dramatic license offered by the use of stories, the wholesale invention of news plots would create enormous strains on the norm of objective reporting. One solution to this tension between the value of dramatic news and the commitment to documentary reporting involves the receptivity of news organizations to events that are staged dramatically by news sources. Even though these events are designed to convey loaded political messages, they do conform in a narrow sense to the norms associated with documentary reporting and story formats. So important is the dramatic element in political performances that they are often judged for newsworthiness on this criterion. Gans observed that

> an exciting story boosts morale; and when there is a long drought of exciting stories, they (reporters) become restless. In the Spring of 1978, some magazine writers, left "crabby" by a drought of dramatic domestic news, joked about their readiness to be more critical of the President and other public officials for their failure to supply news that would "make adrenalin flow."[55]

The use of stories also places another constraint on news content by promoting the use of standardized plots in news reporting. Any communication network based on stories will become biased toward particular themes. For example, criminal trials are dominated by such familiar plots as "mistaken identity," "victim of circumstances," and others relevant to the legal judgment of cases.[56] Storytelling between friends frequently centers on recurring themes that define the relationship and express the identities that the individuals have created in it. In politics, consensus and legitimacy can be promoted through the frequent and plausible use of the dominant values, beliefs, and myths of the political culture.[57] It is common knowledge that elites, leaders, and interest groups define political situations in these familiar themes. These themes, if used repeatedly, strike journalists and ordinary citizens alike as suitable framings of events. Gans has noted the domination of the news by a remarkably small number of recurring themes. These plot devices include "ethnocentrism" (America first, America-the-generous, America-the-embattled, etc.), "altruistic democracy," "responsible capitalism," and "individualism," among others.[58]

Political performances scripted around routine themes legitimize the status quo and severely limit the range of political discourse.[59] However, reporters who are locked into the "formula-story syndrome" are forced to invert the relationship between stories and reality so that formula stories become viewed as exhaustive representations of reality. This naive approach to objectivity gives news writing a mystical quality described by Darnton: "Big stories develop in special patterns and have an archaic flavor, as if they were metamorphoses or *Ur*-stories that have been lost in the depths of time....News writing is heavily influenced by stereotypes and by preconceptions of what 'the story' should be. Without preestablished categories of what constitutes 'news,' it is impossible to sort out experience."[60]

Not only do stories lock in the narrow political messages of routine news events, but the professional commitment to the news story can introduce equally serious distortion into investigative reporting. Stories, by definition, encapsulate events, making them seem to be self-contained and independent of external forces. Since the stories and tips provided by "inside" sources to investigative reporters are often (one suspects, usually) motivated by political considerations on the part of the source, it is possible to frame the information given to reporters in ways that keep the political concerns of the source out of the picture. Recall, for example, the earlier discussion that the Watergate story based on the investigative reporting of Woodward and Bernstein may have been only part of a much larger political scandal (see chapter 2). The source of the inside information necessary to keep the story unfolding seemed to provide only information that would turn the story toward the Oval Office. Epstein noted that there might have been other political actors, like the CIA, who could have been caught up in the Watergate scandal and who would have benefited enormously by trying to encapsulate the issues in a story centered on the president and his men.[61]

We will, of course, never know who provided the information that trapped Nixon within the damaging plot of the story that eventually emerged in the Watergate case. The point here does not depend on knowing who did it. In fact, the point is underscored by the fact that the reporting practices involved make it *impossible* to find out who did it or why. The obvious need to protect the confidentiality of sources is not the only, nor even the most important, reason why the political contexts of news stories are seldom disclosed. The elevation of the story form to a professional practice places an even more subtle prohibition on revealing the politics behind political news. There exists a fundamental contradiction between the pragmatics of story writing and the normative justification for the practice. The normative defense of stories is that they do in fact constitute complete and objective versions of events. It would be devastating to this simplistic view of news reality to show that behind every story lies another story that comes much closer to revealing the true politics of the situation. As Epstein explained, the story-behind-the-story approach to news reporting would blow the cover off the normative claim that objective reality can be encapsulated somehow in stories.

Reporters as Generalists. Stories play another role in journalism by representing a universal reporting "methodology" employed by all reporters whether of politics, sports, or business. Reporters are trained as generalists who are able to write stories on any subject. Although a small percentage end up reporting in specialized areas like science or fashion, the majority change beats periodically and pride themselves on their ability to cover any news story.[62]

The emphasis in the profession on training reporters as generalists has obvious origins and payoffs. As Gans noted, ". . . the news is still gathered mostly by generalists. One reason is economic, for general reporters earn less and are more productive. Beat reporters can rarely produce more than one story per television program or magazine issue, while general reporters can be asked, when necessary, to complete two or more assignments within the same period."[63] Despite these obvious economic advantages, generalism is justified almost exclusively in normative terms. A key element of the journalism code is public service. The news is billed normatively as a democratic service to the mass public. *The use of generalists who employ a standardized story format is justified as the best means of presenting comprehensible information to the average person. If a reporter has any special expertise on a topic, he or she may run the risk of complicating a story or violating the story form altogether by lapsing into technical analysis.* Whether or not there is any foundation to the belief that the general public cannot follow news produced by overly specialized reporters, this belief is widely shared by editors and producers in the news business. For example, Epstein reported the following response of an NBC news executive to a

Justice Department suggestion that the television networks use correspondents with special knowledge of ghetto problems to cover urban riots:
"Any good journalist should be able to cover a riot in an unfamiliar
setting....A veneer of knowledgeability in a situation like this could be
less than useless."[64] In another case Gans reports a comment by an
executive producer to his economic reporter following a good story on a
complicated subject: "You scare me with your information; I think we'll
put you on another beat."[65] Gans also noted the general anxiety shared by
many specialists that they were becoming too knowledgeable for the tastes
of their audiences or their superiors.

*Although generalism is justified normatively as a necessary concession
to a mass audience, the audience may pay a high political price in exchange
for the alleged gains in news comprehension. Generalist reporters are often
at the mercy of the news source. In technical areas generalists are seldom
qualified to ask critical questions.*[66] *As a result, reporters may have to ask
news sources for guidelines about appropriate questions. Even when
generalists are assigned to fairly straightforward political stories, they may
have to fashion their stories almost entirely from official pronouncements
and the story angles pursued by other reporters.*[67] As a result of greater
dependency of generalists on their sources, the odds are even greater that
they will report fabricated events. Moreover, generalists may be less likely
than specialists to spot flaws in performances that would make it possible to
expose the contrived nature of an event. For example, Gans noted of
generalists:

> Not knowing their sources well enough to discount self-serving infor-
> mation, they may report an opinion or a hopeful guess—for example, the
> size of an organization's membership—as a statistical fact. In this way,
> enterprising politicians sometimes get inflated estimates of their support
> into the news....Occasionally, general reporters may cover only one
> side of a story without ever knowing that there are other sides.[68]

Thus generalism, like other reporting practices, is justified as a public
service, but in fact it increases the likelihood of elite control of the news.

The Practice of Editorial Review. It is hard to imagine a criticism that
could be lodged against the journalistic commitment to the practice of
editors' reviewing, checking, and approving reporters' preliminary
accounts of events. The review policies of most news organizations are
represented as insurance that the professional practices discussed above
will be used in reporting the news. In a sense, editorial review does serve
this function, thereby ensuring the news distortion produced by these
journalistic practices. Editorial review also exerts its own influence on the
political content of the news. Editors are not just the overseers of news

production; they are accountable to management for the competitive market position of their news product. As a result of this accountability, editors and owners (or managers) typically formulate implicit criteria that their news product must satisfy in order to be successful and professionally respectable in their eyes. Studies of the internal workings of news organizations make it clear that these implicit criteria are major influences on reporters and on the political content of news.[69]

These implicit editorial criteria would not be a problem if they were idiosyncratic. However, news organizations are businesses driven by the same economic imperative that exists in any large market dominated by a small number of competitors. This imperative, as noted earlier, is the same whether applied to political campaigning in a two-party system, news reporting in a three-network market, or car production in a three-company industry: Standardize the product as much as possible so as to minimize the risk of losing a minimally acceptable share of the market, and compete for greater market share via production efficiencies and market techniques. The consequence of this imperative for the news is twofold. First, most editors find it expedient to take their story leads from the wire services. The reliance on the wire services as implicit standardizing mechanisms applies to both print and broadcast media.[70] Second, editors tend to standardize their product further by bringing it in line with the competition. Due to the conservation imperatives in news production, it is easier to justify similarities in the coverage of stories than to account for differences between organizations. *To put it simply, the transparency of the "objectivity" or "fairness" claim becomes most evident when the coverage of one organization differs from the others and must, as a result, be defended against queries by publishers, politicians, and the public. The best defense of objectivity is contained in the implicit standardization of editorial review practices.*

The obvious political consequence of standardized editorial policies was captured nicely by Edwin Diamond, who noted that editorial practices reinforce the worst tendency in the news business to stereotype stories. News stereotypes conform to the major plot outlines of fabricated news performances and give the news its obvious status quo bias. As Diamond notes, none of this bias can be attributed directly to political motives on the part of reporters. To the contrary, the professional standards of journalists cleanse the news of such motives; yet, somehow, the resulting product does seem to display a particular slant:

> The press isn't "racist," though as the skins of the participants become darker, the lengths of the stories shrink. The press isn't "pro-Israeli," though it is very sensitive to Jewish-American feelings. The press isn't afraid of the "vested interests," though it makes sure Mobil's or Senator Scott's denials appear right along with the charges. The paranoids are

wrong: there is no news conspiracy. Instead there are a lot of editors and executives making decisions about what is "the news" while constrained by lack of time, space, money, talent, and understanding, from doing the difficult and/or hidden stories.[71]

In short, the editorial review standards pointed to as the fail-safe mechanism for preventing news distortion are, paradoxically, the very things that guarantee news distortion.

OBJECTIVITY RECONSIDERED

It is clear that the news does not hold up very well under scrutiny of the normative claims made about it. A number of observers have argued persuasively that whatever the news is, it is not a spontaneous and objective mirror of the world. Nevertheless, it would be a mistake to draw from the contradiction between journalism norms and practices the conclusion that neither the objectivity nor the reporting practices matter. The objectivity norm hides the connection between reporting practices and their economic, organizational, and political contexts. At the same time, the objectivity norm gives the press the look of an independent social institution. Moreover, even though actual reporting practices distort the political content of the news, they fit conveniently into the objectivity code, thereby obscuring their political effects. In this fashion, journalistic norms and reporting practices operate together to create a strong status quo bias in the news—a bias that is well hidden behind a facade of independent journalism.

Beyond the Fairness Doctrine

"Passivity" is a better word than "objectivity" or "fairness" to describe the professional stance of the press. Passivity accounts for the three major modes of newsgathering:

1. Passing along prepared propaganda as news.
2. "Normalizing" spontaneous events by representing them in the most familiar and traditional terms. This "course-of-least-resistance" reporting strategy makes news information seem true (or at least acceptable) by appealing to existing belief, prejudice, and superstition.
3. Reporting conflict and scandal in the terms chosen largely by the parties involved, with minimal analysis of the history and institutional context surrounding the events.

All three of these journalistic modes reinforce the status quo and ignore possible failures of the political system. Yet there is no conspiracy at work between reporters and officials. If anything, the press is guilty of taking its claims of objectivity or fairness too seriously and, therefore, failing to recognize that these professional standards boil down to an extremely passive stance toward news.

Compounding the inability of journalists to recognize the pitfalls of professional passivity is the pervasive assumption that "the system works." It is easier to report whatever officialdom does and call the story "fair" if one assumes that the system usually works the way it should to represent the public interest and to correct its own failures. This assumption allows the press to appear neutral while gathering large amounts of news efficiently and profitably.

The trouble is that the system does not always work to represent the public interest. Even the simple correspondence of policy to public opinion does not occur very often. Interest representation is all the less likely to occur in the presence of a "neutral" media that passes over in silence failures of representation whenever those failures are also passed over in silence by the officials involved. As a presidential advisor once said when an administration policy ran against public opinion, "Well, we certainly aren't going to make an issue of it." The trouble is that in many, perhaps most, cases in which policy runs counter to opinion, nobody in an official position makes an issue of it. And when the officials who are supposed to represent the public don't raise issues, a passive press usually doesn't either.

In a rare candid interview in *Mother Jones* (which he later regretted granting), NBC News anchor Tom Brokaw expressed his frustration at the failures of supposedly responsible public officials and business leaders to represent the public interest. He cited the failure of big business to point out the irresponsibility of Reagan administration "supply side" economic policies due to the short-term advantages those policies offered business. The interviewer, in turn, criticized Brokaw for compounding this failure of public interest representation by not issuing an independent criticism of government and business behaviors. The journalist defended his "silent treatment" in the news by wrapping himself in the "fairness doctrine":

MJ: You just criticized members of the business community for keeping their mouths shut even though they knew Reagan's ideas were idiotic.

BROKAW: Right.

MJ: Now, I suppose you can't say the president is an idiot on national television. But aren't you guilty of the same thing?

BROKAW: You would have been happier if I had just said on that special, for example, "Maybe the business community will finally have the courage to tell his guy to this face that his program is not working."

MJ: That would have been a lot straighter.

BROKAW: But part of what governs our thinking is the whole business of "Is it balanced? Is it fair? Is this a fair and balanced program?" The *Washington Post* said our program was quite tough on the president. I thought it was a fair report on what people are saying.[72]

In cases like the above, the professional code of objectivity or fairness and the supporting assumption that "the system works" leave journalists in a bind. Even if reporters spot a case of bad policy or political duplicity among officials, the journalistic code has no provision for making such observations directly in a story. Introducing a journalistic voice directly into the news would violate professional norms. And so, perceptive reporters must wait for some "newsmaker" to make an issue of public interest problems. Often it is a long wait.

Later in the interview reported above, Tom Brokaw also mentioned his concern that the news had portrayed the civilian elections in El Salvador as a meaningful exercise in democracy in which motivated voters chose between legitimate parties. What didn't make the news even on his own broadcast were many "unofficial" clues about the broader political context of these elections. Brokaw reports sitting outside the house where victorious leaders of the

five right-wing parties were all gathered, striking a deal before they went over to have lunch with [U.S. Ambassador] Hinton. I know pretty well how it works. Having flown out on an airplane with a woman in her red-white-and-blue outfit who said, "Oh yeah, well, we all got together. What you guys don't understand is that we've all worked together for years. We just made up these [political] parties." This was a Salvadoran woman who was flying back to Miami. She had gone down only to vote. She owned a plantation up in the hills. So...I, I think it's a sham.[73]

Yet it was not the image of a "sham" that came across in the media coverage of the 1982 and 1984 elections—coverage that enabled the White House to claim victory in its efforts to transplant American-style democracy to El Salvador. Following the claim of democratic victory, the administration began a "red-baiting" campaign that cast doubts on the loyalty of members of Congress who questioned the wisdom of U.S. policy in El Salvador and elsewhere in Central America. The image of popularly supported democracy in El Salvador had come across so strongly in the news that anyone questioning the wisdom of policies there could be represented as naive, disloyal, or, worse, a supporter of the "Communist" rebellion that the U.S. was fighting militarily. And so, given the choice between hiding behind a convenient news image of popular democracy winning the hearts and minds of Salvadoran citizens, and facing opponents who would raise questions about their loyalty and ideological purity in the next election, the majority in Congress stopped saying anything in opposition to U.S. policy.

The tragedy of situations like the war in El Salvador is that when the legitimate opposition is silenced for whatever reason, critical public debate in the news is also silenced. Despite the escalation of a devastating war against large numbers of civilians and the erosion of popular support in El Salvador for the "democratic" government, the news virtually forgot the Salvadoran story after the elections of 1984. Also forgotten was the fact that U.S. military escalation of the conflict in El Salvador and elsewhere in Central America was opposed consistently by a majority of the American people, according to Gallup and Harris polls between 1982 and 1986.

I had the opportunity to ask Tom Brokaw why U.S. policies opposed by a majority of the public (and bringing such havoc to the already suffering Salvadoran people) had received so little news attention. The likable anchor looked at me as though personally wounded by the question and then proceeded to explain that it was unfortunate that Congress had lowered its voice on the issue. But what could the media do? After all, said Brokaw, "Congress is *supposed* to represent the people, and when there is no opposition in Congress, there isn't that much that we can report."[74]

El Salvador would, of course, make the news again, following a future coup or military disaster or corruption scandal, but these events would not be attributed to failures of U.S. policy. Indeed, the earthquake of 1986 received far more coverage than the U.S.-supported bombing missions, even though the air war drove many more hapless civilians from their homes than did the earthquake. True to form, the crises that pushed the troubled country into the news only reinforced popular stereotypes about "ungovernable little Banana Republics," while giving U.S. officials an opportunity to claim that the solution lay in redoubling our efforts to get existing policies (like the air war) across. Thus, the failure of democracy in a coup, or the failure of military campaigns to stamp out revolution, or the failure of economic development programs to end poverty and depression may only lead to calls for more of the same policies in the future: more well-orchestrated elections, more intense military campaigns, more economic aid cycled through corrupt military and business interests. In the upside-down world of news reality, the image is what counts. When officialdom unites behind a common image (whatever their political reasons may be), the media become trapped into reporting political illusion, no matter how well journalists may understand the political "sham."

This is a dilemma that the media have inflicted upon themselves. Journalists are guilty of taking their professional standards too seriously while failing to recognize that, like most professional norms, they arose through convenience and circumstance more than through great moral vision or some higher law. At the same time, the professional code of "fairness" protects reporters from suffering too deeply the contradictions of their often-silenced condition. At present, journalism is stuck in an untenable position, unable to use its own professional knowledge about situations unless that knowledge can be made to come out of some newsworthy official's mouth. Yet that painful position will be sustained until journalism educators and the management of news organizations begin to recognize a new professional standard of advocacy journalism in which discrepancies between public policy and public opinion (and other indices of the public interest) can be introduced into the news directly by journalists for the sake of open communication and the stimulation of democratic dialogue.

At some level, many journalists know that government is hidden behind veils of secrecy and silence and that the public trust is squandered through efforts to manipulate public opinion through the news. Professional journalism publications like the *Columbia Journalism Review* and the *Washington Journalism Review* are filled with articles on how officials manipulate the media while they fortify the wall of legal secrecy that surrounds many of their activities. Unfortunately this awareness has yet to shatter professional myths about neutrality, fairness, and objectivity— myths that enable journalists to live comfortably with their contradictions. It will take more than an attitude change alone to alter journalistic dependence on government newsmaking formulas; the practices of advocacy journalism will have to be developed through formal education as well as through experimentation in the field. However, a new professional attitude would be a good start on the road to a public-interest press.

NOTES

1. See, for example, the numerous accounts of reporters, including Lou Cannon, *Reporting: An Inside View* (Sacramento: California Journal Press, 1977); Robert Darnton, "Writing News and Telling Stories," *Daedalus* 104 (Spring 1975): 175–94; and Lewis Lapham, "Gilding the News," *Harper's*, July 1981, pp. 31–39.
2. For an excellent discussion of this syndrome, see Gaye Tuchman, *Making News: A Study in the Construction of Reality* (New York: Free Press, 1978).
3. Robert Scholes, "Double Perspective on Hysteria," *Saturday Review*, 24 August 1968, p. 37.

4. For a detailed analysis of how this pattern occurs, see Leon Sigal, *Reporters and Officials* (Lexington, Mass.: Heath, 1973).
5. Tom Bethell, "The Myth of An Adversary Press," *Harper's*, January 1977, p. 36.
6. Quoted in David Owen, "The Best Kept Secret in American Journalism Is Murray Kempton," *Esquire*, March 1982, p. 50.
7. See, for example, Warren Breed's classic study, "Social Control in the Newsroom," *Social Forces* 33 (May 1955): 326–35.
8. Edward Jay Epstein, *News from Nowhere* (New York: Vintage, 1973).
9. *Ibid.*
10. These observations and hypothetical examples are reconstructed from discussions with members of marketing and news production staffs in news organizations that have hired the services of news consultants. For obvious reasons, these people wish to remain anonymous. The reader can read more about the news doctors by consulting the running dialogue about them that has emerged in publications such as the *Journal of Broadcasting* and the *Columbia Journalism Review*.
11. Ben H. Bagdikian, "Fat Newspapers and Slim Coverage," *Columbia Journalism Review*, September/October 1973, p. 17–19.
12. Fred C. Shapiro, "Shrinking the News," *Columbia Journalism Review*, November/December 1976, pp. 23–24.
13. Fergus M. Bordewich, "Supermarketing the Newspaper," *Columbia Journalism Review*, September/October 1977, p. 27.
14. Quoted in *ibid.*, p. 25.
15. See, for example, Philip Meyer's criticism of marketing research and defense of more reliable social science investigations in his article, "In Defense of the Marketing Approach," *Columbia Journalism Review*, January/February 1978, p. 61.
16. See Timothy Crouse, *The Boys on the Bus* (New York: Ballantine, 1973).
17. Mark Fishman, *Manufacturing the News* (Austin: University of Texas Press, 1980), pp. 80–81.
18. *Ibid.*, p. 81.
19. Stephen Hess, *The Washington Reporters* (Washington, D.C.: Brookings Institution, 1981), p. 130.
20. John W. C. Johnstone, Edward J. Slawski, and William W. Bowman, *The News People: A Sociological Portrait of American Journalists and Their Work* (Urbana: University of Illinois Press, 1976). Also: Charles J. Brown, Trevor R. Brown, and William L. Rivers, *The Media and People* (New York: Holt, Rinehart and Winston, 1978); and Hess, *Washington Reporters*.
21. See, for example, Edith Efron, *The News Twisters* (Los Angeles: Nash, 1971); and Doris Graber, *Mass Media and American Politics* (Washington, D.C.: Congressional Quarterly Press, 1980), chap. 10.
22. For a review of these professional norms, see John Tebbell, *The Media in America* (New York: Mentor, 1974); Johnstone, Slawski, and Bowman, *The News People*; Tuchman, *Making News*; and Michael Schudson, *Discovering the News: A Social History of American Newspapers* (New York: Basic Books, 1978).
23. In recent years, the much-touted specialist has entered the reporting ranks.

However, the use of specialists continues to be restricted to a few subject areas like science and economics. Also, specialists are employed by a relatively small number of big news organizations. Since the bulk of political reporting continues to be done by generalists who rotate assignments periodically and who refrain from introducing technical or theoretical perspectives in their reports, the practice of generalism merits inclusion here.

24. For supporting evidence for this claim, see, among others, Meyer Berger, *The Story of the New York Times* (New York: Simon and Schuster, 1951); Frank L. Mott, *The News in America* (Cambridge, Mass.: Harvard University Press, 1952); Edwin Emery and Henry Ladd Smith, *The Press in America* (New York: Prentice-Hall, 1954); Tebbell, *Media in America*; and Schudson, *Discovering the News*.

25. For discussions of the origins and impact of the wire services, see Bernard Roscho, *Newsmaking* (Chicago: University of Chicago Press, 1975); Mott, *News in America*; and Emery and Smith, *Press in America*.

26. Tebbell, *Media in America,* chap. 12.

27. Schudson, *Discovering the News*, chap. 3.

28. Upton Sinclair, *The Brass Check* (Pasadena, Calif., published by the author, 1920). Also, Berger, *Story of the New York Times*; and Tebbell, *Media in America*.

29. For a history of this period and its ideas, see, among others, Harold J. Laski, "The Present Position of Representative Democracy," *American Political Science Review* 26 (August 1932): 629–41; John Diggins, *Mussolini and Fascism: The View from America* (Princeton: Princeton University Press, 1972); and Schudson, *Discovering the News*.

30. See the following books by Walter Lippmann: *Drift and Mastery* (New York: Kennerly, 1914); *Liberty and the News* (New York: Harcourt Brace, 1920); *Public Opinion* (New York: Free Press, 1922); and *The Phantom Public* (New York: Harcourt Brace, 1925).

31. Cannon, *Reporting*, p. 35.

32. Tuchman, *Making News*, p. 87.

33. See, for example, Murray Edelman, *The Symbolic Uses of Politics* (Champaign-Urbana: University of Illinois Press, 1964); Peter L. Berger and Thomas Luckmann, *The Social Construction of Reality* (New York: Anchor Books, 1966); and W. Lance Bennett, *Public Opinion in American Politics* (New York: Harcourt Brace Jovanovich, 1980), chaps. 13, 14.

34. C. Jack Orr, "Reporters Confront the President: Sustaining a Counterpoised Situation," *Quarterly Journal of Speech* 66 (February 1980): 17–32.

35. *Ibid.*, p. 22.

36. See, for example, Harvey Molotch and Marilyn Lester, "Accidents, Scandals, and Routines: Resources for Insurgent Methodology," *Insurgent Sociologist* 3 (1973): 1–11; Molotch and Lester, "News as Purposive Behavior: On the Strategic Use of Routine Events, Accidents, and Scandals," *American Sociological Review* 39 (February 1974); 101–12; Murray Edelman, *Political Language* (New York: Academic Press, 1977), chap. 3; Todd Gitlin, *The Whole World Is Watching* (Berkeley: University of California Press, 1980), chaps. 2, 7; Graber, *Mass Media in American Politics*, chap. 8.

37. David L. Altheide and Robert P. Snow, *Media Logic* (Beverly Hills: Sage,

1979), chaps. 3, 4.

38. See, for example, Howard Simmons and Joseph A. Califano, Jr., eds., *The Media and Business* (New York: Vintage, 1979).

39. Henry Beck, "Attentional Struggles and Silencing Strategies in a Human Political Conflict: The Case of the Vietnam Moratoria," in *The Structure of Social Attention: Ethological Studies*, ed. M. R. A. Chance and R. R. Larson (New York: Wiley, 1976).

40. It is not hard to understand why politicians often become personally embittered over their treatment by the press. Although it often seems that politicians adopt a "sour-grapes" attitude about the adversarial norm itself, it is worth considering the validity of the politician's typical complaint that news coverage is arbitrary, gratuitous, and unpredictable. These may be reasonable perceptions of journalists' ritualistic behaviors.

41. It is worth considering the depth of overlapping constraints imposed by this ritual on news content. For example, politicians who are personally threatened by the arbitrary adversarialism of news coverage are likely to be even more guarded in their definition and presentation of public statements. Thus the ultimate paradox of adversarialism may be that it fuels what is already a major source of news distortion: the use of propaganda as the everyday medium of political communication. When politicians regard reporters (in a sense, correctly) as people who are out to get them, politicians may treat reporters, in turn, the way Lyndon Johnson did, as "people who had to be bamboozled, bullied, cajoled, or bribed with entertainment." Quoted in George E. Reedy, "The President and the Press: Struggle for Dominance," *The Annals* 427 (September 1976): 67.

42. See Jacques Ellul, *Propaganda* (New York: Vintage, 1973).

43. Quoted in *Rolling Stone*, 7 October 1976, p. 57.

44. For these and other editors' responses, see Priscilla S. Meyer, "Hello, Rolling Stone? What Did Butz say?" *Wall Street Journal*, 7 October 1976, p. 18.

45. When the national press finally acknowledged the incident, Ford had little choice but to fire Butz. However, one suspects that Butz's desire to exit the situation gracefully, and Ford's wish to minimize his political losses, could not have been satisfied any better than through the delicate treatment accorded to the episode by the journalistic community.

46. This moralism of the press makes less sense as an enhancer of news content than as a spinoff of the economic base of the media. As mentioned earlier, a key part of the market strategy of the turn-of-the-century press was to appeal to the moral sensibilities of the most affluent, rapidly growing, and untapped mass news market: the middle class. From these beginnings, the news has helped create a restricted picture of American society in two ways: First, by representing the world through middle-class values, the news became an implicit model for social propriety; second, by introducing selective moral perspectives into news coverage, the press tacitly became the legitimator of the same values it helped to promote.

   The strength of middle-class moralism in the news business is formidable. For example, even a semisensationalist paper like the *New York Daily News* did not print the word "syphilis" until 1931. One suspects that the phenomenon to which this word refers was an important social problem long before the respectable reading public was exposed to it in print. Similarly, the prototype of the highbrow family newspaper, the *New York Times*, refused to review Kinsey's landmark study of sexual behavior until it had been certified by the academic community, long after the publication date, as a serious scholarly work (see Tebbell, *Media in America*, p. 141). One also suspects that human sexual behavior was a significant and widely practiced phenomenon long before the *Times* endorsed it as a subject worthy of discussion.

47. "AIDS and the Family Paper," *Columbia Journalism Review*, March/April 1986, p. 11.
48. Daniel Boorstin, *The Image* (New York: Atheneum, 1961).
49. See Edwin Diamond, *Good News, Bad News* (Cambridge, Mass.: MIT Press, 1978).
50. See W. Lance Bennett, "Storytelling in Criminal Trials: A Model of Social Judgment," *Quarterly Journal of Speech* 64 (February 1978): 1–22; and W. Lance Bennett and Martha S. Feldman, *Reconstructing Reality in the Courtroom* (New Brunswick, N.J.: Rutgers University Press, 1981).
51. Bennett and Feldman, *Reconstructing Reality in the Courtroom*, chap. 4.
52. James David Barber, "Characters in the Campaign: The Literary Problem," in Barber, ed., *Race for the Presidency: The Media and the Nominating Process* (Englewood Cliffs, N.J.: Prentice-Hall, 1978).
53. Epstein, *News from Nowhere*, pp. 4–5.
54. Herbert Gans, *Deciding What's News* (New York: Vintage, 1979), p. 173.
55. *Ibid.*, p. 171.
56. Bennett, "Storytelling in Criminal Trials," and Bennett and Feldman, *Reconstructing Reality in the Courtroom*.
57. See Murray Edelman, *Political Language* (New York: Academic Press, 1977); and W. Lance Bennett, *Public Opinion in American Politics* (New York: Harcourt Brace Jovanovich, 1980).
58. Gans, *Deciding What's News*, chap. 2.
59. See Tuchman, *Making News*; and Fishman, *Manufacturing the News*.
60. Robert Darnton, "Writing News and Telling Stories," *Daedalus* 104 (Spring 1975): 189.
61. Edward Jay Epstein, "The Grand Cover-up," *Wall Street Journal*, 19 April 1976, p. 10.
62. Johnstone et al., *News People*.
63. Gans, *Deciding What's News*, p. 143.
64. Epstein, *News from Nowhere*, p. 137.
65. Gans, *Deciding What's News*, p. 143.
66. *Ibid.*
67. *Ibid.*; also, Crouse, *Boys on the Bus*.
68. Gans, *Deciding What's News*, p. 142.
69. See, for example, Breed, "Social Control in the Newsroom"; Walter Geiber, "Across the Desk: A Study of 16 Telegraph Editors," *Journalism Quarterly* 33 (Fall 1956): 423–32; Epstein, *News from Nowhere*; Crouse, *Boys on the Bus*; and Gans, *Deciding What's News*.
70. For discussion of the impact of wire services on newspaper coverage, see Crouse, *Boys on the Bus*; and Sigal, *Reporters and Officials*. The impact of the "wires" on television news is discussed extensively in Epstein, *News from*

Nowhere; and Gans, *Deciding What's News*.
71. Diamond, *Good News, Bad News*, p. 228.
72. Frank Browning, "Tom Brokaw Is Mad as Heck," *Mother Jones*, April 1983, p. 37.
73. *Ibid.*, p. 38.
74. Breakfast Seminar, University of Washington, September 15, 1986.

CHAPTER 5

The Public: Prisoners of the News

We're living in the future
Tell you how I know
I read it in the papers fifteen years ago.

—John Pryne

It should be clear by now that the news is neither made nor reported primarily for the purpose of providing citizens with useful political information. Both politicians and journalists are concerned with more immediate goals than the problem of how to give people an accurate and useful picture of the world in which they live. As a result of the political and journalistic factors that shape the news, the public is placed in a difficult bind. On the one hand, those who pay serious attention to the news run the risk of absorbing its subtle political messages, accepting its familiar stereotypes, and adopting its rigid modes of thinking. On the other hand, people who avoid the news may suffer the social stigma of ignorance, the guilt of being poor citizens, and the confusion of not knowing what is happening in the world. Between the true believers and the truly ignorant are the majority of citizens who accept what the media give them as the best, most believable version of reality. As noted earlier, this latter group must live somehow with the knowledge that the same news that seems so believable is created in the image of the political agendas and policy directives of business, government, and military elites. Beyond this conflicted majority there are also a few perceptive souls who manage to penetrate the screen of stereotypes and propaganda that dominate the news. Most of us have encountered those rare people who can bring a news story into clear focus by adding a bit of background information or political analysis to the report.

Since the news must be judged ultimately in terms of its political effects on the people who consume it, there are two important questions to be addressed at the outset of this chapter:

1. What enables a comparatively small number of people to make insightful and independent interpretations of the news?
2. Why do most people remain prisoners of the news, either forced to accept its simplistic political messages or resigned to a life of confusion about the world around them?

ESCAPING THE NEWS PRISON: HOW PEOPLE SEE BEYOND THE WALLS

A small percentage of people stand in sharp contrast to the majority who absorb and expel news information as though they were contestants in a lifelong trivia match. Some people seem to have an inside line on the politics behind news reports. If, by this stage in the book, you are not such a person, at least you have all the information you need to figure out how these people come into the world.

Consider two facts that help explain who becomes liberated from the political confines of the news. First, we already know that the news consists overwhelmingly of "objective" (or at least "fair") "documentary" reports that pass along, with little analysis, the political messages of official spokespersons. As noted in chapter 3, less than 1 percent of mass media coverage contains any sort of independent analysis from the reporter's perspective, while around 90 percent of the news originates from circumstances that give officials substantial control over political content. Second, consider the fact that most Americans who are politically active, system-supporting citizens have been socialized in environments (family, school, workplace) that discourage analytical or ideological political thinking. This combination of nonanalytical news with nonanalytical people does not bode well for much analytical thinking in response to political messages in the news.

A third factor further undermines the critical thinking of the public. Also noted in chapter 3, political actors tend to construct simplistic political messages that appeal to myths and unquestioned beliefs held by large segments of the public. Such messages are seldom brought into focus because of the absence of analysis in the news and the lack of analytical dispositions in the audience. As a result, most news messages appeal directly to unconscious myths and unquestioned beliefs. In short, the propagandistic, nonanalytical qualities of mass news mesh smoothly with the well-conditioned, nonanalytical orientation of the citizenry.

This profile of the news prisoner contains an obvious clue about those who escape. *In order to escape the news prison, people must develop some*

independent, analytical perspective from which to interpret the news. So
much for the obvious. More difficult is to identify the sort of perspective
that helps people understand the news more clearly. There are actually
several orientations that would enable people to break through the layers
of subtle persuasion in the news and think sensibly about what might be
going on behind the stories. For example, *a grasp of American history
would provide a perspective on the patterns of myth and rhetoric in political
events.* A common technique of political propaganda is to blur the
relationship between past and present. When historic disasters like foreign
involvements or economic collapses seem to be on the verge of recurring,
public officials can be expected to persuade the public that important
differences distinguish present circumstances from the past. At other
times, when the signs of change seem entirely clear, threatened elites may
try to persuade the public to avoid the fearsome future and step back into
the comforting shadow of the past. The repeated and successful use of
these communication patterns suggests that the American people can be
led easily to see differences where none exist and to ignore distinctions
where they are apparent.

A firm grasp of political history would provide people with a more
secure foundation than they now have from which to resist political
pressures and with which to develop alternative understandings. Unfortunately, most school boards look with disfavor on history curricula that offer
coherent interpretations of American politics. As a result, the majority of
American children suffer through several years of the same history
course—a course that emphasizes disconnected facts and events, reinforces
basic myths that leave people vulnerable to political rhetoric, discourages
people from developing a secure understanding of power and politics in
American society, and, above all, emphasizes the deeds of great national
heroes. This "hero history" not only brings myths to life but also
encourages people to trust contemporary hero-leaders to do their thinking
and acting for them. There are, to put it bluntly, few Americans with an
adequate grasp of their country's history.

*Another possible frame of reference for the news would be the sort
provided in this book, namely, a theoretical grasp of how politicians and
journalists act together to make the news.* Such a perspective would help
people to locate and interpret the gaps and biases in mass media coverage.
When diplomatic talks are called "cordial and productive," people could
assume immediately that nothing had happened and that the leaders
involved had some other political reason to hold the conference. Flags
would go up cautioning people to discount unverified rumors spread by
"unidentified" officials. Similar skepticism would apply to "doublespeak"
statements like this one in the news: " 'We've made no secret of our views,'
said a U.S. official who insisted on anonymity."[1] People could recognize
political manipulation in the news through the use of leaks, pseudo-events,

and various image-making techniques. After hearing "both sides of an issue," people might even begin to wonder what the third side looked like and why it was not reported.

Unfortunately, people are not required to take courses on how to interpret the news. To the contrary, most people are encouraged by every trusted authority, particularly parents and teachers, to take the news seriously and at face value. The majority of us are taught to ingest large quantities of news and wait for an objective understanding of events to strike as if by revelation. Waiting for objective revelations from the news may be more satisfying than waiting for Godot, but it is surely as pointless. Children are quizzed in school on the content of classroom news supplements as though they represented the most accurate and comprehensive coverage of the known world. By memorizing the "right answers" to news quizzes, these children grow up thinking that knowing the facts in the news is equivalent to understanding something about the real world.

The news worship that begins in childhood is continued in adult life by the widespread support for the ideal of objective reporting. The notion that events can and should be presented without values or interpretation feeds the image of the good citizen as a concerned seeker of truth. At the same time, the widespread belief in objective reporting obscures the possibility that most "truths" that emerge from the news are likely to be the result of subtle political messages that appeal to subconscious beliefs and prejudices. People can hardly be blamed for thinking that they have found truth under such circumstances. After all, few things seem as objectively true as having one's deepest prejudices confirmed by respected authorities. Presenting two sides of every story with no critical "bridge" to transcend the differences between the sides only invites people to choose the version closest to their existing beliefs. Studies of newspaper readers (presumably the most critical information-seekers) have shown that newspapers primarily reinforce preexisting political attitudes.[2]

In the absence of a grasp of newsmaking theory or political history, the only other obvious source of independent news judgment is political ideology. Ideologies are formal systems of belief about the nature, origins, and means of promoting values that people regard as important. Not only do ideologies provide people with a clear sense of life's purpose, but they provide a logic for interpreting the world by giving rules for translating real-world events into illustrations of how those values are promoted or damaged. Thus, people who view the news through the lens of an ideology are likely to spot hidden political messages and translate them into independent political statements. The trouble with ideologies is that they can become rigid and limiting frames of reference, leading people to select only the information that fits them while rejecting all other input. For example, many people in the United States continue to hold a "cold war" ideology that views the appearance of socialism or communism anywhere in the world as inherently threatening to democracy, freedom, and the American way of life. For those who cling rigidly to the "cold war" belief system, many important distinctions about world politics may be lost. The emergence of Socialist governments in Europe may seem to be a threatening step along the road to world totalitarianism. Socialism in the Western hemisphere ("our backyard") seems intolerable. Lost in this ideological view is the understanding that all Socialist and Communist governments are not alike, and that most of them do not pose threats to democracy, freedom, or the American way.

Since the news seldom explains how other political systems work from the standpoint of the people who live in them, we tend to hear mostly U.S. official and expert opinion about other systems. And when it comes to Communist or Socialist systems, the chances are pretty good that equal time will be given some venerable "cold warrior" quick to predict the end of democracy, and communism on our doorstep. News consumers with kindred and rigid ideological views can use these familiar pronouncements to reinforce existing beliefs rather than learn something new about the world from the another viewpoint.

If people recognized this vicious circle of news and popular belief, they might be more inclined to build an imperative for learning into their belief systems, turning ideology into a dynamic rather than a static outlook. *If used constructively, ideologies could create challenging understandings of the world by enabling people to find the inconsistencies, puzzles, and paradoxes in events.* Thinking through the puzzles in political events can broaden an ideology by adapting it to resolve the puzzles. This process of adaptation simultaneously creates new ways of seeing the world. For example, Richard Nixon and Henry Kissinger were able to see beyond ideology to recognize the advantages of opening political and economic relations with once-dreaded "Communist" China. After high political authorities had pronounced China safe to think about, journalists began to cover Chinese events from a less rigid ideological viewpoint. If it is possible to do business with a one-party Communist state like China, why not a multiparty Socialist country like Nicaragua? The answer depends largely on whether one's ideology is open or closed to learning new things about the world.

In a perfect world, people would supplement their ideologies with a command of history and a theoretical grasp of news politics. Such a combination of perspectives would enable people to combat news propaganda with their own conclusions. This is not, as you probably guessed, a perfect world. It is unlikely that more than a tiny fraction of the public has an understanding of American history or news politics, and by even the most generous estimates, few people can be called self-reflective ideologues.

Even those few people who manage to construct a political worldview may find it a mixed blessing. On the one hand, they are able to understand political communication in comprehensive and personally satisfying ways. On the other hand, their ideological insights are likely to be discredited by the majority of their fellow citizens, who have been taught to wait for "objective" revelations to emerge from the news. Hence, another paradox: People who espouse a stance of objectivity toward the news are likely to accept blindly the institutional bias of the news media (if, indeed, they are able to form any political conclusions at all), while those who manage to form clear political perspectives are likely to be condemned for being "opinionated."

In order to understand the differences between the ways in which news prisoners and the relative handful of "escapees" react to the news, it will be helpful to explore the responses of some real people to a typical news report. The case study that follows involves an actual news story and the reactions it produced among members of a representative news audience. After thinking about this case, the reader might find it interesting to conduct a similar study to see if the results can be replicated.

THE CASE OF THE KILLER SATELLITES

The example I have selected to illustrate the effects of familiar news messages on the average person comes from my own research on how people "process" the political content in the news.[3] An initial sample of 2,000 people was drawn at random from a commercial mailing list of the residents of a large (pop. 750,000) U.S. city. Such lists are used in marketing research and sales campaigns based on direct-mail contact. Although commercial mailing lists are not perfectly representative of the general population, they tend to be distorted only at the very rich and very poor ends of the economic spectrum. The people included in this initial sample received an introductory letter from the "News Research Project," a news study center at a local university, inviting them to participate in a detailed and somewhat time-consuming study of political attitudes and reactions to the news. A total of 375 people returned a preliminary screening questionnaire indicating that they had the combination of time, interest, and news contact required for participation in the study. These respondents were then sent a long, two-part questionnaire, the first part of which covered general attitudes about politics and journalism, while the second part asked for their reactions to actual news stories that appeared at the time of the study.

Participants were instructed to make contact with their usual news source on a specified day. They were instructed to evaluate up to four stories of their choosing. The evaluation sheet provided for each story allowed participants to respond to the news in the following terms: (1)

whether they learned anything new or useful from the report, (2) whether there was a message or a moral in the story, (3) whether there were actors in the story that produced positive or negative reactions, and (4) if anything reassured or disturbed them about the story.

A total of 268 people completed the questionnaires and news evaluations. The group broke down roughly along the lines of media use in the general population, with about half getting their news from television, a third from newspapers, a tenth from radio, and the rest from news magazines or specialized publications. Since people were exposed to a variety of sources for different lengths of time and at different times of day, there was some overlap and some divergence in exposure to the various stories of the day. The story about the "killer satellites" broke late in the day and appeared in the evening paper and on two of the network evening newscasts. Out of the estimated seventy-five people exposed to the story, twenty-five chose to evaluate it.

The killer satellite story had two equally dramatic plots. First, there was the revelation of a security leak by a member of Congress who was present at a closed-door briefing by a Defense Department expert. The congressman quoted from parts of the secret testimony at a subsequent open committee meeting. The second dramatic aspect of the story involved the topic of the secret briefing. According to the Defense expert, the Soviet Union had developed the capability of launching laser-equipped satellites that could destroy U.S. satellites and space stations. This science fiction motif prompted one of the television news programs to advertise its version of the story as follows: "Killer Satellites in Outer Space...Coming Up Next."

All in all, it was a perfect news story with two great plots: a member of Congress on the hot seat and a new twist on the arms race. The link between the two plots was provided by the Department of Defense, whose spokesperson said that it was "impossible to tell" how much damage had been done to the delicate U.S.-Soviet military balance by the leak of top intelligence information. The implication of the Defense Department statement was that the existence of laser satellites was bad enough but that letting the Russians know that we knew about them was even worse. An uneasy situation seemed to be complicated further by turning it into a public issue.

The security leak somehow added a sense of urgency to the latest twist on the old plot of conflict between the superpowers—if, indeed, the prospects of a war in outer space needed any embellishment. It is probably not surprising to learn that the overwhelming majority of those who evaluated this story indicated high levels of distress and concern about the arms race and U.S. military preparedness. People were able to respond to these thirty-year-old themes as though they had just encountered them for the first time. Not only does this response illustrate the power of news to continually breathe new life into familiar political messages, but it also illustrates the propensity for people to take political news at face value even when there are many clues to suggest that propaganda is at work. Before exploring the actual responses of these "news prisoners" to the story, let's review the evidence for the possibility that the entire story was staged by government officials for propaganda purposes.

Consider some interesting facts that were available to anyone who had made contact with the killer satellite story in particular and the day's news in general. Any "news detective" should have found these facts puzzling:

1. The story originated with a Defense Department statement to the effect that it was impossible to tell how much "damage" had been done by the leak. If the Defense Department was afraid of whatever unspecified damage might follow from the leak, why did it go out of its way to issue such an inflammatory statement? Common sense would suggest a no-comment strategy, or an attempt to specify and minimize the possible damages, if, of course, the Defense Department had any interest in keeping the information secret.

2. The secret testimony was delivered at the time of crucial defense budget deliberations in Congress. The Defense Department typically offers such briefings in order to help members of Congress "understand" the true need for increased defense spending.

3. There was strong public resistance to the Defense Department's proposals for huge spending increases as the country was in the midst of a serious recession and the defense increases would come in exchange for cuts in social programs.

4. The member of Congress read the secret testimony aloud at a public meeting. This is not the sort of anonymous release that usually accompanies leaks. Even though the representative claimed that reading the testimony was an accident, it is hard to imagine how anyone could quote directly from classified material without knowing what he was doing. Moreover, had the representative admitted to leaking the information on purpose, he might have been subject to legal or ethics charges. All in all, it seems reasonable to suspect that he wanted the public to know about the latest Soviet military menace. Whether he leaked the information after consulting Defense Department officials is of course impossible to tell.

5. The only reporter present at the time the secret was leaked represented the *Army Times*. While it is true that the *Army Times* is not "owned" by the Defense Department, it is not clear that it is such an independent publication that it would have rejected the

Defense Department's pleas not to publish secret information. A Defense spokesperson said that strong pressure was applied to the *Army Times* but that the paper published the story anyway.

6. If, as the Defense Department claimed, it wished to minimize the impact of the story, why did it then respond to the *Army Times* article by talking about "unknown damage" in U.S.-Soviet relations and "impossible to assess" effects on the U.S. military posture? Such ominous comments escalated the story into a mass media news item the next day. Government officials generally refuse comment or issue statements minimizing the significance of events when they truly want to downplay a news story.

All of the above clues were available to everyone who read the story in question and who had even a passing familiarity with surrounding headlines proclaiming the political controversy over the proposed defense spending increases. The six clues, when put together, add up to an obvious hypothesis about the story: The "leak" was a ploy to lend immediacy and credibility to standard Pentagon scare tactics designed to win public support for defense allocations every year around budget time. A second-party leak that is then condemned by the original source of the information makes the information seem all the more credible and compelling. When the Defense Department condemned the leak, it became hard to prove that they were simply playing budgetary politics with a new and rather deadly twist.

Even if caution would warn against leaping to conclusions, surely it would be hard to suppress doubts about the authenticity of this story! Unfortunately, most people are prisoners of the news who find it difficult to think analytically or critically about news events. As noted earlier, it is difficult to suspect ulterior motives on the part of public officials when we are taught to accept what authorities tell us. It is also hard to reconcile the possibility of news manipulation with our widely conditioned acceptance of news as a believable, face-value rendering of reality. Finally, it is difficult to make connections between news stories (e.g., linking the satellite story to stories on the defense budget) when most news reports are both fragmented and lacking in analysis. When all these factors are taken into account, it is perhaps disheartening but hardly surprising to find that most people took the killer satellite story at face value.

The overwhelming majority of people responded as though their lines had been scripted by the same authors who wrote the story. People were angered by the security leak, but this anger was overshadowed by genuine concern about the latest Soviet military advantage. A total of twenty-five people evaluated the story. Of these, eighteen accepted, without question, the basic political messages of the story, while only five raised any questions about the honesty of the leak or the credibility of the message that "the Russians are ahead of us again." Two evaluations were too sketchy to be coded as either accepting or critical of the report.

Among the eighteen people who accepted the report and its message without question there was not the slightest hint of doubt. These people were able to generate a remarkable degree of emotional distress about this latest episode in the U.S.-Soviet conflict. Even though the American people have been exposed to the same scare about Soviet domination over the past thirty years, it still seemed terribly real in its latest plot incarnation. Consider the following excerpts from the reactions of the eighteen "believers" (their news sources for the story are in parentheses following their comments):

> Soviets will have space systems capable of attacking targets from space in less than 10 years....We ought to be more concerned about Soviet capabilities....People in responsible positions need to take extra precautions not to make public any secret testimony. (daily newspaper)

> Testimony that was inadvertently made public implies that Soviets have a lead in development of killer satellites....Peaceful purposes of U.S.-USSR space cooperation agreement seem far away. ("NBC Nightly News")

> A leak of information by a Congressman of secrets relating to Soviet space weapons capable of destroying our (or any) other satellites.... Whole report disturbing....Congressman who talked—DUMB! (ABC-TV)

> USSR will have a laser satellite in space by next year, capable of destroying U.S. satellites with lasers....The USSR is quite advanced in its space technology....Having weapons in space disturbs me. (NBC-TV)

> By 1983—Soviets will have laser-equipped space station. By 1990—Space station will be manned military operation....Disturbing that a Congressman could "unwittingly" leak information by national security. (ABC-TV)

> Russian arms in space can destroy U.S. satellites and land installations. ...More care should be taken with the handling of secret information. (ABC-TV)

> A general was shown advocating a U.S. system of 432 killer satellites.... U.S. may move into new arms race to build killer satellites, and despite earlier Soviet-U.S. agreements on use of space for peaceful purposes— the reality may well be different....Idea of new arms race in space is most disturbing. (NBC-TV)

> The Soviets are apparently very interested in pursuing the military advantages of space technology....I'm concerned that we will most likely follow suit with technologies of our own. (newspaper)

Defense Department scientist's secret testimony concerning Soviet laser weapons inadvertently leaked by Rep. Ken Kramer. . . . The fact that the Soviet Union appears to be so far ahead of the U.S., and that Kramer's leak could be damaging to our national security—makes me tend to agree that defense spending is necessary, and wonder why more precautions aren't taken to preserve the confidentiality of such information. (newspaper)

Disturbing that the proliferation of new weapons continues with no apparent sign of abatement. (newspaper)

It was interesting to learn that laser beams could be used for this purpose. . . . The build-up of arms for war is disturbing. (NBC-TV)

We are behind in developing this technology. The disclosure came about on the public reading of classified information during a congressional investigation. . . . The Soviet Union could orbit a laser weapon system that could strike at our orbiting communication satellites. (newspaper)

Geosynchronous satellites may be threatened by Soviet space-based lasers by 1983–88. . . . How imminent such potential is I found extremely upsetting—the potential of such a manned space station is frightening to say the least. (newspaper)

There is evidence that the Soviets may have weapons in outer space. The Soviets seem to be ahead of us in outer space weaponry. (ABC-TV)

A new dimension of warfare is coming of age. Facts were new to me. (NBC-TV)

The Soviets are basically exploiting outer space as a platform for military operations. (ABC-TV)

Some congressman leaked the information that the Soviets have a weapon satellite in space which can launch rockets at our satellites. By 1990 they will be able to launch a manned space craft with weapons to cover all earth targets. . . . The message is that we are behind at this time regarding weapons in space. (ABC-TV)

Russia is starting a weapon in space program and the American public found out because of a leak in Congress. . . . I did not know before that anyone was working on a space weapon program but I always felt it would come about. (ABC-TV)

As the above responses indicate, most people who evaluated the "killer satellite" story believed that the leak was an accident, and they expressed genuine alarm over the news that the Soviet Union was ahead of the United States in a new and deadly arms race. Only a small minority (20 percent) expressed any doubts about the sincerity of the story or the motives behind its message. It is also worth nothing that only one of the skeptics had the strength of conviction that characterized all eighteen of the "true believers." As noted earlier, well-crafted propaganda does not provide the critic with much solid evidence to support doubts. Thus the voices of the doubters, already muffled by their small numbers, were weakened further by their tones of uncertainty:

> Russians may be ahead of us in space research....Russians want to control space....Are we really behind the Russians? Is this a controlled leak, i.e., set up by the U.S. government? (ABC-TV)

> ...the arms race is getting completely out of control....I also wondered if the leak was an intentional scare tactic. (newspaper)

> The Soviet Union is ahead of the U.S., in satellite weapons....Rep. Ken Kramer, the committee member who read aloud the secret testimony, is either incredibly stupid or is deliberately trying to arouse fear in U.S. public....It is disturbing to be given a small bit of information without other confirmation or refutation. (newspaper)

> Nothing remains a secret in Washington, D.C., if somebody wants it leaked....The D.O.D. is still up to their old game of trying to terrify Congress with the worst threat that the Soviets may (someday) be capable of mounting. I imagine the D.O.D. is not unhappy the leak happened; it will tend to help them in their budget battles in Congress. (newspaper)

> Was it a "slip" in having the story come out, or was it a planned "leak" to help continuing increased defense (budget) spending? (newspaper)

These responses indicate that not only are those who spot possible deception in the news few in number but they are less assertive than those who accept news messages without question. It may be that the sheer ambiguity that accompanies suspicions about news messages is unpleasant enough to turn doubters into believers. Although it is hard to tell precisely what separates the doubters from the believers, several features of the group profiles are worth nothing. For example, the two groups did not differ in terms of the left-right leaning of their political views. The average person in both groups described his or her political views as "moderate." Neither was there much difference between the groups in terms of political activities, although the believers tended to be somewhat more active politically than the doubters. Believers felt slightly less able to change things that bothered them in their personal lives than doubters did, but the difference was not significant statistically. An interesting but not easily interpretable difference between the two groups involved the much higher levels of life stress reported by the doubters. Perhaps being a doubter is inherently more stressful than being a believer, or perhaps high-stress people tend to be more critical of information in their environments than do low-stress people, or maybe stress is produced by the feeling that the government is lying to you and nobody else sees it that way.

Fortunately, we do not have to untangle the mysterious web of stress differences in order to identify an obvious distinction between the believers and the doubters. The two groups differ along two very fundamental dimensions. First, the believers reported that they were exposed to half again more news every week than the doubters! To be exact, news contact averaged 8.83 hours per week for the believers and only 5.20 hours per week for the doubters. Causality probably runs in both directions here, with people who find the news credible consuming more of it, while increased news contact reinforces the tendency to accept news messages at face value. Second, it is worth nothing that 80 percent of the doubters read the story in the newspaper, while 67 percent of the believers watched the story on television. For some reason, people think they are less likely to be fooled by a news report that they can see with their own eyes. It would seem that people have fooled themselves by adopting this "seeing-is-believing" attitude about televised news. Televised news stories may seem more credible because they contain pictures, because they are more dramatic and absorbing, or merely because the actors in them make more of a semblance of human contact with the viewer. Far from being indicators of truth, these features of television would seem to undermine basic human judgment. Television news may seem more objective, not because it enables people to judge stories better for themselves, but because it inhibits their judgment!

Whatever the differences between the believers and the doubters, one thing is clear: A dominant effect of the news is to continually dress old political messages in new story plots. Since the news is so vulnerable to political manipulation, the ulterior purposes behind the ongoing stream of new stories and plot twists are seldom exposed. As a result, the majority of the people exposed to political messages in the news are likely to take them seriously and respond as appropriate with alarm, feelings of reassurance, increased activity, or continued passivity in the political arena.

BEYOND POLITICAL INFORMATION:
OTHER REASONS WHY PEOPLE FOLLOW THE NEWS

The reassurance of hearing familiar messages and the comfort of having basic beliefs reinforced are both important reasons why people may follow the news. There are also other effects worth knowing about. As should be clear by now, the news is a rich symbolic medium. Events are presented in dramatic terms with an emphasis on emotional themes and the exploits of a colorful cast of heroes, villains, prophets, and fools. Such rich symbolic content in communication lends itself to multiple human uses that go far beyond the simple quest for information. People also may receive a broad range of rewards or "gratifications" from such communication that far outweigh the occasional satisfaction of using news information to make political choices and life decisions.

Research on the various "uses and gratifications" associated with the news can be summarized under three broad categories:[4]

1. *Curiosity and Surveillance.* Even though the political messages in the news are fairly predictable, the events, plots, and characters are constantly changing. Human curiosity is engaged by new events and novel twists on old themes. Moreover, some of the events in the news may have an impact on the people who follow them. Thus, many people find it useful to scan the news just to keep potentially important events under surveillance.

2. *Entertainment and Escape.* It is easy to become engaged by the drama of news events. The news makes everyday happenings seem larger than life. Most news reports invite us to escape for a minute or two into a story world filled with pathos, tragedy, moral lessons, crisis, mystery, danger, and occasional whimsy. The escape into this dramatic world is made all the easier when the happenings involve people like us or people about whom we have strong positive or negative feelings.

3. *Social and Psychological Adjustment.* The emphasis on drama, emotional themes, powerful images, and strong personalities makes the news a convenient medium for working out psychological tensions and social conflicts. People do not even have to leave their living rooms in order to encounter real people about whom they have strong feelings and issues that seem to affect their well-being. By making connections between personal concerns and events and personalities in the news, people can express feelings and think about their problems in uninhibited and often satisfying ways. This vicarious resolution of social and psychological strains is all the more effective because the realities of news stories are usually too distant for people to experience directly—thus the feelings and understandings people develop in response to the news are seldom subjected to reality testing.

Since all these uses and gratifications have important personal and political consequences, they are worth exploring in more detail.

Curiosity and Surveillance

People are blessed with curiosity—both as a source of sheer pleasure or amusement and as a means of spotting new information that might be useful in coping with everyday reality. Research has shown that our curiosity is piqued by things (e.g., situations, ideas, scenery, films, art, and news) that contain a mixture of familiar and novel features.[5] It is not surprising that human curiosity requires a combination of new and old stimuli in order to be satisfied. On the one hand, the repeated exposure to completely familiar stimuli results in the formation of subconscious mental "scripts" that make it possible to respond to situations without really thinking about them.[6] Curiosity and attention are minimized in such "scripted" situations. On the other hand, stimuli that are completely foreign may be so dissonant and hard to assimilate that people tend to ignore, avoid, or misinterpret them.[7] Partially familiar stimuli, by contrast, enable people to utilize existing mental categories and understandings while provoking people to modify or change those categories to accommodate anything that is new, different, or slightly out of focus.

News is the perfect blend of the familiar and the novel. The basic political messages in the news remain much the same, but they often appear in new settings and under different circumstances. There is an intrinsic satisfaction that comes from seeing how a familiar theme will develop in a new plot or whether an old plot will develop a new twist. For example, how will "freedom of choice"—a theme familiar to every American—be adapted to fit comfortably into such contexts as abortion, drug use, pornography, or the regulation of cigarette smoking in public places? Will the tired old plot of confrontation between the United States and the Soviet Union end in impasse as usual, or will there be a new twist this time? Perhaps a breakthrough in nuclear arms control? Perhaps a misunderstanding that will lead to human extinction? As long as new events keep happening in the world (and chances are pretty good that they will), people will be drawn to the news as a means of applying, testing, and adjusting their understandings about reality. However, the news may be a dangerous object of curiosity due to its often distorted images of reality. People who regard mass media news as a satisfying source of objective information may be led astray by their own curiosity. For example, if the news persists in portraying the problems of the Third World in terms of the virtues of "development" versus the stigma of "underdevelopment," the news audience may fail to perceive many of the problems associated with rapid economic development in Third World societies—problems like the destruction of culture, the growing dependence of poor countries on the economies of rich countries, the political problems that accompany economic growth in repressive regimes, and so forth. All these problems contribute to the political and economic instability of those Third World countries that have entered the seemingly endless process of "development."

Despite its limitations, the development metaphor is written into each chapter of the "development saga" by government officials and co-operative reporters. Thus the latest collapse of a one-crop economy in an African nation may be attributed to a failure to diversify in the world marketplace. The failure to diversify is, of course, a symptom of underdevelopment. Never mind that the one-crop economy was forced on the nation by a former colonial regime, and never mind that the country's economic weakness may have been compounded after colonialism by wealthy countries that exploit one-product economies even more ca- priciously than the colonial powers did. The development metaphor needs no explanations; underdevelopment is at once the cause and effect of an ill- defined economic condition. The solution, of course, is "development." In the case of our hypothetical Third World country, it is easy to imagine a subsequent news story describing a "development plan" for the troubled country—perhaps a massive infusion of loan funds offered by the World Bank. The money will be used to develop foreign-sponsored economic projects in the country. Even though the conditions of such loans, combined with the chronic dependence of indebtedness, will probably produce further setbacks in development, the immediate story now has a happy ending. Curiosity has been aroused by a new crisis in the world economy, and curiosity has been satisfied by resolving that crisis in terms of a familiar political concept. All just part of a day's work in the news world.

As long as the news continues to employ familiar but misguided themes in portraying the real world, and as long as people attempt to satisfy their curiosity about the world through the vicarious medium of mass media news, this syndrome of political misinformation disguised by psychological gratification will continue to exist. The fact that massive doses of misinformation can prove so satisfying is just a small indicator of the degree to which the news removes people from the actualities of politics.

Before the reader concludes that I have overstated the case here, let me offer a qualification. Not all the news is as remote from everyday personal experience as the coverage of Third World development problems probably is. Some stories arouse curiosity because they contain information that is immediately relevant to people. Not all curiosity is for the sake of sheer amusement. Even though people have the capacity to be curious about very abstract things, few people can live by idle curiosity alone. The news is all the more satisfying when it contains periodic information that is directly relevant to people. The reactions to such reporting differ in two interesting ways from reactions to more abstract stories. First, people are more likely to think in action-oriented terms about personally relevant stories. The more distant world of political news often leaves people with little option but to exercise their beliefs in a purely private fashion. Second, people express much less confusion and dis- pleasure about news stories that satisfy curiosity with information that can be applied to immediate life concerns. Consider, for example, some typical reactions to different kinds of news stories from the News Research Project.

One of the stories in the news at the time of the study was a report on the financial troubles faced by four major airlines. The report outlined the various consequences for travelers, employees, and the economy if the airlines went bankrupt. Such information would seem to be of interest to a broad range of people. As a sign of the relevance of the information, everyone who filled out an evaluation of the story was able to find some personal use for the information. The range of uses was quite broad. For example, some people were alerted to possible difficulties in future travel arrangements, as indicated by this person's reaction: "I was disturbed by the fact that the failure of several airlines could result in increased inconvenience in travel." People who had already made travel plans were moved by the report to take direct action, as this response explains: "I found the story disturbing, as I have plane reservations in the spring with one of the airlines that may go bankrupt, so I plan to check with my travel agent about possibly changing airlines." Others found even more intimate applications for the information in the story, as revealed in the following reactions:

> I found the story disturbing as I have a friend that's been employed for several years by another of the airlines mentioned....

> ...reassuring that I am employed by an airline that is doing very well. Their loss is our gain.

It is significant that the airline story did not lead anyone to question its relevance or newsworthiness. Stories that are less personally relevant, by contrast, produce less satisfaction, as indicated by the comparative absence of stated uses for the information and the increased level of complaints about newsworthiness. For example, one of the stories in the study involved an incident between Nancy Kissinger (wife of former Secretary of State Henry Kissinger) and a political demonstrator at an airport. The demonstrator had filed a lawsuit alleging that Mrs. Kissinger assaulted her. Mrs. Kissinger claimed that she was simply defending her husband against a terrible insult from the demonstrator. None of the participants in the study who evaluated the story was able to find a direct personal application for the information it contained. At best the responses reflect an interest in trivia:

> I learned a little about Nancy Kissinger's personality.

> I learned that Henry Kissinger had a heart operation.

> How easy it is for someone to sue another person!

Nearly half the respondents were unable to find even such trivial meaning in the story. Many questioned its newsworthiness:

I did not feel that this article should appear on the front page of the newspaper.

No, I didn't learn anything, and it didn't rate the front page, except for its eye-catching function as a sales aid—à la *National Enquirer*.

I am angry at how people involved resorted to verbal and physical attacks, but more importantly, that the article was placed on the front page—I doubt if the article has much significance—other than sensationalism.

Most news falls somewhere between the airline story and the Nancy Kissinger saga in terms of personal relevance. Most political stories, for example, are regarded as legitimate news in the sense that people react emotionally to them and believe them to be important. Nevertheless, few political stories provoke the sort of reaction or behavior that the airline story did. In fact, few stories about political issues and government activities contain any more food for action than the Kissinger story did. A case in point was the major political story on the day that participants in the News Research Project were instructed to follow the news. President Reagan was on a speaking tour around the country trying to drum up public support for this budget. Despite his campaign promises of a balanced budget, the proposed budget contained the largest deficit in history. Much of the deficit was the result of increased defense allocations. A major section of the speech contained frightening references to the likelihood of war if America's defenses were not strengthened. So gripping were these images that over half the people exposed to this story chose to comment on it. Nearly all the respondents expressed a strong emotional reaction to the talk about war, and most people stated their opinion about the president's claims. Despite these strong psychological reactions, there was a nearly universal absence of ideas about personal actions that might grow out of the information in the story. In fact, only one person mentioned an action in response to the story, and it was not a very realistic one at that: the possibility of quitting work in order to campaign full-time against the president and his dangerous ideas.

The news world, in short, is rich in emotional triggers yet poor in guidelines for actions that might provide meaningful outlets for those emotions. The citizen who centers his or her political life on the distant world of news politics is a citizen by political proxy—at best, registering support through public opinion polls for the various issues and leaders that have been served up on the political agenda. As the next section shows, media politics is vicarious politics.

Entertainment and Escape

Speaking of vicarious involvement in the news raises the obvious issue of news as a source of entertainment and easy escape from mundane concerns. The news may represent itself as fact, but it is communicated to the public with all the trappings of fiction: short, intense scenes; literary rather than analytical treatments; the nearly uniform uses of the story form; and the emphasis on drama, emotional conflict, and larger-than-life characters. The news may portray real events, but it does so in ways that discourage analytical or instrumental uses for the information it carries.

The news is, in short, a perfect medium for escape. Each day's news menu offers a large supply of complete minidramas for our entertainment pleasure. We can step into one fascinating fantasy for a minute or two—experiencing a brief sense of other lives and other worlds—and then move on to the next one. In one moment we are a member of a guerrilla band on maneuvers in El Salvador, the next minute we move in with the survivors of an earthquake in Iraq, suddenly we are transported into the nightmare of a bank robbery-murder that was captured on the bank's closed-circuit video system. At last, the string of high-tension episodes is broken by a commercial that gives us a chance to regain our bearings, grab a snack, and get ready for the next installment of our evening's journey into real-life adventure.

Vicarious involvement in the news is often even more compelling than more conventional forms of escape via drama and literature. News dramas, after all, are represented as real, serious, important, and worthy of everyone's attention. Fiction, by contrast, does not involve real spies, real robbers, or real earthquakes. Fiction can at times command our attention, but fiction seldom combines the mixture of intensity, universality of appeal, and realism that characterizes the news. A best-selling novel may sell a million copies during its lengthy run on the bestseller list, while 80 million people may tune into the news on a single day.

The seriousness or realism of the news is, paradoxically, a key to understanding its power as an escape medium. The general acceptance of the news as factual, important, and objective makes it easy for people to give themselves over to serious involvement with it. Once this easy surrender has taken place, the individual is then swept away by images and ideas that are often both stranger and more dramatic than fiction. For example, few novels contain plot twists like the news story about a band of thieves posing as police officers who were forced by circumstances to try to arrest a group of policeman disguised as a gang of thieves. The real police were—you guessed it—on the trail of the thieves who were posing as police. If a novelist were to submit such a plot to a publisher, it probably would be rejected as incredible or unrealistic. When it becomes news, however, no plot is too incredible to be engrossing. All plots are credible by virtue of the very fact that they are news. Thus the issue of credibility or realism, a major obstacle to involvement in fiction, is transcended easily by stories in the news, no matter how bizarre they may be.

The fact that news stories are thought to represent real situations adds to their entertainment value in at least one other respect. When dramatic incidents involve real people—people who feel, suffer, think, and die—a direct bond of human sensibility is created with the audience. Whereas fiction writers struggle to create such bonds through words and imaginary actions, the news generates them routinely by simply recording dramatic excerpts from real lives. Thus, few novels or movies about the horrors of war can rival the routine nightly installments on Vietnam witnessed by the American people between 1965 and 1970. Fictional accounts of political power and intrigue may achieve a measure of credibility, but few can match the daily revelations about power and corruption in the White House that filled the news during the time of the Watergate scandal.

In fact, the news is so dramatic that it increasingly supplies the plot material for novels, films, and new entertainment forms like the "docu-drama." Novels have been written about murders, robberies, hijackings, and kidnappings, subjects that first captured the popular imagination in the news. Journalistic treatments of terrorism, political corruption, military operations, and spy escapades have spawned movies by the score. Even the journalistic practices behind the news have inspired entertainment fare, as in the case of Woodward and Bernstein's literary and film versions of *All the President's Men*—a highly dramatized account of how the two daring reporters conducted their famous Watergate investigation.

With the action news format gaining in popularity among those who run mass media news, we can expect the news to move ever closer to the routine distillation of "faction," that is, factualized fiction or, if you prefer, fictionalized fact. Such a trend will only enhance the news as an escape medium and further undermine its potential to inform us realistically about contemporary life.

As Walter Lippmann pointed out over fifty years ago, the world of politics, as viewed by the public, will always be somewhat dramatized and fictionalized.[8] Politicians who control the flow of information will attempt whenever possible to shape news to their advantage. However, when the media actively seek dramatized reality to feed to a receptive audience, the only check on the representation of political reality is removed. *When politicians, press, and public all judge political performances more in terms of dramatic criteria than moral standards, the conscience of the polity will be lost.* Politicians will be free to lie and deceive at will (for it will no longer be thought of as lying and deception), and if they are challenged, they need only muster appropriate dramatic displays of oversight, regret, misunderstanding, or good intentions.

If people become slowly conditioned to judge political performances for dramatic qualities rather than other features like truth, principle, or observable consequences, minor annoyances like inconsistency, duplicity, or failure on the part of the political actor may be forgiven in exchange for compelling dramatic performances. For example, despite the evident failure of his economic policies during his first two years in office, Ronald Reagan maintained a much higher level of popular support than less skilled presidential actors could have expected under similar circumstances. Many people seemed willing to grant Reagan large measures of sincerity and good intentions. How can people make such attributions about the offstage character of a public actor except by exercising implicit judgments about the quality of his onstage dramatic performances? Can such judgments really differ greatly from similar public attributions of sincerity and goodwill that made Reagan, earlier in his career, a successful television salesman for home appliances and soap powders?

In the world of political drama, the performance counts more than the success or failure of action, for, as noted in chapter 3, the performance "is" the action as far as the public is concerned. Consider some cases of similar actions that were either made or broken by the quality of the surrounding dramatic performances. When John Kennedy admitted to botching the Bay of Pigs invasion, he was forgiven by a majority of Americans on the strength of his compassionate and convincing apology. Yet when Jimmy Carter took responsibility for the aborted attempt to rescue the American hostages from Iran, his popularity plunged. Carter, unlike Kennedy, had failed to script a dramatic performance that fit his role properly into the surrounding adventure saga. In short, Carter gave a bad performance. When Richard Nixon was a candidate for vice president in 1952, he faced the nation on television to address charges of political corruption. He won millions of voters' hearts with his careful script, his calculated stage setting, the fine supporting role of his faithful wife, and his emotionally delivered reference to his innocent little dog, Checkers. By contrast, when Nixon again faced corruption charges over two decades later, his performance was flawed, petulant, personal, and poorly rehearsed. He failed to produce the all-encompassing script and well-rehearsed supporting cast that represented his only conceivable salvation from the otherwise tawdry reality of the Watergate affair.

If the dramatization of political reality is a key to understanding the fortunes of public life, it is no less important for understanding the private political worlds of individual citizens. Vicarious political experience may be different from direct participation, but it is nonetheless a form of experience. Escape and entertainment are far from being meaningless pursuits. Whatever their other effects may be, political dramas can help people open up their fantasies and subconscious feelings with the result of relieving psychological tensions and easing social strains. The escape and entertainment functions of the news thus pave the way for important social and psychological adjustments.

Social and Psychological Adjustment

When people escape into the world of drama found in the news, they do not necessarily leave all their concerns behind them. Although our inclinations for direct action may be inhibited by the one-way communication channels of the mass media, we respond psychologically to the people and issues in news reports. It is, in fact, remarkably easy to identify with actors in the news, respond to them emotionally, and imagine that we are somehow part of their experiences. This sort of response to the news is possible because we have the capacity to generate fantasies.

Human beings spend a good deal of their waking and sleeping time creating imaginary scenarios in which they explore wishes, hopes, fears, and desires. Through fantasies we can rehearse unfamiliar social roles and anticipate encounters with other people. Fantasies also enable us to contain powerful feelings like anger, sexual desire, or fear when they are inappropriate to express openly in a particular situation. In other situations, fantasies help in making choices about how best to express those feelings in public.

A healthy fantasy life is essential for adjusting to the conditions and people we encounter in real life. The news, with its powerful images, emotional themes, and colorful characters, is a rich source of fantasy material. It is possible to step into a news plot and imagine what it would be like to be rich, poor, powerful, weak, female, male, sexy, brave, or intelligent. By taking the real world into the privacy of our minds via the news, we can explore feelings in ways that might not be comfortable in real life. We can relate to people in ways that would not be possible in real life.

Fantasies require very little anchor in reality in order to thrive. In fact, since fantasies involve by definition the suspending of ordinary reality, they can spring from the barest of suggestions and the least substantial of images. As far as our fantasy life goes, what does it matter what our favorite newscaster is really like in private life? As long as he or she displays the right style, manner, or looks, we feel comfortable inviting him or her into our home and listening as we would to a trusted friend imparting all the "news" that has transpired since we last got together. CBS anchor Dan Rather probably changed very little as a result of adding a sweater vest to soften his video image, but that small change of image apparently helped many viewers incorporate him into their fantasy lives.

Since fantasies feed from such minimal information, and since the news transmits such condensed, ambiguous images, it should not be surprising to learn that different people can generate very different fantasies from the same story. Who knows what it is really like to be the guerrilla fighter dashing through the jungle, locked in a life-or-death struggle for the freedom of her country? Some might imagine that she is a romantic figure, with virtues like bravery, charisma, morals, and intelligence—the sort of person they would secretly like to be. Others might imagine her as a bloodthirsty heathen—an immoral Communist who threatens their values and life-styles. Same news story, different fantasies.

Part of the fantasy element in the news is caused by the heavy emphasis in politics on "fantasy themes" having to do with power, community, order, and security.[9] Such concerns are central to the social and emotional well-being of the average person. Find a political speech without an emphasis on power, community, order, or security, and you have found an atypical and in all likelihood ineffectual political statement. These fantasy themes of politics would never make it to the mass audience if the news did not transmit them.

It is hardly surprising that the news transmits fantasy themes from political performances to audiences. In fact, mass media journalism tends to focus on fantasy themes. These themes, after all, represent the most dramatic and universally appealing components of political performances. Fantasy themes are about the only medium through which a lengthy political performance can be condensed into a meaningful news-length capsule.

In many cases, the news even emphasizes powerful images and fantasy themes more than they may have been in the actual political performance. Various techniques of storytelling, scene setting, and audio and visual display can be used to upgrade the fantasy level of an event. Consider, as an example, television news coverage of the Reagan inaugural. High rituals of state like inaugurations, campaigns, funerals, state-of-the-union addresses, and the like offer a good vantage for viewing fantasy themes in action. These rituals are designed to appeal to the popular imagination with images of strength, community, security, and new beginnings. Inaugurals are always occasions for calling the people together, reminding them that they are one nation with common bonds, and calling for renewed commitment to the goals of prosperity, harmony, peace, and security.

Since most people are preoccupied at some level with concerns about prosperity, harmony, peace, and security, it is comforting to have related fantasies evoked time and again by each new leader chosen to preserve and protect these elements of the American fantasy, more commonly referred to as the "American dream." Inaugural speeches are open invitations for new presidents to pull out all the symbolic stops in an effort to kindle the deepest fantasies that define the political community.

Ronald Reagan was faced with a challenge when he mounted the platform to address the nation in 1980. The country was plunging into recession, national pride was at an ebb, and people saw a future with little promise. Drawing on the themes that got him elected, Reagan exhorted the country to step back into the past as a means of finding the values and spirit with which to face the future. He chose the perfect setting for such a speech. Standing at the West Front of the Capitol, Reagan could point to the great gallery of monuments that fill the national shrine of Washington,

D.C. As he mentioned great heroes and episodes from the nation's past, he could evoke their physical presence at the same time. Mentioning George Washington is one thing, but filling the mind with the dramatic image of the Washington Monument and its stunning reflecting pool is an even more effective means of engaging the imagination of the audience.

In order to realize the full potential of the images in his speech, Reagan needed a little help from the media. He could, of course, talk about the great monuments and symbols of state that surrounded him, but how much more effective it would be if the media incorporated pictures of those things as though they were part of the script for the performance. Reagan and his media advisers must have anticipated what the journalists would do. All the White House needed to do was announce the time and place of the performance and issue an advance copy of the script, and the media could be relied on to do the rest. As the following excerpt from Ernest Bormann's analysis of inaugural coverage by CBS television indicates, journalist and political actor joined forces smoothly to maximize the fantasy potential in the event:

> Toward the close of the speech Reagan noted that this was the first time the ceremony was held on the West Front of the capitol, then he said, "Standing here, one faces a magnificent vista (The director called up a long shot of the magnificent vista), opening up on this city's special beauty and history. At the end of this open mall (The director had the camera pan up the open mall) are those shrines to the giants on whose shoulders we stand. Directly in front of me, the monument to a monumental man: (Cut to a shot of Washington monument) George Washington, father of our country...." After an encomium to Washington Reagan said, "Off to one side (Cut to a shot of the Jefferson Memorial), the stately memorial to Thomas Jefferson." After some words of praise for Jefferson, Reagan continued, "and then beyond the reflecting pool, the dignified columns of the Lincoln Memorial (Camera moves to Lincoln Memorial)." When Reagan next directed his audience's attention to the "sloping hills of Arlington National Cemetery with its row upon row of simple white markers bearing crosses or Stars of David...." the director had the camera focus on the cemetery.[10]

With this kind of interplay between political images and news emphasis, it is little wonder that news represents a rich source of fantasy. Indeed, the responses of participants in the News Research Project indicated a good deal of fantasy and emotional resonance with issues and actors in the news. Two characteristics of such fantasy play are the formation of strong expressions of feeling and opinion (stronger than would ordinarily be acceptable in real-life situations) and the development of vicarious relationships with the actors in news stories. Communication theorists have used the term "parasocial relationship" to refer to the often intimate emotional bonds that people can establish with the distant actors on the other end of one-way, mass media relationships.[11]

The responses of participants in the News Research Project indicated that people had developed highly personalized relationships with actors in the news, relationships that had blossomed safely over the vast distances of the mass communication wires. The level of emotional expression in many of the news evaluations was as intense as might be expected in the most intimate of real social relationships. Also indicative of the fantasy level on which parasocial relationships operate was the stream-of-consciousness form of many responses. For example, an evaluation of a presidential speech included the following statement about the speaker: "President Reagan—Wealthy-Elitist-Bigot Friend-of-the-Rich Foe-of-the-Poor and Handicapped Poorly Read—Always the Mediocre Actor."

"Wealthy-Elitist-Bigot." Those strong terms are both emotionally expressive and representative of social bonds and antagonisms that have been established with the outer world. Such reactions to people and issues in political reporting can be important for emotional adjustment and maintaining a sense of emotional belonging in a vast and alienating society. Whereas people often feel pressure not to express their true feelings in real-life settings, they can rail against injustice and political folly through private interactions with the media. Similarly, although it may be hard for people to take the measure of their group memberships in real life, a range of clear-cut, simplified, and easily accessible social ties and antagonisms is displayed on a daily basis in the news. The social and emotional adjustment functions served by media politics may be more satisfying than the corresponding outlets for emotional expression and social bonding in everyday life.

WHAT PRICE MASS MEDIATED REALITY?

Convenient as it may be for people to invest emotions and social commitments in neatly packaged media dramas, some costs are part of the bargain. These costs are reflected partly in the quality of the social communities in which people live. If the mass audience increasingly invests feelings and social bonds in media relationships because they are less threatening than real relationships, the quality of social life is likely to decline. People may increasingly remove important values and beliefs from the foundations of relationships. While it may be true that relationships built on things people value and care about are risky and emotionally volatile, the alternative is empty and meaningless. Friendships and associations based on nothing more than life-styles, sports, games, or convenience are liable to dissolve as quickly as they were formed. People in such relationships cannot count on one another for support or trust. In fact, the withholding of true feelings about politics and society can become grounds for mutual paranoia, alienation, and suspicion.

People in modern society often work at maintaining social distance and cultivating casual relationships. At the same time, if talk shows, bestseller lists, and the latest human-development fads are any indicator, people seem preoccupied with how to restore meaning and feeling in their social lives. It would seem that people are in a bind. The convenience of fantasy relationships may be too tempting to resist, yet the poverty of real society is too painful to ignore.

Beyond the social consequences of a mass mediated reality there lie some important political effects. *If people find emotional and social significance in the distant world of news politics, the media and the government are in possession of a powerful mechanism of political and social control. The temptation always exists for political actors to propose magical solutions and fantastic political scenarios through the use of myths, stereotypes, scapegoats, and other symbolic devices. When the media legitimize such techniques and in the process condition the public to accept them, there are no restraints on the fabrication of political reality. Under such circumstances, political actors can manage issues, conflicts, and crises by simply throwing symbols at them—symbols that may be irrelevant to the matters at hand yet provoke powerful emotional responses from the public.* For example, during the public debate in Congress over U.S. policy toward El Salvador, the State Department continued to make alarming statements that the civil war was promoted by outside Communist intervention. Senators spoke of the need to help our "friends" in the Salvadoran government in their struggle for freedom. Such statements persisted even after no conclusive evidence of massive outside Communist assistance was produced. The Secretary of State claimed that such evidence existed but could not be presented for national security reasons having to do with the protection of intelligence sources. The Salvadoran government continued to be called a "friend" in the struggle for freedom, even though it perpetrated the murder, rape, or torture of more than 10,000 innocent civilians each year (a rather large terrorism program for a small, freedom-loving country). The White House even issued repeated reports to the effect that there had been significant improvements in the human rights policies of that "democratic" government—reports that must have been regarded as empty symbolic statements by those who issued them.

Nevertheless, what may be an empty symbolic statement to the authority who issued it can become filled with feeling and meaning by a confused public looking for simple and satisfying solutions for political and social problems. Even though opponents in Congress were heard, in the early years of the war, to attack the government propaganda campaign on El Salvador as a sham, the news audience was faced once again with its standard dilemma: the acceptance of unprovable accusations against the authorities who control information and manufacture propaganda to suit their policies, versus the acceptance of the propaganda. The propaganda has the attractions of being officially endorsed, represented in the news as at least one legitimate alternative, and, above all, emotionally satisfying. It is so much simpler to cast one's sympathies on the side of "democracy" and one's social antagonisms against the "Communists" than it is to work out a personal understanding of the situation, particularly when such an understanding will be rejected by the authorities elected to handle the problem and condemned by fellow citizens who find it easier to follow the course of least emotional resistance.

Eventually, the illusion of democracy in El Salvador won out over the contradictory reality. As that small, war-torn country entered the list of the top five U.S.-aid recipients in the world, U.S. news coverage all but disappeared. Given the fantasy themes of democracy and economic development, continued reporting of troublesome facts would have been strained. Using the excuses that congressional opposition died and that nothing about the situation had "changed" (see the comments by Tom Brokaw in chapter 4), the media abandoned the story.

A group of media experts (editors, journalists, and journalism school faculty and deans) calling themselves "Project Censored" placed media silence on El Salvador at the top of their list of the Ten Best Censored Stories of 1985.[12] According to the group, nothing short of self-censorship could account for the universal failure to tell the Salvador story with an independent, critical eye. In the words of Alexander Cockburn, one of the few investigative journalists who persisted in covering the mess in America's "backyard": "How is it that over the past two years the United States has been organizing, supplying, overseeing and in many cases actually executing the heaviest bombing and most ferocious aerial war ever seen in the Americas and not one coherent report of the extent, viciousness or consequences of this campaign has appeared in any major U.S. newspaper or magazine?"[13]

The answer lies in the interplay of propaganda, professional journalism norms, and public information-use habits discussed throughout this book. Not a small part of this answer involves the increasing disconnection of public information from political action and the substitution of passivity-producing fantasy themes that go by the name of news. If these two trends toward the suppression of feelings in real life and the displacement of social and emotional ties onto distant political symbols continue, the most unsettling effect of all may result. People may grow gradually to expect, and even depend on, the media to provide them with outlets for their social and emotional needs. If people find satisfaction in the fantasy scenarios of mass media politics (not to mention television programs, movies, commercials, etc.), it may cease to matter how far removed from reality those fantasy objects may be. The public may become conditioned to the emotional manipulation that oppresses them. George Orwell may have been a few years too hasty in making his terrifying predictions about 1984, but the seeds of what he was talking about already exist in the psychological bonds that join government, media, and the people in their current political union.

NOTES

1. AP wire story, "U.S. Complains to Algeria over Visit by Hijack Fugitive."
2. See review of research in David H. Weaver and Judith M. Budenbaum, "Newspapers and Television: A Review of Research on Uses and Effects," *ANPA News Research Report* no. 19, 20 April 1979. See also specific studies by Leo Bogart, "Measuring the Effectiveness of an Overseas Information Campaign: A Case History," *Public Opinion Quarterly* 21 (1957–1958): 475–98; and Maxwell E. McCombs and David Weaver, "Voters and the Mass Media: Information-Seeking, Political Interest, and Issue Agendas" (Paper presented to the American Association for Public Opinion Research, Buck Hill Farms, Pennsylvania, 1977).
3. The "News Research Project" was the first phase of a larger study of political issue-formation funded by the National Science Foundation under grant #SES80–25046, W. Lance Bennett, principal investigator.
4. For an introduction to the "uses and gratifications" concept, see Jay G. Blumler and Denis McQuail, *Television in Politics: Its Uses and Influences* (Chicago: University of Chicago Press, 1969). Also, Lee B. Becker, "Two Tests of Media Gratification: Watergate and the 1974 Elections," *Journalism Quarterly* 53 (1976): 26–31.
5. See, for example, Dan Berlyne, *Conflict, Arousal, and Curiosity* (New York: McGraw-Hill, 1960).
6. For an explanation of how such scripts are formed and how they work, see Roger Schank and Robert Abelson, *Scripts, Plans, Goals and Understanding* (Hillsdale, N.J.: Lawrence Erlbaum, 1977).
7. For a discussion of how new stimuli become incorporated into a mental picture, see W. Lance Bennett, "Perception and Cognition: An Information-Processing Framework for Politics," *The Handbook of Political Behavior*, vol. 1, ed. Samuel Long (New York: Plenum, 1981).
8. Walter Lippmann, *Public Opinion* (New York: Free Press, 1922).
9. "Fantasy theme" is a concept coined by Ernest G. Bormann in his article "The Eagleton Affair: A Fantasy Theme Analysis," *Quarterly Journal of Speech* 59 (1973): 143–59.
10. From Ernest G. Bormann, "A Fantasy Theme Analysis of the Television Coverage of the Hostage Release and the Reagan Inaugural," *Quarterly Journal of Speech* 68 (1982): 137–38.
11. See, for example, Donald Horton and R. Richard Wohl, "Mass Communication and Para-Social Interaction," *Psychiatry* 19 (1956): 219–29; see also

Mark R. Levy, "Watching TV News as Para Social Interaction," *Journal of Broadcasting* 23 (Winter 1979): 69–80.

12. Carl Jensen, "The Ten Best Censored Stories of 1985," *Utne Reader*, Oct./Nov. 1986, pp. 84–91.

13. *Ibid.*, p. 84.

CHAPTER 6

Freedom from the Press:
Solutions for Concerned Citizens

NEWS FROM THE PAST
Where the press is free, and every man able to read, all is
safe.
—*Thomas Jefferson*

NEWS IN THE FUTURE?
The critics say it's a new art form—a mixture of news,
documentary and drama serial....Part of what excites
people is that they never know if what they're watching is real
action...or if it's staged. You can think whatever turns you
on the most....[I]t's the last stage of the spectacle—a sort of
living room bread-and-circuses with the copout of letting you
pretend it's not real.
—*Marge Piercy*

Appealing to ideology, prejudice, fear, and faith, the images dispensed
by political insiders limit the terms of political debate and turn democracy
into a spectator sport. The resulting "political spectacle," as Edelman[1]
calls it, creates a dilemma: Either we reject the simplistic images of
politics, thereby suffering isolation from opinion and debate, or we
accept the symbols of politics and live much of the time caught in webs
of crisis, stereotype, and drama, watching powerful actors decide our
fates from afar.

Mind-filling images can grow from very small suggestions if we let
them. People who prefer to run with the tide of opinion can build an
illusory world from the tiny image fragments filling the news: "Communists
on our borders," "standing tall for America," "welfare cheaters," "special
interests," "big government," "freedom," "democracy," "the right to
life," "fat cats," "America, the poor helpless giant," "America, the
brave," "big-spending liberals," "Make my day." Whether these symbols
are planted by candidates posturing in political campaigns or government
officers seeking to preserve the arms race in spite of a skeptical public, the
result is the same: the blurring of issues and the removal of choice and
accountability from popular grasp. These effects are normally associated
with propaganda systems.

PROPAGANDA, AMERICAN STYLE

The U.S. propaganda system differs from the stereotype most Americans are taught about propaganda: mind-warping doublespeak and Soviet-East European–style censorship requiring centralized communication and totalitarian political control. The variety of propaganda practiced in the United States is simple, straightforward, easy to grasp, and anything but totalitarian. It works like this:

First,   political authorities plant simple, vivid, ideologically and culturally popular images with the press.

Then,   journalists, searching for quick dramatic angles, choose the safest political course, emphasizing centrist ideology, ethnocentric and egocentric concepts, and official rhetoric.

Finally,   the passive public, looking to resolve new situations in easy terms, complete the cycle either by tuning out the drone of politics altogether or by having their prejudices confirmed once again.

And so, an information system based on mind-numbing stereotypes is sustained by all the parties involved (including enough people who regard the news as "believable" to allow politicians and journalists to trumpet the virtues of a free society).

It is true that our propaganda system differs from the totalitarian brand in the sense that two sides are heard on most issues. Yet the key to propaganda is not necessarily the suppression of all opinion, but the control of behavior. Despite the alleged superiority of "two-sided news," the American public remains ignorant and passive on most issues, foreign and domestic. *What difference does it make if the information system is totalitarian (like "theirs") or pluralistic (like "ours"), if the result in either case is an ignorant, passive public?*

The twin threats of passivity and ignorance that undermine the foundations of democracy chase each other in a vicious circle which is sustained not by some mysterious force like "apathy" but by real, in-the-world structures of power, participation, and mass communications. The conditions that support the propaganda system and its behavioral outcomes can be described as follows:

• Since opportunities to participate directly in decision making are severely limited, people are unlikely to demand more critical information from the mass media or seek out existing alternative sources outside the mass media.

- Yet without critical information it is hard even to imagine (much less demand) participating directly in the political process.
- Instead of disrupting this cycle, the highly profitable media merely point to a generally satisfied if lamentably "apathetic" public as their excuse for feeding more of the same information into the system.

This system satisfies the basic propaganda imperative of all large-scale centralized states, whether totalitarian or pluralistic: getting most of the people most of the time to accept (or at least put up with) the status quo, even when it is not working to their advantage.[2]

True, "our" propaganda is folksier and friendlier than "theirs." Ours does not emanate from some secret and sinister "Thought Committee of the Ministry of Truth." In place of Big Brother, we have The Great Communicator who channels the latest opinion research on popular fears and prejudices through the news and tells people what they want to hear. In America, the propagandist is our friend. We buy used cars from folksy dealers who promise us, time and again, a "real deal" on a "good clean used car." We form subliminal attachments to shampoos, deodorants, and cough remedies because these and other products are endorsed by movie, sports, and TV personalities with whom we identify. Politics is no different. Loyal Americans routinely accept major policy decisions like arms buildups and recurring wars against little countries because trusted, homespun leaders have mastered the soft sell. Although we may later regret acquiescing to those policies just as we may regret buying that used car or some other product, what real choice is there? Will the next leader bring us closer to truth, the next commercial closer to reality? It is no wonder that most people just shrug their shoulders and live with it. The only other alternative seems to involve joining the hard core of people who really believe that the illusions of democracy and economic choice are real, meaningful facts of life. But perhaps there is a third way.

How to get beyond the illusion? How to see the structures that limit choice and participation? How to create a demand for critical information? These are the questions before us. *What follows is a general strategy for citizens and journalists alike to free themselves from at least some of the unhelpful illusions about our political condition in order to begin forming more useful and critical insights about the American political system and how it works.* The strategy is developed in three parts:

First,   "freedom from the press" begins by understanding how the realities of political power and mass communication differ from the ideal of a "free press and a free people" that drives many of our illusions about the political system and how it works.

Second,   a review of factors contributing to the "free press" myth
          helps explain why the myth is so difficult to dispel.

Third,   for those who wish to go beyond political myth and the
          daily illusions it promotes, a set of critical information-
          processing guidelines will be helpful. One set of guidelines
          is offered in the following pages to help concerned citizens
          "decode" the news as it currently exists. A second set of
          guidelines is offered for journalists who would like to
          make the news more useful as a stimulus for informed
          citizen participation.

NEWS AND POWER IN AMERICA:
THE IDEAL VERSUS THE REALITY

In the ideal civics-book version of American democracy, power rests with
the people. The people, in effect, are the voice of the political system.
Leaders are supposed to take cues from the people and express their voice
politically. The journalist in this scheme occupies the role of the
independent "monitor" who reports to the people on how well leaders
handle the public trust. In simple picture form, this ideal version of power
in America looks like figure 1.

It is obvious that the reality of power in America does not look much
like this ideal picture. *As numerous examples in the book have indicated,
leaders have usurped enormous amounts of political power and reduced
popular control over the political system by using the media to generate
support, compliance, and just plain confusion among the public.* People
may be given some range of choice by the ruling elite, but the substance of
that choice is determined more by politicians and media than by the public.

The media also occupy a different role in the reality of American
politics than the one they are supposed to play in the ideal version. Far
from being monitors of the elite, the media have become political
transmission lines to the people. The media not only send political
messages to the public but also screen the reactions of people to those

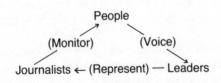

FIGURE 1

messages. Thus, even when people attempt to respond to their leaders, those responses are translated into standard reporting formulas that redefine public reactions, underplay fundamental dissatisfactions, exaggerate short-term frustrations, and move issues out of the range of public attention as rapidly as possible. *The media thus reinforce the legitimacy of power from above while defusing the demands for power from below. The roles of elites and the media in this power structure clearly relegate the power of the people to the bottom of the heap. The public is exposed to powerful persuasive messages from above and is unable to communicate meaningfully through the media in response to those messages.* A more realistic picture of American political power looks something like figure 2.

In the modern world of politics, power depends so much on the control of information that information is manufactured to suit the political designs of its users. The hierarchy of power becomes unshakable when leaders do not have to worry about hiding the truth because they have gained control over the bureaucracies and intelligence organizations that manufacture the information on which the truth rests. An uncritical media then cements the hierarchy of power. Consider an example of this sort of information control. Both during and after the Vietnam War, it was rumored that the U.S. Army had falsified its estimates of enemy troop strength and enemy battle deaths. The underestimation of enemy troop strength and the overestimation of body counts would have been useful ways of boosting the morale of the American public, who grew ever more weary of the endless war. Reports of higher death rates among fewer enemy troops gave cause for optimism and shored up public support for government war policies.

It wasn't until fourteen years after the first rumors of intelligence falsification began to appear that a CBS news documentary gave them legitimate news coverage. In a 1982 exposé titled "The Uncounted Enemy—A Vietnam Deception," former intelligence personnel reported that they encountered pressures to manufacture unrealistic figures on

FIGURE 2

enemy strength. The documentary was immediately attacked by both the government and former Army commander William Westmoreland, who was accused of directing the intelligence falsification. Westmoreland brought a multimillion-dollar slander suit against CBS. Even though it came far too late to affect public input into the war policy, the documentary was a rare example of critical reporting—the news at its best. Although the lawsuit was eventually dropped, CBS suffered years of costly legal preparation and adverse publicity.

Let's interrupt the story at this stage to draw two points from it. First, we have here a classic case of government power (in this case, the power to wage a war) depending on information control that worked long after the policy of the government had ended. The American people can hardly be expected to participate in their government when they are kept in the dark both during and after the events that affect their lives. Second, even this rare, after-the-fact news report on information control elicited a massive political and legal reprisal from the parties involved. It is, to say the least, costly for news organizations to reveal the true workings of power and information in American politics.

But our story is not over. There is still the matter of whether, in the final analysis, the charges of falsification of figures can ever be made to stick. If in the end the issue boils down to a few former low-level officials saying that facts were falsified and a few high-level officials saying that the figures were simply the best available estimates—who is to say who is right? Former State Department official Hodding Carter III provided a key insight into this problem of information verification when he noted that by the end of the war, all the government intelligence agencies were coming up with virtually identical estimates of enemy troop strength. Carter noted in a *Wall Street Journal* editorial that in the early years of the war, the Central Intelligence Agency had disagreed with Army Intelligence estimates. The CIA even argued its case with the president but quickly realized that the point of intelligence wasn't always to produce accurate information. As Carter (and CBS) noted:

> The CIA's analysts repeatedly challenged the [army] figures during much of 1967, but when a showdown on the figures arose, the CIA's top brass apparently decided that sticking with the truth made for bad bureaucratic politics, since it put the agency at odds with the President, and they backed away temporarily. The military analysts who knew better decided to play good soldier. The American people knew nothing of this and instead were fed a stream of statements claiming that the enemy's ranks were being steadily depleted.[3]

The problem hidden in this scenario is that when intelligence-gathering procedures begin to fit information to the needs of government policy, there is no longer any hard information with which to prove the case against the government. In fact, just the opposite is true: All the "best" information produced by the "best" intelligence methods is perfectly in line with what the government told the people. The most thorough investigative reporting can do no more than pit one person's word against another's. Such high-level shouting matches are seldom satisfying, for they cannot fully resolve the doubts of an "objectivity-minded" public who suspend their judgments about truth until they see hard, undisputed facts. *The days of independent and conclusive facts are rapidly coming to an end in the modern information state. Yet the ideal of objectivity lingers on.*

Consider another example that foretells the "end of objectivity." In his discussion of the CBS Vietnam documentary, Hodding Carter went on to draw a parallel with more recent government actions in El Salvador. One of the conditions attached to U.S. grants of military and economic aid to El Salvador was that the Salvadoran government had to distribute farmland to thousands of hungry, powerless, and exploited citizens. The U.S. government estimated that there were some 125,000 families eligible to receive farmland. Following two years of "rumors" that the land-reform program was a sham, the U.S. State Department released a report stating that the program was working smoothly. The report concluded that nearly one-third of all eligible families had received land. The only problem was that the alleged success of the program was based on a government revision of its estimates of eligible families from 125,000 to 67,000. When questioned about the revision, the State Department (speaking through Deane Hinton, the ambassador to El Salvador) said simply that the new figure reflected "subsequent analysis based on the best available data."[4] To which Carter mused in his editorial: "Perhaps, and perhaps not. It may be only coincidental that the new arithmetic makes our policy position in El Salvador, and our client government there, look good. . . . Whence come the new figures? Not from U.S. officials, because the Agency for International Development has discontinued field checks on the land reform program because of dangerous conditions in the countryside."[5]

The most telling statement in Carter's commentary on the El Salvador land-reform question is one that can be applied equally well to dozens of government policy areas:

> Does that mean this is another case of making the facts fit the policy? We have no way of knowing based on the available evidence. But if a scam is being pulled on us in the name of national policy once again, it would be nice if we didn't have to wait 14 years before those who know better come forward and blow the whistle. Great television exposés after the fact help us understand history, but in the meantime we're stuck with lousy policy.[6]

Carter might have added that even if we find out about such information scams fourteen years too late, we almost never have enough hard evidence to convincingly prove the case anyway—even if people cared that much about the facts of "ancient history."

At some point, it must be recognized that the use of information to control political reality is an everyday occurrence. Information is the basis of power, and as a result, any change away from "objective" news reporting will be resisted by leaders who understand the subtle points of the information game. As Thomas Powers noted in a discussion of how intelligence agencies have fueled the international arms race:

> Dishonesty in the intelligence business is not personal but institutional. In effect, the analysts are advocates. The Air Force wants to build planes and missiles; the Navy wants to build ships; the army wants more tanks and fully equipped divisions. All tend to think that the Russians see things the same way, and all "interpret" the evidence according to their own lights. The scantier the evidence—and it is always scanty at the beginning—the wilder the extrapolations. Since no one knows what the evidence means for sure, every National Intelligence Estimate is subject to negotiation, an intensely political process reflecting the realities of life in Washington.[7]

Are journalists truly trapped in a set of power relations that makes it impossible for them to see the contradictions in their commitment to "objectivity" and adopt a more realistic reporting strategy (such as ideological critique, theoretical analysis, or simple, logical political interpretation)? In some ways it would seem that journalists have the greatest margin of flexibility within the power structure. After all, this is still a liberal political system. The state does not own and operate the press. Freedom of speech is still protected by the courts. Dissident journalists are unlikely to be shot, tortured, or to simply "disappear." In most respects the elite could not operate in its current fashion without the tacit cooperation of the press. So why will the media not take the monitor role seriously and provide information to the people in ways that might liberate them from the political communication trap discussed earlier?

There are, of course, a number of obvious reasons why the media do not monitor government actions in an adequate way. To begin with, the news as it currently exists is a successful, profit-making enterprise; news organizations have little incentive to change what they do. Moreover, journalists derive a large measure of professional success and personal life-satisfaction from their jobs. Where is the incentive to rock the boat? It also must be noted that critical reporting often brings both subtle and overt forms of political pressure to bear on reporters and their organizations. As noted, for example, the political and legal responses to the CBS Vietnam report were imposing.

Even routine news reporting is constantly criticized by members of the political and economic elite for not being sufficiently "objective." Powerful people who are as secure and influential as Walter Wriston, the chairman of Citibank, act as if the best defense of their power is a good offense against the media:

> The media, supported by some academic "liberals," would have us believe that things are not just going badly, they are growing progressively and rapidly worse. The dominant theme is the new American way of failure. No one wins; we always lose. Jack Armstrong and Tom Swift are dead. If an individual says anything important, it is either ignored or nitpicked to death by commentators....Let one scientist resign and say that nuclear power is a lethal accident waiting to happen, and he is awarded front page with pictures. He has unlimited interviews on television. The massive achievements of hundreds and hundreds of scientists and the comfort of millions of citizens who enjoy the products of nuclear power go for nothing. We daily see illustrated a point made by the jurist Oliver Wendell Holmes: "When the ignorant are taught to doubt, they do not know what they safely may believe." The media should beware of sowing the dragon's teeth of confusion.[8]

The world must look like a pretty rosy place from atop the Citicorp tower. From that vantage, it must be frustrating to think that the public has the capacity to doubt. However, it is not clear that the rich and powerful see (or even live in) the same world that the rest of us live in. Yet the members of the corporate and political ranks spend a good deal of time convincing the public that we all share the same interests and that it is the press who have led us astray through doubt and confusion. When the authorities accuse the press of not being fair or objective, they put journalists in the bind discussed in chapter 4—the bind created by exposing the fragile nature of "fairness" or "objectivity." Even though these same authorities may be the ones guilty of sowing the seeds of doubt and confusion, the media must cave in ultimately as long as they wish to maintain the illusion of an objective world.

AND SO, THE MYTH OF A FREE PRESS PERSISTS

Somewhere in the back of the mind of almost every citizen is a collection of inspiring images of the press. These images are based on the dramatic events and guiding sentiments of American history, sentiments like the ones expressed in these words of Thomas Jefferson: "The people are the only censors of their governors [and they must have full] information of their affairs through the channel of the public papers....[Were] it left to me to decide whether we should have a government without newspapers or newspapers without a government, I should not hesitate a moment to prefer the latter."[9]

Ideas like these have been echoed by every generation of journalists, educators, and politicians throughout American history. When such guiding principles are passed down from generation to generation, they come to represent the spirit of a nation and a people. It ceases to matter much what those sentiments really mean, or whether they are even true. Ideas given such powerful reinforcement and endowing people with such noble purpose take on a life of their own. They are inspirational, hopeful, and ennobling. They give substance to a national history that would otherwise become vague in the minds of new generations. Such are the characteristics of myths. Unfortunately, myths like "the free press" stand in the way of seeing realities of power like the Vietnam deception story.

Myths require little empirical proof to sustain them. They are taught to the children of a society long before the children are old enough to think or reason critically. They are reinforced throughout life with the words and acts of the most respected people in society. They are uttered by one and all as much out of a sense of abiding duty and social solidarity as out of any conviction based on evidence of their validity. In some cases, the powerful climate of opinion established by the universal proclamation of a myth is enough to force people to utter the words of a myth even when they may not believe them in private. It is likely, for example, that many citizens of Nazi Germany had little private commitment to the myth of Aryan superiority, and yet the powerful climate of opinion in the country induced virtually everyone to act as if they believed the superiority myth. When the majority acts as if they believe in something, it matters little what their private thoughts may be. The private doubts of millions of Germans did nothing to prevent the holocaust of World War II.

The point here is not to suggest that our most profound social beliefs rest entirely on a foundation of psychological conditioning, celebrity endorsement, and social pressure. Nevertheless, it would be a mistake to underestimate the importance of conditioning, authority, and social pressure in the construction of our social and political worlds. Beyond these social and psychological forces, myths also depend on some sort of functional payoff to keep them alive for long periods of time. Without some tangible benefits, the "free press, free people" myth (with its related beliefs about objective information) could not have endured as long as it has in American politics.

The acceptance of myths becomes even more universal when the myths offer something tangible for everyone. For example, different advantages go to different groups that accept the myth that America must defend world freedom. Cozy ties with Third World governments make for lucrative business climates that benefit the corporate and financial elite. The commitment to military strength makes for big industrial profits and provides jobs for many working people. The idea of doing good in the world gives some people a sense of pride and self-worth. While the same benefits do not go to everyone, many different groups get something out of their acceptance of the myth.

The myth of a "a free press and a free people" and its guiding principle of objective reporting provide different but compelling benefits for different groups. However, there is a catch: The groups at the top of the power structure gain the material advantages of power and control, while the groups at the bottom trade real power (since the myth works in reality to limit their political involvement) for psychological reassurances. The irony of this situation is that the broader the support is for the idea of "fair" or objective journalism, the more firmly established the inequalities of power become. A brief overview of the interests of politicians, journalists, and the public illustrates how different (and even contradictory) the bases of loyalty to a myth can be.

Politicians and the News Myth

The reasons are obvious why political actors display such universal support for the free press, free people myth. The regular proclamation of the myth is both useful and necessary. It is useful to invoke the myth because it is much easier to hide political deception behind a convincing show of support for truth and popular sovereignty. It is necessary for politicians to endorse the news myth because the American public would never tolerate a leader who did not keep up the outward appearances of commitment to democratic ideals. Even if the information agencies of government work overtime to engineer public opinion, the public demands at least the illusion that the government represents their will. The news myth helps create the illusion that the ideals of popular government are still viable.

The more the politician proclaims the public importance of the news myth, the more he or she serves personal interests and the interests of the state on which his or her power depends. It matters little whether politicians are conscious of the contradiction between their public support for the myth and their private efforts to control information. The private political benefits accrue to the true believer in news objectivity as surely as they flow to the cynical politician who takes the news myth in vain.

Journalists and the News Myth

The benefit of the news myth for the journalist is not power but professional credibility. Without a public commitment to objective or "fair" reporting, the journalist would lose any claim to professional status or political access. As in the case of the politician, the reporter is provided a ready-made role in the ideal picture of American democracy. Since that role is so easily dramatized with the help of the politician, it would be hard to imagine many reporters not embracing the part. Rather than engage in futile efforts to expose the news game, most reporters who become frustrated with mass media objectivity simply leave the major news organizations to become free-lance writers or reporters for news channels outside the mainstream.

Some journalists, like some politicians, may adopt the cynical attitude of mouthing the news myth while harboring full knowledge of its emptiness. However, it is reasonable to suppose that many journalists fail to see the contradiction in their pursuit of news objectivity. At some point, most career journalists accept the fact that reporting what officials say and do is really the highest form of professionalism. The line between objectivity and political distortion in the news is further eroded when one adopts the reporting formulas that mark the journalist's craft. Thus it is a small step from participation in the activities of professional, objective journalism to the assumption that these activities really are the keys to revealing the truth about politics. "Telling it like it is" can become equated, however erroneously, with telling the truth. For example, it is hard to imagine any lack of sincerity in these words of Walter Cronkite, the former dean of American newscasters: "...we are all *professional* journalists, dedicated to truth, honesty, to telling it as it is without fear or favour—and...there is no politician or bureaucrat who can make that claim."[10] At the time that Cronkite made this statement, he was regarded as the most trusted public figure in the country.[11] Journalists, like politicians, receive their benefits from endorsing the news myth whether or not they are conscious of its contradictions.

The People and the News Myth

But what about the public? What can people gain from deceiving themselves about the quality of information in their lives? In order to answer this perplexing question, we must return to the two pictures of power in America presented earlier in the chapter. In the second picture (figure 2)—the reality of power in America—the people are locked into a weak power position with their choices structured for them and their efforts to respond politically filtered through the distorting lens of media formulas. Such a plight would naturally leave most people helpless and wishing for a return to the ideal version of American politics in which press and politicians served the public, rather than the other way around.

People who wish hard enough for an escape from their political reality have that wish granted by the magic of the media. Both journalists and politicians continually dramatize the illusory appeal of figure 1, the free press, free people myth, for the benefit of the public. Most news stories are offered as reports to the people about some choice or problem that faces them. Leaders appeal in the news for popular support and understanding. If people can suspend their concerns about such nagging questions as where media issues come from, how the proposed solutions are chosen, and what the limits of public involvement really are, then it is possible to escape into a world of political drama. In this political fantasy world the people do seem to have choices, leaders do seem to respond to popular input, and the news does appear to monitor the activities of government in the name of the people.

When confronted with a choice between escaping into the satisfying ideals of democracy and facing the unpleasant realities of politics, it is not surprising that many people prefer the former alternative. Nor is it surprising that many people who opt for fantasy politics over more realistic political involvement are able to treat the fantasy world seriously. After all, the public too can call up the myth of a free press and a free people. The public affirmation of the myth is a way of asserting that, in effect, the world of media politics *is* the real world of politics. As long as the news scripts contain suitable roles for the public, and as long as politicians, journalists, and the public endorse the news myth, then it is possible for people to treat the news world seriously.

People may harbor secret doubts about the honesty of government or the authenticity of news, but what good would it do to express those doubts? Who would listen? What could be done? It is unpleasant for people to admit their own helplessness, particularly when comforting social illusions are available. Thus the public, like politicians and journalists, reap certain benefits from endorsing the news myth. It is unfortunate that the "benefits" in the case of the public are so counter to the real interests of the people.

IS THERE A SOLUTION? CRITICAL GUIDELINES
FOR CITIZENS AND JOURNALISTS

At this point in the book it is tempting to call for sweeping news reforms. If the problems with the news were not caught in the tangle of power and national belief described above, there would be any number of changes that would improve the quality of public information. For example, the journalism profession could advocate the use of interpretive political reporting based on ideology, historical analysis, social theory, or just plain political reasoning. Journalists trained in these interpretive methods could educate the public about politics through the news. The mass media could break out of its enslavement to "two-sided" news and present diverse, provocative political views. The rejection of hidden reporting formulas in favor of grounded interpretive frameworks would give the news audience a basis for developing an active, thinking, reasoning relationship with the political world. For the reasons discussed throughout this book, the media are unlikely to take up the challenge of a sweeping reform program.

Despite the lack of media leadership, the current state of news politics is too serious to tolerate helplessly. If the problems discussed in this book persist, the American people will become ever more isolated from their government and ever more confused about politics. The United States could move toward a sort of "media oligarchy" in which a smaller and smaller number of elites, with increasingly shared interests, dominate the political arena. These media-made elites would, of course, proclaim themselves to be competitive under their familiar guises as liberals and conservatives and Republicans and Democrats. The media, for their part, would continue to legitimize the claims of political competition through the tradition of objective journalism. All the while, the true range of political competition, real debate, and meaningful public participation would grow narrower and narrower. Something must be done. But what is it?

The path to change begins when people like you and I recognize a problem and become convinced that something must be done about it. Expecting change to come from within the political establishment is asking for an unusual degree of selflessness from the average politician. However, it is not unreasonable to think that students and teachers of politics and communications might initiate changes in the U.S. information system. *Movements for change spread most rapidly when they have an institutional base, and the citizens and journalists of the future are passing through institutions of higher education today. An important part of the general college curriculum should include instruction in "reading between the lines" in the mass media and evaluating the daily information flow more critically.* Toward this end, the next section proposes a set of basic guidelines for becoming a better-informed citizen. Even without a revolution at the corporation level, journalists could, of course, make the citizen's task easier by supplementing personalized, dramatized, fragmented, and normalized reporting with more critical, historical, and analytical perspectives. The section after next suggests ways in which reporting can be improved without abandoning such basic givens as the story format or the daily deadline.

Becoming a Better-Informed Citizen

Becoming better informed entails more than just memorizing the "who, what, where, when, and how" of the isolated events of the day. Understanding the political causes and social consequences of public affairs is also useful for clarifying feelings and deciding how to respond. Such understandings would be easier to reach after some preliminary reading of history. However, most people are too busy keeping up with the present to devote much time to the past. Armed with the basic introduction provided in this book, it is possible to recognize and "decode" the most common information biases in the news. The following guidelines should help in becoming a more critical news consumer.

1. *Recognize and discount the use of stereotypes, loaded descriptions,*

and standard plot formulas in the news. When new information is translated into old formulas there is no challenge for people to replace their prejudices with new insights. Yet the easiest stories for journalists to write and politicians to tell are based on familiar images of the world. Unless these warmed-over schemes are detected and discarded, the news remains an unhelpful forum, reinforcing superficial understandings and rigid ideologies.

Loaded descriptions and buzz-words are important to detect and discard. Terms like "leftist," "right-winger," "Communist," "freedom," and even "well-placed" or "informed" sources can set up information for very selective interpretations. For example, "well-placed" and "informed" sources are often high officials acting irresponsibly under the cover of anonymity to plant rumor and innuendo in the news. Despite the unsupportability or political nature of such leaks and plants, their attribution to an "informed" or "well-placed" source can lend credibility to the information. *In general, more weight should be given to those "informed sources" who take the risk to be at odds with their organizations than those who are cleverly advancing general policy and propaganda.*

In the case of "leftists," "right-wingers," and "Communists," the news critic should remember that people so labeled probably do not go out of their way to plant such descriptions with reporters, but their enemies and opponents do. When powerful and popular figures use loaded references to refer to their political enemies, the terms often stick and become used in the media as though they were objective descriptions. This is not to say that there are no leftists or rightists or other "ists" in the world, but that once a group or person has been described in such terms, many people don't want to know anything else about them. When meaning becomes condensed into the images triggered by a single word, it becomes irrelevant what real people may be saying or doing here or on the other side of the world.

It may be true, for example, that some people really are the crazed, vengeful sociopaths that the word "terrorist" connotes. However, other "terrorists" may be members of disenfranchised groups who have resorted to violence as a last desperate measure to make themselves heard and their problems addressed. If they are dismissed as terrorists, their legitimate claims will once again be stifled, and their anger at being ignored may lead to an escalation of their violent behavior in the future.

It is bad enough when politicans and the true believers who follow them champion warped images of the world. However, when journalists write such terms into their own news copy, it becomes all the more compelling for people to see the world through them. Yet the independent standing conferred by the media is based only on the perception that a particular term is popularly accepted. This becomes a vicious cycle in which reality is defined by popular prejudice, and it becomes difficult to think critically or act creatively because people are convinced that they are already seeing things clearly.

A look into the news of the past provides painful confirmation of how many images in the news are tied to the popular prejudices of the moment—prejudices that are cultivated by opportunistic leaders in the first place. For example, a reading of U.S. newspapers during World War II finds the headlines and the stories filled with blaring references to the "Japs." True, most people may have adopted this and other derogatory language to refer to a national enemy. However, when the press legitimated the use of the term, it became all the more difficult for people to see the damage being done to the thousands of loyal Japanese-Americans who had their property confiscated and were thrown into concentration camps during the war. These Americans were also "Japs" as far as the prejudiced public and its mirror-conscience media were concerned. And would it have been so easy to accept dropping the atomic bomb if the victims hadn't been "Japs"?

With a little practice, entire plot outlines in formula news stories can become as easy to spot as glaring buzz-words and stereotypes. As discussed in chapter 2, for example, a common story formula begins with conflict between people, building to some sort of climax (scandal, election, resignation, winning or losing a key vote, etc.). Following the resolution, the situation is returned to normal and the story, or at least its latest chapter, is closed. Since this and other easily recognized plot formulas have little to do with the political causes and effects underlying an event, the critical news consumer should avoid building an interpretation of the event around them.

2. *Once the standardized plot has been discarded as an interpretive frame, the news critic can begin looking for "loose facts" that help make sense of the story.* For example, reporters often mention seemingly extraneous facts that don't fit the dominant story line but which could become the basis for an entirely different story. Building an interpretation around these "loose facts" can help illuminate the underlying political issues that are worth paying attention to. It is always easier to latch onto stray facts and see what can be made of them when one is not trying to fit them into the surrounding plot. A case in point is *Newsweek*'s coverage (mentioned in chapter 2) of a presidential "victory" over Congress on a funding bill to aid the "Contras" in their fight against the Sandinista government in Nicaragua. The clear plot outline in the story was written around the personal victory of the president, who "pulled out all the stops," "worked his septuagenerian magic," and won by virtue of his contagious "optimism and commitment." Needless to say, none of this had anything to do with the larger political implications of escalating the war against Nicaragua. However, two stray sentences in the *Newsweek* article provide an important clue about some of the important consequences of the event. Apparently attached to the bill (although poorly explained by *Newsweek*) was a go-ahead for direct CIA involvement in the war. *Newsweek* said of the vote that "...it will once again unleash the CIA, which has been barred from military involvement with the contras since 1984: *Newsweek* learned the agency is preparing to provide the rebel forces with covert logistical support, training, communications and intelligence with the equivalent of $400 million."[12]

In light of the larger sum of money coming from the CIA ($400 million) than Congress ($100 million), and the resumption of direct and escalating U.S. involvement in the war, it is tempting to think that the headline should have read: "CIA Given Go-Ahead in Escalating U.S. Confrontation with Nicaragua." Yet the press dwarfed the institutional commitment of U.S. personnel and large sums of money behind the misleading image of a "Reagan victory." *The critical citizen should, by now, expect the underlying issues to be deflected by such melodramatic puffery.* When not caught off guard by the melodrama, the alert critic can go straight to the underlying issues and form an interpretation independent of the plot offered up by the media.

Once an independent interpretation has been started, subsequent "stray facts" in future news reports will make a lot more sense. In the case of the war against Nicaragua, it would be possible to understand the institutional basis for official U.S. involvement, the path toward escalation, the reasons why the public did not protest sooner (even though the majority opposed U.S. involvement), and other important features of the developing political situation. Above all, the news critic is in a position to think and talk intelligently about the situation when it seems appropriate to take political action. It will, of course, never seem appropriate to take action as long as the war in Nicaragua is viewed as a White House soap opera. In this manner, reaching independent understandings of the news opens the doors to citizen participation, and effective participation, in turn, is enhanced by critical interpretation of the news.

Sometimes there just don't seem to be any "loose facts" on which alternative interpretations can be built. The mark of successfully controlled news is the presence of just the right number of facts to document the image intended by the political script. When politicians get their "pseudo-events" across successfully, the press will report only the documentary "facts" that were planted to lend credibility to the story. What to do in this case?

3. *The critic must learn to recognize the characteristics of pseudo-events or controlled political performances and decipher the political messages they convey. The first clue, of course, is that successful pseudo-events don't contain any stray facts.*

Consider an example of how to see through a pseudo-event. When a president announces a "war" on anything, the news consumer should begin looking immediately for signs of a well-planned political drama with a clear political purpose. Such political staging was plainly in evidence when Ronald Reagan declared war on crime after nearly two years in office. He announced his support for a complete package of legislation that would make it tougher for criminals to get away with terrorizing the majority of law-abiding American citizens. The entire performance was designed to rally the support of a fearful, economically troubled citizenry around a strong leader. It was not incidental that the entire performance was staged just two days after Reagan suffered his first major political defeat (Congress overrode his veto of a major federal spending bill). Could the president have had a prepared political diversion waiting in the wings for just such an occasion? What do you think? An attentive news critic should be able to detect the signs of scripted political performances and note how they fit the political needs and circumstances of the actors who perform them.

Whether the story in question contains "loose facts" or is an immaculate "pseudo-event," the directive of these interpretive guidelines is to look beyond the immediate plot to see what may be going on in the political world beyond. *The basis for news interpretation thus lies in the institutional processes of the real world, not in the stage settings of a dramatized news world. Once connections are made between news events and the workings of political institutions, patterns begin to emerge—patterns that overcome news fragmentation and make it easier to interpret future reports.* In the case of the war on Nicaragua it becomes clear how the resources and agencies of the executive branch were used to expand the scope of conflict against another nation despite the (passive) disapproval of the public and without (technically) violating Constitutional limits on the president's war powers. In the case of the war against crime, it is possible to understand why the issue dropped from sight so quickly without engaging any notable institutional operations in the process. The crime issue, in this case anyway, was created largely to distract public attention from a potentially image-damaging "loss" suffered by the president. As these sorts of evaluations develop, one learns to place events in their institutional contexts and by doing so to assess their relative importance.

Still, you may have reasonable doubts about how to make these sorts of judgments. Like any "judgment call," news criticism contains an element of risk and uncertainty. How can we be sure that familiar plot formulas are always irrelevant or misleading? Aren't they appropriate some of the time—particularly when there are facts to back them up? Are we to discount the facts in the news just because they support a standard, stereotypical interpretation of an event? Here we encounter another guideline for critical news interpretation, a guideline pertaining to the facts that *do* fit the plot formulas.

4. *When judging the "central facts" in a story, evaluate critically the*

factual claims offered by officials to support their policies. This interpretive maxim should be applied strictly in cases where the only source of "facts" is the political organization or official promoting a particular image of the situation—an image that just happens to be supported by those facts. It is useful to remember the maxim that "There are lies, damn lies, and then there are statistics." Documentary evidence including statistics and pictures can be taken out of context to suit the image of the moment. *Evidence often seems true or factual simply because it fits so neatly with a powerful image, a familiar plot, or a deeply help belief. An equally useful reminder about "reality," by contrast, is that it is never neat and clean.* Raw data are always messy and ambiguous. The ambiguity of data is its real advantage—it makes us think critically and probe for new patterns. When facts fit perfectly, they don't serve the purpose of a reality check but instead provide an "image confirmation."

The first issue in applying this guideline is to decide whether the facts really say anything new about the world or whether they are used primarily to lend credibility to a staged political performance. Consider, for example, the role of facts in a presidential crusade against crime. Without citations of rising crime rates, the recurring call for a war on crime might seem entirely transparent. The listing of facts about the crime problem gives the issue a certain measure of credibility even if the facts sound virtually identical each time the issue is revived. Even a critic of the president's motives might find it hard to deny the legitimacy of the issue. Yet why should the same old facts about crime be taken seriously just because the president calls attention to them at a particular time and proclaims that they represent a serious problem? After all, the facts have always been there, and the problem has always been there. If the facts represent a serious and enduring problem, then it makes little sense to take them seriously as support for a short-term "crisis issue." If they are to be useful at all, the standard facts about crime must be taken entirely out of the context of a fragmented, short-lived news story and placed in broader interpretive frameworks. This means, for all practical purposes, that the repetitive facts in familiar news stories are of little value, since the news critic must discount the immediate context of the story in order to make sense of them.

In contrast to the number of seemingly unchanging facts that rise and fall with issues in the news, some facts appear to be both new and pertinent to understanding the specific topic of a news story. These story-specific facts present a different interpretive problem. For example, when the government announced that the land-reform program in El Salvador was successful, based on the best available statistics, what was the public to think? *The first thing the news critic should ask about such a case is "Who was the source of the information?" If the same agency that is advocating a political position also has control over the gathering and release of supporting information, then the news critic should discount that information.* When the State Department cannot show that its information was independently and reliably gathered, then there is no point in regarding the information as "factual" in nature. To the contrary, the news critic should put more stock in competing claims about the facts in question. If "rumors" are reported to the effect that official facts have been inflated, then those rumors should be taken seriously. It is so difficult for even the hint of skepticism about official pronouncements to enter the news that such hints should be weighted heavily by the news critic.

The key in the examples above is to recognize when the facts fit perfectly with the propaganda message of the moment, with no loose ends and no ambiguities. The subordination of facts to image and ideology has become a routine part of political life. In many cases officials abandon supporting evidence altogether in favor of bold assertions, allegations, and charges. Thus, many things that seem like facts dissolve upon close inspection into unsupported claims that are believable primarily because they fit neatly with the surrounding political scenario. During its lengthy campaign against Nicaragua, the Reagan administration maintained that U.S. intervention was warranted by the fact that Nicaragua directly threatened the sovereignty of its neighbors. A typical assertion was made at the time of the above-mentioned contra-aid vote. *Newsweek* quoted a State Department spokesman as saying that "Nicaragua is engaged in a substantial, unprovoked and unlawful use of force against its neighbors."[13] During the years in which it leveled this charge, the administration never produced a picture, a documented incident, or a substantiated claim from a "neighbor" that suggested unprovoked Nicaraguan belligerence. On the rare occasions when challenged by the press on this lack of evidence, the officials in charge claimed that the evidence was contained in top-secret intelligence reports that were too sensitive to make public. This is stretching the idea of a "fact" about as far as it can go. By saying, effectively, "there are facts, just trust us," officials ask the public to view a situation through pure imagery and to accept that vision on the authority of the officials who have a tremendous stake in promoting it.

5. *Whether they are explicit or, as in the last example, only implied, it is important to bear in mind that facts are "constructed" by the contexts in which they appear. Their relevance and credibility depend on how well they fit an emerging image of a situation.* The news is anything but a scientific medium in which theories about reality are tested and falsified against critical evidence. In the news, the image becomes predominant by appealing to prior beliefs and dispositions held by substantial segments of the public. There is nothing like prejudice to seek out the facts that support it.

In order to counter this "news psychology," the facts must be weighed carefully before accepting them. First it is important to peer through the rhetorical smoke to seek if there are any documented claims at all or only unsupported charges and assertions. Next, the source of the facts should be examined. People with a political axe to grind should not be trusted to make up an impartial set of facts. Finally, the facts that seem tailor-made to support the political points of the various sides should be "cancelled out." After these various screenings have been made, any "facts" left over should be seized upon and used as the basis for building an alternative interpretation. There may not be much left after such an evaluation. For example, screening the *Newsweek* story on Nicaragua in terms of these interpretive guidelines left only two lines of significant text. Yet those two lines were more helpful in building an independent interpretation than anything in the surrounding page-and-one-half! It is quality, not quantity, that counts when it comes to weighing the facts.

6. *If this "cancelling out" procedure seems too harsh, there is an exception that can be made: Additional sources of information can be sought out and independent checks can be run on various claims.* This doesn't mean consulting *Time* as a reference on *Newsweek*'s presentation of the facts. It means consulting publications and documentaries that provide richer, more historical accounts that are told, above all, from the standpoint of a broader range of people—not just the officials—involved in the situation. There is, of course, no reason why the news couldn't provide historical and sociological cross-checks on official versions of events—it just doesn't do so very often. Thus, the recommendation is to use the "cancelling out" method unless one has the time to do additional background research.

At this point you may be concerned that these guidelines will turn you into a cynic rather than a critic. Who or what can be trusted? The goal of news criticism is not to reject everything—it is to think confidently and independently about world events in the face of a lot of pressure to think like everybody else. Nor is the point to distrust all authorities—it is to trust your own judgment.

Becoming a news critic involves more than just taking six easy lessons. The path to informed, active citizenship is a lifelong process that should be nurtured and enjoyed as an opportunity for self-discovery. Frustrations along the way can be minimized by recognizing that we all have prejudices and blind spots that are hard to overcome all at once. Overnight change should not be expected, or even desired—it is too easy to become "born again" into an equally limiting perspective of another ideological color. This brings us to the final interpretive guideline: recognizing the importance of our own belief systems in interpreting political information.

7. *Recognize the importance of prior beliefs in screening and accepting news information, and wherever possible challenge those beliefs with information that is at odds with them.* Since the news contains two sides to most stories, people can simply select the version of reality that comes closest to their prior beliefs and never change their thinking about the world. But what if neither side represented in the news is the most useful way to think about an issue? What if both sides have some merit? Where will new solutions come from if we don't actively challenge our beliefs about old problems? The point is that escaping our current political dilemmas requires the will to challenge existing political beliefs. And there is no better way to challenge beliefs than by resisting the daily temptation to look to the news for confirmation of what we already hold to be true about the world (or for reassurance that someone else is taking care of problems for us).

The point of being conscious and critical of the interplay between old beliefs and new information is not to get rid of beliefs altogether or to tear them down as fast as we build them up. The point is to recognize that some beliefs are better able to handle more information than others. Some beliefs are more open to change than others. The goal of examining prior beliefs is to make sure that they do not stand as a wall against reality. Beliefs are most useful when they help us engage constructively in the activity of society and the ongoing solution of social problems. When beliefs are proclaimed as absolutes to be defended against all evidence to the contrary, they become the causes of social problems.

It is sometimes painful to look back at the stands we have taken and the commitments we made on the basis of blind belief—so painful that the inclination may be to cling all the more stubbornly to those beliefs. I recall a conversation with a person who had supported all of the wars that America had fought in his lifetime: World War II, Korea, Vietnam, and, more recently, the growing involvement in Central America. Vietnam was the most painful, not just because America lost (although he felt we could have won with a bit more of that "Rambo" mentality), but because so many Americans opposed it. How could loyal Americans abandon their country in its time of greatest need? And they didn't just abandon the country, they also abandoned him, leaving him an isolated minority supporting an unpopular war to the bitter end. The bitterness was still with him years later. I suggested another way of looking at it. Perhaps the majority didn't abandon the country—perhaps they *became* the country in that moment when they abandoned blind loyalty in favor of a critical look at what was happening. Perhaps people came to their senses in time to keep the United States, on that occasion at least, from going the way of all empires: marching blindly to its demise over a lost and misguided cause. But, he persisted, how could people abandon their president when he needed their support? I suggested that, perhaps, it finally became inescapable that President Johnson had misled the public from the beginning as to the justification for the war, the international support for U.S. involvement, the honesty of the government we were supporting, and the levels of popular Vietnamese resistance to a U.S.-imposed solution.

But, he asked, why would my president ever lie to me? To this question he was unable to hear an answer.

And so the discussion went. The man had been taught as a child, as we all were, to support the country and trust the president. Yet throughout his adult life that is just where he remained: in a childlike state of blind faith in the inherent honesty of all authorities. "Why would my president lie to me?" It is really beside the point whether presidents lie or whether governments embark consciously on paths of public deception. What is important to recognize is that presidents and governments can make serious mistakes and, worse yet, fail to recognize or admit them. When citizens blindly accept the pronouncements of "infallible" authorities (or passively withdraw from politics), the whole enterprise can be lost in a tragicomedy of the blind leading the blind. And there is, historically speaking, no moment riper for the unconscious demise of a civilization than when it sits at the pinnacle of power and accomplishment. The sense of invulnerability can be contagious. Yet when probed, that sense of righteousness rests on nothing more (but nothing less) than a host of unexamined beliefs about loyalty, authority, human nature, and the supposed causes of political problems.

The continuing health of a political system rests on the capacity for critical thought and creative action in its citizens. *Thus, the overall point of becoming an information critic emerges from this final critical guideline: In the process of sharpening one's beliefs and opening them to change, one becomes an active participant in the political process.* Political passivity is fed by the daily confirmation of prior belief as well as by the resignation that things are always the same and therefore cannot be changed. Even when new information somehow gets through these belief barriers, it only produces confusion if it isn't clear how to work it into the existing belief system. A readiness to accept challenging information and to change beliefs makes it possible to assimilate new information and think about new strategies for action. There is nothing like seeing how things can be done differently to motivate people to participate in the change process.

But how to be open to new information without being confused by every new pronouncement that one hears? That is a good question. Many people are so open to different views of situations that they just don't know what to believe. Some of the most conscientious citizens, in fact, become paralyzed and confused by the conflicting information they hear in the news. The longer they wait for more information to emerge and bring them to an "objective" understanding, the more confused they become. Clearly the process of challenging one's beliefs doesn't mean accepting everything one hears as equally valid. This is where the first six guidelines come into play. Much of the confusion in the news can be sorted out by looking beyond old plot formulas and by discounting the "facts" that have been produced to support them. These steps will remove much of the "noise" from the daily information flow and make it possible to look for new details that are genuinely thought-provoking.

This process of *selectively* challenging one's beliefs will result in broader understandings of the political world and how it works. It will become possible to see how issues that once seemed isolated or "fragmented" are really quite closely connected. It also will become more evident which solutions to problems get at root causes and which ones fail time and again. As these perspectives broaden, an important change will take place—a change that makes it both easier and more satisfying to develop an independent political point of view. *As more of the outer world comes into focus, it is hard not to change one's sense of what really matters in life. In short, as beliefs change, so do values—the things we care about and that help us sort out feelings and guide actions.*

The most significant value change associated with becoming a more critical and involved citizen is that *egocentrism* (self-centeredness), which is our natural first orientation to the world, is replaced by a more *sociocentric* (society-centered) view of things. That is, we come to see that long-term personal well-being is enhanced by political solutions that work for the good of all. Egocentric (me-first) and ethnocentric (my-people-first) values promoted by personalized news formats become replaced by broader social concerns that allow us to look beyond the often contradictory solutions proposed by the warring factions of the moment. Developing a general sense of what is fair and just for society enables one to escape the constant pressure to "choose sides"—a choice that often proves difficult and confusing. Some situations do, of course, call for choosing sides and joining the fray, but it is always more satisfying to make these choices knowing why they have been made.

As a self-conscious belief and value system develops, it becomes easier to evaluate the issues and information of the day without being thrown into political confusion and paralysis. We know who we are and what we stand for, and we can think about problems in a socially concerned rather than a self-centered way. *An emerging political orientation like this one is preparation for citizenship in the best sense of that term: A citizen is one who sees the connection between self-interest and promoting the public good.* The process of developing more critical understandings of the "news world" prepares one for active citizenship in at least three ways: first, by being able to see what social values are at stake in developing political situations; second, by understanding how those situations "work" politically (i.e., what institutional processes are engaged in them); and third, by seeing a path for citizen action that promotes one's values by engaging effectively with the institutions involved.

Before leaping directly into the political fray, it is a good idea to "practice" new political insights by talking to others. It is best to be prepared for occasional blank stares or discouraging words in return, for most other people have not been through a course on becoming an informed citizen. Persistence will pay off, however, through sharpened arguments and expanded understanding of problems. Eventually other people will be found who are receptive to critical and creative thinking about the world around them. From such encounters, good ideas are born and effective citizen participation takes shape.

One example of effective citizen action emerging from news criticism occurred among a group of friends in a large American city. The group included people from various walks of life: several students, a lawyer, a landscaper, an artist, a writer, and a service representative for a business machine company. At their social gatherings politics was a frequent topic of conversation. Again and again people lamented how misguided, "officialized," and generally unhelpful the local papers were when it came to foreign-affairs coverage (sound familiar?). Members of the group were particularly concerned about growing U.S. involvement in Central America at a time when the larger political questions were going unanswered behind media images of an apathetic public and a "winning" president. Convinced that public apathy was as much a product of public information as anything else, the group discussed ways of responding to the general disinformation problem. Slowly, the idea emerged to conduct a study of the content of Central America coverage in the local papers and, if the results were consistent with their preliminary hypotheses, to discuss their findings with the editorial boards of the newspapers.

After reading about content analysis and drawing up a set of questions, the group sampled news stories on Central America and analyzed their information content. A local college class on the news helped code and analyze the data. The results were interesting. First of all, there wasn't much Central America coverage at all compared to various local and national issues, and compared to other parts of the world like Europe and the Soviet Union that are automatically on the "news map." Yet, the group argued, things were happening in Central America, and an important chapter in history was in the making unbeknown to most Americans. A second finding was even more troubling: when stories appeared on places like El Salvador, Nicaragua, or Honduras, they were usually based on copy written in the White House or the State Department. What about the story from the viewpoint of the people who live in El Salvador, Honduras, and Nicaragua? And why were the people in the region who opposed U.S. policy dismissed as Communists? Shouldn't they at least be given an opportunity to speak for themselves and explain their own positions? In addition to these and several other conclusions, it was also found that one of the two local papers fared considerably worse than the other in terms of these information problems. The group, which decided to call itself the "Media Project," agreed that the paper with the worst coverage should be contacted first.

An appointment was made with a senior editor for the newspaper (believe it or not, such things are quite easy to arrange). The group sent a delegation who explained the study and suggested a number of things the paper could do to improve its coverage. The editor was receptive to the constructive criticism and agreed to take the matter up at a forthcoming meeting of the editorial board. Within a couple of weeks the Media Project had a response from the paper: The editors would try to give more news- and feature-article coverage to Central America, and the group was invited to commission an expert analysis piece on a key Central American issue for the paper's op-ed page each month.

From this important beginning the group went on to other projects designed to boost the quality of news coverage in the local area (which was the major metropolitan center in the state). The concerted action of the Media Project along with other citizen action groups in the area helped create greater public awareness and political representation on issues related to Central American policy. As one indicator of the impact of this informed citizen participation, the congressional delegation for the state better represented constituent views on the various policy questions relating to Central America than did most other state delegations, who tended to yield to presidential arm-twisting when they received little input from passive citizens.

The task of becoming an informed citizen would be considerably easier if the news required less "decoding" and provided more challenging perspectives to begin with. It is unlikely that the mass media will undergo an "information revolution" and proclaim their independence from formula reporting and the daily pronouncements of government officials. However, there is much that journalists can do within the current constraints of the profession to improve the quality of their product.

What Can Journalists Do?

Reporters and editors often argue that they would like to do more with the news, but time and space limits (not to mention an easily bored public) just won't permit it. In response to these journalistic laments, consider the following challenge: *It is the responsibility of the press to prepare the citizenry for participation and this task can be accomplished without changing current limitations of time and space.* Here's how:

1. *Downplay personalized story angles and set the dramatic scene with more substantial references to historical and institutional factors.* As suggested in chapter 2, the use of drama could be a help rather than a hindrance in communicating short, interesting, and powerful messages about the world. Current news formats, however, are more melodramatic than seriously dramatic, sacrificing the enduring issues and questions surrounding events for momentary glimpses into the trials and tribulations of political actors. It would be relatively easy for journalists to reduce the melodramatic overtones of the news by developing the historical and institutional contexts in which action is played out. This does not mean getting rid of the actors involved—it is hard to tell a story without characters. It simply means placing the actors clearly within the political context in which the enduring effects of their actions will be felt. Thus, crime stories could be removed from the realm of the bizarre, grotesque, and sinister and placed in the social world of poverty, loss of community, alienation, group conflict, and psychological disorders that breed crime. Budget deficits could be removed from the clutches of big-spending politicians and placed in the context of the bureaucratic and social forces that create them. Arms races could be taken out of the personalized world of tough talk, belligerence, and mistrust at the "summit" and shown in the context of economic, military, and international institutional structures that sustain them. And so virtually every issue could be depersonalized in favor of more useful social, historical, and institutional analyses. Such journalistic shifts would make it possible for the general news audience to grasp the larger political implications of events without resorting to so much laborious decoding.

But wouldn't this require an impossible amount of research from reporters on the scene? In some cases, reporters would have to ask different questions about the historical origins of events and the institutional effects of current developments. However, it might prove surprising to find that people on the scene are excellent informants on such matters if only they are asked the right questions. Some journalists do, of course, ask the right questions but simply find it hard to work the answers into standard news formulas. Many "beat" reporters, for example, acquire good background understandings of the events they cover but find that the daily news hole is too small to accommodate these insights. Even when background facts are added to a story, they are likely to be placed at the end where they will be cut by copy editors operating under space constraints. This is particularly true for wire-service copy, where many of the most useful details buried toward the back of stories never make it into print in the subscribing papers. As this description of the problem suggests, there are at least two places where the problem of sacrificing the big picture for melodramatic moments could be corrected. Either reporters could build more of the political context into the front end of stories, or editors could rewrite their copy to accomplish this result.

Many reporters and editors seem reluctant to pursue this strategy because they believe that personal melodrama is what people really want. Another popular belief among journalists is that more attention to social, institutional, and historical factors would only make the news more complicated and confuse people even further. It is not clear what, other than journalistic superstition, supports either of these beliefs. It is hard to imagine people being any more confused about the world than most news consumers are at present. It is also worth considering that current levels of confusion are the direct result of melodramatic news formats that fail to provide intelligible contexts for developing events. Yet news professionals opt for ever more simple-minded coverage and wonder what to do with an ever more simple-minded public.

Consider an example of how this first reporting guideline could have been applied to an actual story. During the mid-1980s Nicaragua pursued a case against the United States in the World Court, charging that U.S. aggression against Nicaragua violated international laws respecting national sovereignty. Big news? No, but it could have been when the Court ruled in favor of Nicaragua and the United States refused to accept the ruling. However, the coverage in most of the American media offered little understanding of what the lawsuit was all about or what the U.S. rejection of the ruling meant for institutions of international law. For the most part, news coverage centered on the blusterings and personal charges of the actors involved, most notably presidents Reagan and Ortega. When details were reported in articles they were usually technical legal arguments designed to justify the U.S. position, not general background information on the legal issues and procedures involved in the conflict. Thus, when the court issued its ruling and the United States refused to accept it, it really wasn't at all clear what was going on or why it mattered. All but the most perceptive news critics in the audience were left with little recourse but to ignore the situation entirely or to simply choose sides based on little understanding of what the issues were, what the World Court is, or what might be the effect of a U.S. rejection of the ruling. Yet all of these matters could have been addressed easily by applying the first reporting guideline above.

The following article illustrates how a lot of background political context can be provided in a short space without sacrificing the basic dramatic form of the news story. It is worth nothing that this article was compiled from the same international wire services available to any big-city U.S. newspaper—it just happens that it appeared in a paper not published in the United States:

> The World Court gives its verdict this week in a Nicaraguan case against the United States which brought rare drama to the UN body, but also dealt a historic blow to its standing.
>
> For two years the left-wing Nicaraguan Government has been arguing before the international panel of judges that US President Reagan's support for its rebel "Contra" opponents is illegal.
>
> It is one of the few cases of strategic importance to come before the World Court in its 40-year history, but instead of advancing its claim for wider recognition as a forum for settling international disputes, it brought a set-back.
>
> Halfway through the proceedings the United States, a pillar of support

since the institution was established, renounced its recognition of the court's jurisdiction saying it was being used as a propaganda stage.

That decision means that if 16 judges at the World Court declare on Friday that President Reagan has broken international law, he is free to ignore them.

The move also robbed the court, which is properly known as the International Court of Justice (ICJ), of an important share of the moral authority which is its only means of enforcing decisions, said diplomats and legal experts.

"This case has been an unfortunate experience for the World Court. It is not very pleasant when a powerful country like the United States withdraws its recognition," said Paul De Waart, Professor of International Law at Amsterdam's Free University.

Founded in 1946 as the legal arm of the new United Nations organization, the court is still looking for an effective role in world affairs.

In all, 48 judgements have been handed down at the towering red-brick peace palace in The Hague, on disputes between states covering offshore rights, borders, citizenship cases and a variety of other issues.

Notice that in nine short paragraphs the copy editor who compiled this article from the wires was able to include references to the history of the World Court, the basis for its institutional authority, and the possible consequences of the current incident. The article also states clearly what the immediate conflict is about and what the positions of the actors are. All this, without sacrificing the dramatic imperatives of news writing (note the opening paragraph). This illustrates what can be accomplished in limited space using ordinary wire-service copy when the editorial focus is shifted away from personalized melodrama.

In order to follow this guideline, reporters must become comfortable with introducing their own "voice" more often in writing the news. This doesn't mean that one must air "active-voice" opinions or personal views about what is going on. Rather, journalists should learn to use "passive-voice" descriptions to explain what they, as expert witnesses, have come to know about the workings of a situation.

Current reporting practice leans heavily toward letting the actors tell the story. While this may make sense in principle, it is of dubious value in practice. Actors at the center of conflict tend to hide background information behind strategic images that advance their political causes. The movement away from actor-centered narrative toward observer-centered narrative can be stated as a second general reporting guideline.

2. *Reporters should rely less on the actors involved to provide background political context on an event while relying more explicitly on what they, as journalists, have observed about the situation. When writing a story, the reporter should set the scene with the intention of introducing the larger political issues involved, not with the intent of introducing various* *actors who will then take over the narrative duties. This places control over the development of a news story with the journalist, where it properly belongs, not with politicial actors who have an interest in manipulating the story to their own advantage. Only rarely will actors reveal what reporters often know to be the important issues behind the scenes.*

A rare case in which an actor did provide revealing background information illustrates why it is so important for reporters to take the narrative lead more often. Toward the end of the first Reagan administration, journalist William Greider had the unusual opportunity to conduct a series of probing and personal "on-the-record" interviews with White House budget director David Stockman. At the time the young budget forecaster was the boy wonder of Washington who promised to solve budget deficits and federal income problems by applying a new theory called "supply-side economics." In the Greider interviews, as in his public press conferences, Stockman talked about how deeply he believed in the supply-side theory as the solution to the government's economic difficulties. However, in a candid moment that would never have occurred at a press conference or a congressional hearing, Stockman told Greider that government revenues had just not increased the way the theory predicted they would. As a result, he had thrown out the actual figures and reconstructed a set of "data" more likely to convince Congress to adopt his theory-based budget proposals.[14]

Stockman's admission that he had, in effect, thrown out the data in order to save the theory created quite a furor. The issue was discussed in newspaper editorials and on talk shows and debated by the friends of supply-side theory and by its foes, who took pleasure in calling it "voodoo economics." The most interesting feature of the whole uproar over Stockman's candid revelation was that there was one person who was not surprised at all: William Greider. In fact, Greider expressed surprise that everyone else seemed so surprised.

As a keen observer of the White House-Congress "budget ballet," Greider had known all along that Stockman was playing fast and loose with the figures. However, since no one had made an explicit admission or accusation to that effect, the daily news about the budget battle did not raise the issue directly. Yet Greider felt that reporters covering the issue had dropped enough hints about possible White House statistical deceptions that the attentive public should have caught on. Obviously, given the reaction, the attentive public did not catch on until the situation was made clear by a rare admission from the culprit.

It is instructive that professional reporters like Greider often feel that the clever "news critic" should be able to decode the "deep background" information that lurks "between the lines." The trouble is that precious few news critics are trained at the levels of cryptography required to decipher most of the news. On the other hand, many journalists understand the workings of political situations and could introduce such knowledge into their reports if only they could shift from actor-voiced description to reporter-introduced situational analysis.

3. *Avoid the use of buzz-words and stereotypes that stand in the way of new insights.* It is tempting to "peg" stories on themes that trigger instant recognition from the audience. However, the more familiar the vocabulary used in a story, the less informative the content will be. Even a few loaded symbols can undermine new learning while reinforcing old prejudice and ideology. For example, the otherwise excellent story on the Nicaragua case at the World Court (used to illustrate the first guideline) contains an unfortunate reference to the "left-wing" Nicaraguan government at the beginning of the second paragraph. It is true that the government in question was socialist in philosophy, but the prominent display of that fact invites an ideological reading of the story—a reading that might stand in the way of other understandings.

Placing the World Court story in the context of the ideology of the disputants invites "left-wingers" in the news audience to ignore the legal issues involved, while "right-wingers" may discount the importance of the case to World Court legitimacy. Consider, for example, the impact on reactions to U.S. Supreme Court proceedings if cases were discussed in terms of ideology rather than constitutionality. What if pro-abortionists were stereotyped as "left-wing atheists" while anti-abortionists were described as "right-wing religious fanatics"?

Moreover, consider the additional bias created by the absence of buzz-words to describe the U.S. government. Why wasn't the United States called the "right-wing U.S. government"? Arguably the Reagan administration had as much claim to right-wing credentials as the Sandinistas of Nicaragua had to the left-wing title. In most instances, the use of buzz-words makes one side seem reasonable and mainstream while another side appears extremist. Such one-sided labeling may tempt people, at least subliminally, to accept the proposition that the non-stereotyped side has some greater justification for its position. If this perception results, the news has played into the propaganda campaign of one of the parties in conflict. It is worth noting, for example, that the Reagan administration was single-minded in its efforts to justify its aggression against Nicaragua on grounds that the Sandinistas were left-wing. When the news uses similar labels as though they were natural descriptions, propaganda is transformed into legitimate discourse. There are many "left-wing" governments in the world that are not labeled as such in the news (e.g., France, Sweden, Norway, Denmark, etc.). The chances are good that when journalists start to use loaded terms without thought, they have succumbed to partisan propaganda. Here's an experiment: Try rewriting the story on the World Court so that prejudices about the parties involved are minimized and issues related to problems of international justice are emphasized.

4. *When terms and concepts related to a situation are defined clearly, the tendency to project prior understandings onto the news may be reduced.* Once buzz-words are minimized, reporters face the difficult task of explaining clearly what is going on. It is helpful to define technical terms, procedures, groups, and demands that distinguish the situation. Definitions should be carried over in continuing installments about a developing situation. New information is hard to assimilate under the best of circumstances. In fragmented, fast-paced news, definition and repetition of new information are essential to comprehension.

Pointing out that TV viewers miss the main ideas in two-thirds of all stories, Levy and Robinson urge a revamping of current formats. They conclude that TV news is "produced for people already in the know, it's filled with the jargon of policymakers and riddled with cryptic references to continuing stories. What TV journalists forget is that most viewers need some help in understanding the news, no matter how often the story has been told."[15] The absence of useful definitions is cited as a major reason why people fail to grasp the point of stories:

> One reason TV news fails to inform is that too often it uses language and concepts that are outside the viewer's normal vocabulary. Terms such as Gramm-Rudman, electronic countermeasures, rights of passage, and War Powers Act popped up regularly in three programs we sampled— and just as regularly they went unexplained.
> Most viewers need some kind of translation. On one newscast Tom Brokaw showed what can be done by taking the phrase "Contadora observers" and immediately explaining it as "a group of people from Central American and South American countries to go in to make an independent observation of the so-called battle site." Too often, though news might just as well have been written in Tagalog.[16]

After personality and human-interest angles have been diminished, background information has been enhanced, buzz-words eliminated, and key terms defined—that is, after guidelines 1–4 have been observed—one important reporting task remains. Although reporters may understand perfectly well why a story is important, the significance may be lost in the presentation of the story. Journalists should be explicit about what matters in a story. Levy and Robinson suggest that reports must pass the "so what?" test:

> It's used implicitly all the time in the newsroom to decide if something is newsworthy. Why, for example, was it important that a space suit had been recovered from the shuttle wreckage; or what impact was the Nicaraguan incursion into Honduras having on the Contra aid debate? The TV journalists who covered that news knew the answers; they had to

in order to get their stories on the air. But most reports in our March sample never explicitly conveyed that "so what?" element of the news. Sometimes it was there—between the lines. But in our experience, information reported between the lines tends to remain there.[17]

Making explicit the importance of the issues, events, and conflicts in a report is the fifth and final reporting guideline.

5. *Journalists should be explicit about the highest social values and consequences at stake in newsworthy situations. Where there are values in conflict, attempts should be made to bridge the gap between competing viewpoints by showing how they rate on various value dimensions.* For example, the early debates about U.S. involvement in Central American wars were filled with competing references to "fighting communism," "promoting democracy," and "protecting human rights." Not only was news coverage personalized, loaded with buzz-words, and poorly defined, but the relative importance of the various issues in conflict was seldom clear.

The term "human rights" appeared frequently in reports about death, disappearances, and torture perpetrated by governments receiving U.S. assistance. However, there was almost never an attempt to explain exactly why human-rights concerns were relevant to U.S. efforts to fight communism and establish democracy in the region. It may seem obvious why governments that torture their citizens don't deserve American support, but it is likely that the significance of the human-rights debate was lost on many people. In three years of network TV coverage of Guatemala and El Salvador between 1981 and 1983, not a single story took pains to explain why governments that violate human rights cannot be termed democracies in any meaningful sense of the word. It would have been useful for answering the "so what?" question to be reminded constantly in the news that fighting communism does nothing to promote democracy if the tactics used in the fight destroy human rights in the process. Making the connection between human rights and democracy as explicit as the connection between democracy and fighting communism might have gone a long way toward educating the public and involving them meaningfully in the national debate.

To their credit, the media did a good job bringing the "human-rights" debate into the news in the early years of Central American coverage, but they did a poor job of defining what the term meant or explaining why it really mattered. Without a clear sense of why the issue mattered, it was easy for the administration to wear down the human-rights advocates and eventually drive the issue out of the news altogether. The majority of the public continued to have doubts about U.S. policy in the region, but the news failed to educate people enough about the issues so that those doubts could be articulated with a common voice that carried any moral force.

Failing to grasp the higher social values at stake, the majority opposed to U.S. policy remained isolated and generally silent.

Whether propaganda actually changes minds or simply renders people passive and silent, it accomplishes the same result: the elimination of a united, articulate opposition. When the news can be counted on to neglect the "so what?" test by failing to make value-linkages explicit, propaganda does not have to be very sophisticated to accomplish its goal. By observing the reporting guidelines described above, journalists could turn the news from a system where propaganda has relatively free reign to one in which propaganda is held in check by critical information.

CONCLUSION: INFORMATION, CITIZENSHIP, AND DEMOCRACY

Despite the pressures to accept mass-communicated political reality, people have the capacity to resist. The capacity to reject distorted pictures of the world is greatest in a liberal political system like that of the United States, which has not yet taken the final turn toward the totalitarian world of *1984*. American citizens are still free, within limits, to think what they like and say what they think. Nevertheless, the degree of freedom that remains in American society is deceptive in that it leads people to doubt the need for vigilance and personal courage. It is tempting to think that there are more important things in life than politics. It is tempting to trust our political affairs to a government that spends a great deal of energy inviting our trust and presenting political issues as too complex and technical to warrant our concern.

Although it may be tempting to leave our political thinking to others, it would be a disaster to do so. The tacit acceptance of the reality presented in the news is equivalent to abandoning the most basic right on which all our freedoms depend: the right to formulate independent judgments about political affairs. Each individual has a personal stake in thinking critically about events in the news and in forming an independent perspective on the political world.

People cannot continue to let journalistic formulas and political melodramas dictate their views of reality, views that are confirmed only when the individual looks back into the distorting lens of the media for support and reassurance. As Lapham observed, the final victory of government and media over the minds of the people can occur only with the cooperation of the people:

> If the media succeed with their spectacles and grand simplifications, it is because their audiences define happiness as the state of being well and artfully deceived. People like to listen to stories, to believe what they're told, to imagine that the implacable forces of history speak to them with

a human voice. Who can bear to live without myths? If people prefer to think that drug addiction causes crime, that may be because they would rather not think that perfectly ordinary people commit crimes, people not too different from themselves, people living in the same neighborhoods and sending their children to the same schools.

The media thus play the part of the courtier reassuring their patrons that the world conforms to the wish of the presiding majority. The media advertise everything and nothing. Yes, say the media, our generals know what they're doing (no, say the media, our generals are fools); the energy crisis was brought down on our innocent heads by the Arabs (the energy crisis is the fault of our profligacy and greed); Vietnam was a crusade (Vietnam was imperialism); homosexuality is a "lifestyle" (homosexuality is a disease); the Kennedys were demigods (the Kennedys were beasts); the state is invincible (the state has lost its nerve); yes, Virginia, there is a reality out there, and not only can it be accurately described, but also it looks just the way you always wanted it to look.[18]

If people are content with these, to borrow Tom Wolfe's phrase, "Vicks-Vapo-Rub" world views, then they also must content themselves with the eventual loss of freedom, value, and meaning. These are heavy prices to pay for the convenience of a ready-made reality full of instant controversy, disappearing problems, and reassurance around every corner. There is an alternative. The reader is equipped at this point to escape from the news prison. Even though the news distorts the political world and inhibits critical thinking, it should be evident by now how it does these things. Armed with this information, it should be possible to break the "news code" in virtually any news story and produce a better, more sensible, and more useful interpretation of the reality behind the story. With a little help from the press, we might even create democracy in the process.

NOTES

1. See Murray Edelman, *Constructing the Political Spectacle* (Chicago: University of Chicago Press, 1988).
2. The need for propaganda in modern society is discussed extensively in Jacques Ellul, *Propaganda* (New York: Vintage, 1965).
3. From Hodding Carter III, "Time to Trust the Government Again, Right?" *Wall Street Journal*, 28 January 1982, p. 23.
4. *Ibid.*
5. *Ibid.*
6. *Ibid.*
7. Thomas Powers, "But Never Danger Today," *Atlantic*, April 1982, p. 106.
8. Quoted from Howard Simons and Joseph A. Califano, Jr., eds., *The Media and Business* (New York: Vintage, 1979), p. xiii.

210 FREEDOM FROM THE PRESS

9. Quoted from Frank Luther Mott, *The News in America* (Cambridge, Mass.: Harvard University Press, 1952), p. 5.
10. Quoted in Marvin Barrett, ed., *The Politics of Broadcasting, 1971–1972* (New York: Crowell, 1973), p. 49.
11. According to an Oliver Quayle poll reported in *ibid.*
12. "Rekindling the Magic: Reagan Wins a Congressional Victory to Aid the Contras," *Newsweek*, 7 July 1986, p. 33.
13. *Ibid.*
14. William Greider, "The Education of David Stockman," *The Atlantic*, December 1981, pp. 27–40.
15. Mark R. Levy and John P. Robinson, "The 'huh?' Factor: Untangling TV News," *Columbia Journalism Review*, July/August 1986, p. 48.
16. *Ibid.*, p. 49.
17. *Ibid.*, p. 50.
18. Lewis Lapham, "Gilding the News," *Harper's*, July 1981, p. 37.

Index